Access to History
for the IB Diploma

vil rights and social movements in the Americas

Vivienne Sanders

HODDER
EDUCATION
AN HACHETTE UK COMPANY

The material in this title has been developed independently of the International Baccalaureate®, which in no way endorses it.

The Publishers would like to thank the following for permission to reproduce copyright material:

Photo credits: p10 © 2012 Banco de México Diego Rivera Frida Kahlo Museums Trust, Mexico, D.F./DACS. The Art Archive/ National Palace Mexico City/Gianni Dagli Orti; **p20** Reuters/Corbis; **p23** Credit: 'So That All Shall Know'. Photo: Daniel Hernández-Salazar © 1992. www.danielhernandezsalazar.blogspot.com; **p25** AFP/Getty Images; **p60** John E. Phay Collection, Southern Media Archives; **p71** Time & Life Pictures/Getty Images; **p74** Bettmann/Corbis; **p106** Topfoto/AP; **p113** Yanker Poster Collection/Library of Congress; **p124** akg-images; **p130** AFP/Getty Images; **p152** Reproduced with the kind permission of Kevin Siers and Kind Features Syndicate; **p166** AFP/Getty Images; **p179** Bettmann/Corbis; **p183** Michael Ochs Archives/Getty Images; **p210** Bettmann/Corbis; **p214** From the private collection of Marjorie Agosin; **p229** Yanker Poster Collection/Library of Congress.

Acknowledgements are listed on page 252.

Every effort has been made to trace all copyright holders, but if any have been inadvertently overlooked the Publishers will be pleased to make the necessary arrangements at the first opportunity.

Although every effort has been made to ensure that website addresses are correct at time of going to press, Hodder Education cannot be held responsible for the content of any website mentioned in this book. It is sometimes possible to find a relocated web page by typing in the address of the home page for a website in the URL window of your browser.

Hachette UK's policy is to use papers that are natural, renewable and recyclable products and made from wood grown in sustainable forests. The logging and manufacturing processes are expected to conform to the environmental regulations of the country of origin.

Orders: please contact Bookpoint Ltd, 130 Milton Park, Abingdon, Oxon OX14 4SB. Telephone: +44 (0)1235 827720. Fax: +44 (0)1235 400454. Lines are open 9.00a.m.–5.00p.m., Monday to Saturday, with a 24-hour message answering service. Visit our website at www.hoddereducation.co.uk

© Vivienne Sanders 2013

First published in 2013 by
Hodder Education,
An Hachette UK company
338 Euston Road
London NW1 3BH

Impression number   10 9 8 7 6 5 4 3 2
Year   2017 2016 2015 2014 2013

Cover image © George Gardner/The Image Works/TopFoto
Illustrations by Gray Publishing
Typeset in 10/13pt Palatino and produced by Gray Publishing, Tunbridge Wells
Printed in Dubai

A catalogue record for this title is available from the British Library

ISBN 978 1444 156621

Contents

Dedication   l

Introduction   2

  1 What you will study   2
  2 How you will be assessed   3
  3 About this book   6

CHAPTER 1   Native Americans and civil rights in the Americas   9

  1 The indigenous population in Latin America   9
  2 Native Americans in the USA   27
  3 First Peoples in Canada   38
  Examination advice   51
  Examination practice   52

CHAPTER 2   African Americans and the Civil Rights Movement   53

  1 African Americans to 1945   53
  2 Short-term causes of the Civil Rights Movement 1945–55   57
  3 Key debate: When did the Civil Rights Movement begin?   67
  4 The end of segregation in the South 1955–65   68
  Examination advice   86
  Examination practice   89

CHAPTER 3   Martin, Malcolm and Black Power   90

  1 The role of Martin Luther King Jr in the Civil Rights Movement   90
  2 Key debate: Who or what played the most important role in the Civil Rights Movement?   100
  3 The Nation of Islam and Malcolm X   101
  4 The rise of Black Power in the 1960s   108
  5 Key debate: How new and successful was the Black Power movement?   117
  Examination advice   121
  Examination practice   122

CHAPTER 4 Afro-Latin Americans   123

1 Afro-Latin Americans in the nineteenth century   123
2 Afro-Latin Americans in the twentieth century   124
3 The impact of the Afro-Latin American Civil Rights Movement   133
4 Key debate: Have Afro-Latin Americans attained equality through agency and
   racial democracy?   138
   Examination advice   140
   Examination practice   141

CHAPTER 5 Role of governments in Civil Rights Movements in
                the Americas   142

1 The US government and civil rights   143
2 The Bolivian government and civil rights   154
3 Key debate: Were Latin American constitutional guarantees of indigenous rights due
   to activism?   169
   Examination advice   171
   Examination practice   173

CHAPTER 6 Youth culture and protests of the 1960s and 1970s   174

1 Youth culture and protests in the USA   174
2 Key debate: How 'new', effective and widespread was 1960s' US student radicalism?   185
3 Youth culture and protests in Canada   186
4 Youth culture and protests in Latin America   188
   Examination advice   194
   Examination practice   195

CHAPTER 7 Feminist movements in the Americas   196

1 Women's movements in Canada   196
2 Women's movements in Latin America   202
3 Women's movements in the USA   221
4 Key debate: When and why did the modern women's movement start?   234
   Examination advice   235
   Examination practice   238

   Timeline   239
   Glossary   241
   Further reading   245
   Internal assessment   248
   Index   249

Dedication

Keith Randell (1943–2002)

The original *Access to History* series was conceived and developed by Keith, who created a series to 'cater for students as they are, not as we might wish them to be'. He leaves a living legacy of a series that for over 20 years has provided a trusted, stimulating and well-loved accompaniment to post-16 study. Our aim with these new editions for the IB is to continue to offer students the best possible support for their studies.

Introduction

This book has been written to support your study of HL option 3: Aspects of the history of the Americas: Civil rights and social movements in the Americas of the IB History Diploma Route 2.

This introduction gives you an overview of:

✪ the content you will study for Civil rights and social movements in the Americas

✪ how you will be assessed for Paper 3

✪ the different features of this book and how these will aid your learning.

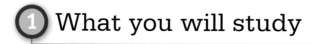

① What you will study

After 1945 and the end of the Second World War, growing political and social movements had an effect on every country of the Americas. Groups that had been ignored for centuries began to organize and push for greater inclusion in their respective countries. These included native peoples, African Americans, Afro-Latin Americans and women. These groups challenged traditional power élites and sought rights that others possessed and took for granted. How they were able to make progress and to overcome enormous obstacles is the focus of this book. In many cases, advancement was slow. Civil disobedience, violence, mass marches and the use of the courts all marked this process of change.

This book covers the civil rights and social movement post-1945.

- Chapter 1 examines the situation of the native or indigenous peoples in North and South America and how they organized themselves to win greater rights.
- The origins, tactics and organization of the Civil Rights Movement in the USA is examined in Chapter 2. The fight against segregation, particularly in the South, is explored, as are the various organizations that pushed for change both in the courts and at grass roots level.
- Chapter 3 traces the various strategies employed by Dr Martin Luther King Jr, Malcolm X and the Black Power Movement as they challenged the *status quo*.
- Afro-Latin American movements are investigated in Chapter 4 and compared and contrasted with African American movements in the USA.
- The role of governments in assisting or holding back change in the Americas is considered in Chapter 5.

- Chapter 6 looks in detail at the youth movements in the 1960s and 1970s in the region.
- Finally, Chapter 7 analyses the growth of feminist movements in the Americas.

② How you will be assessed

The IB History Diploma Higher Level has three papers in total: Papers 1 and 2 for Standard Level and a further Paper 3 for Higher Level. It also has an internal assessment which all students must do.

- For Paper 1 you need to answer four source-based questions on a prescribed subject. This counts for 20 per cent of your overall marks.
- For Paper 2 you need to answer two essay questions on two different topics. This counts for 25 per cent of your overall marks.
- For Paper 3 you need to answer three essay questions on two or three sections. This counts for 35 per cent of your overall marks.

For the Internal Assessment you need to carry out a historical investigation. This counts for 20 per cent of your overall marks.

HL option 3: Aspects of the history of the Americas is assessed through Paper 3. You must study three sections out of a choice of 12, one of which could be Civil rights and social movements in the Americas. These sections are assessed through Paper 3 of the IB History diploma which has 24 essay questions – two for each of the 12 sections. In other words, there will be two specific questions that you can answer based on Civil rights and social movements.

Examination questions

For Paper 3 you need to answer three of the 24 questions. You could answer either two on one of the sections you have studied and one on another section, or one from each of the three sections you have studied. So, assuming Civil rights and social movements in the Americas is one of the sections you have studied, you may choose to answer one or two questions on it.

The questions are not divided up by section but just run 1–24 and are usually arranged chronologically. In the case of the questions on Civil rights and social movements in the Americas, you should expect numbers 21 and 22 to be on this particular section. When the exam begins, you will have five minutes in which to read the questions. You are not allowed to use a pen or highlighter during the reading period. Scan the list of questions but focus on the ones relating to the sections you have studied.

Remember you are to write on the history of the Americas. If a question such as, 'Discuss the impact of the student movements on the society of one country of the region' is asked, do *not* write about Chinese student movements. You will receive no credit for this answer.

Command terms

When choosing the three questions, keep in mind that you must answer the question asked, not one you might have hoped for. A key to success is understanding the demands of the question. IB History diploma questions use key terms and phrases known as command terms. The more common command terms are listed in the table below, with a brief definition of each. More are listed in the appendix of the IB History Guide.

Examples of questions using some of the more common command terms and specific strategies to answer them are included at the end of Chapters 1–7.

Command term	Description	Where exemplified in this book
Analyse	Investigate the various components of a given issue	Pages 51–2
Assess	Very similar to evaluate. Raise the various sides to an argument but clearly state which are more important and why	Pages 121–2
Compare and contrast	Discuss both similarities and differences of two events, people, etc.	Pages 235–8
Evaluate	Make a judgement while looking at two or more sides of an issue	Pages 171–3
In what ways and with what effects	Be sure to include both ways and effects in your answer – that is how an event took place and what the repercussions were	Pages 194–5
To what extent	Discuss the various merits of a given argument or opinion	Pages 86–9
Why	Explain the reasons for something that took place. Provide several reasons	Pages 140–1

Answering the questions

You have two-and-a-half hours to answer the three questions or 50 minutes each. Try to apportion your time wisely. In other words, do not spend 75 minutes on one answer. Before you begin each essay, take five to seven minutes and compose an outline of the major points you will raise in your essay. These you can check off as you write the essay itself. This is not a waste of time and will bring organization and coherence to what you write. Well-organized essays that include an introduction, several well-supported arguments and a concluding statement are much more likely to score highly than essays which jump from point to point without structure.

The three essays you write for Paper 3 will be read by a trained examiner. The examiner will read your essays and check what you write against the IB mark scheme. This mark scheme offers guidance to the examiner but is not comprehensive. You may well write an essay that includes analysis and evidence not included in the mark scheme and that is fine. It is also worth remembering that the examiner who will mark your essay is looking to reward well-defended and well-argued positions, not to deduct for misinformation.

Each of your essays will be marked on a 0–20 scale, for a total of 60 points. The total score will be weighted as 35 per cent of your final IB History. Do bear in mind that you are not expected to score 60/60 to earn a 7: 37–39/60 will equal a 7. Another way of putting this is that if you write three essays that each score 13, you will receive a 7.

Writing essays

In order to attain the highest mark band (18–20), your essays should:

- be clearly focused
- address all implications of the question
- demonstrate extensive historical knowledge
- demonstrate knowledge of historical processes such as continuity and change
- integrate your analysis
- be well structured
- have well-developed synthesis.

Your essay should include an introduction in which you set out your main points. Do not waste time copying the question but do define the key terms stated in the question. The best essays probe the demands of the question. In other words, there are often different ways of interpreting the question.

Next, you should write an in-depth analysis of your main points in several paragraphs. Here you will provide evidence that supports your argument. Each paragraph should focus on one of your main points and relate directly to the question. More sophisticated responses include counter-arguments.

Finally, you should end with a concluding statement.

In the roughly 45 minutes you spend on one essay, you should be able to write 3–6 pages. While there is no set minimum, you do need explore the issues and provide sufficient evidence to support what you write.

At the end of Chapters 1–7, you will find IB-style questions with guidance on how best to answer them. Each question focuses on a different command term. The more practice you have writing essays, the better your results will be.

The appearance of the examination paper

Cover

The cover of the examination paper states the date of the examination and the length of time you have to complete it: 2 hours 30 minutes. Please note that there are two routes in history. Make sure your paper says Route 2 on it. Instructions are limited and simply state that you should not open it until told to do so and that three questions must be answered.

Questions

You will have five minutes in which to read through the questions. It is very important to choose the three questions you can answer most fully. Remember that two questions will be on civil rights and social movements after 1945. After mastering the material in this book, you may well decide to choose the two questions that focus on this topic. That is certainly permissible. After the five minutes' reading time is over, you can take out your pen and mark up the exam booklet:

- Circle the three questions you have decided to answer.
- Identify the command terms and important points. For example, if a question asked, 'Analyse the aims and impact of the Black Panthers in the 1960s and 1970s', underline the words 'aims' and 'impact'. This will help you to focus on the demands of the question.

For each essay take 5–7 minutes to write an outline and approximately 43–5 minutes to write the essay.

③ About this book

Coverage of the course content

This book addresses the key areas listed in the IB History Guide for Route 2: HL option 3: Aspects of the history of the Americas: Civil rights and social movements in the Americas. Chapters start with an introduction outlining key questions they address. They are then divided into a series of sections and topics covering the course content.

Throughout the chapters you will find the following features to aid your study of the course content.

Key and leading questions

Each section heading in the chapter has a related key question which gives a focus to your reading and understanding of the section. These are also listed in the chapter introduction. You should be able to answer the questions after completing the relevant section.

Topics within the sections have leading questions which are designed to help you focus on the key points within a topic and give you more practice in answering questions.

Key terms

Key terms are the important terms you need to know to gain an understanding of the period. These are emboldened in the text the first time they appear in the book and are defined in the margin. They also appear in the glossary at the end of the book.

Sources

Throughout the book are several written and visual sources. Historical sources are important components in understanding more fully why specific decisions were taken or on what contemporary writers and politicians based their actions. The sources are accompanied by questions to help you dig deeper into the history of civil rights and social movements in the Americas.

Key debates

Historians often disagree on historical events and this historical debate is referred to as historiography. Knowledge of historiography is helpful in reaching the upper mark bands when you take your IB History examinations. You should not merely drop the names of historians in your essay. You need to understand the different points of view for a given historiographical debate. You can bring these up in your essay. There are a number of debates throughout the book to develop your understanding of historiography.

Theory of Knowledge (TOK) questions

Understanding that different historians see history differently is an important element in understanding the connection between the IB History Diploma and Theory of Knowledge. Alongside some of the debates is a Theory of Knowledge style question which makes that link.

Summary diagrams

At the end of each section is a summary diagram which gives a visual summary of the content of the section. It is intended as an aid for revision.

Chapter summary

At the end of each chapter is a short summary of the content of that chapter. This is intended to help you revise and consolidate your knowledge and understanding of the content.

Examination guidance

At the end of Chapters 1–7, you will find:

- Examination guidance on how to answer questions, accompanied by advice on what supporting evidence you might use, and sometimes sample answers designed to help you focus on specific details.
- Examination practice in the form of Paper 3 style questions.

End of the book

The book concludes with the following sections.

Timeline

This gives a timeline of the major events covered in the book, which is helpful for quick reference or as a revision tool.

Glossary

All key terms in the book are defined in the glossary.

Further reading

This contains a list of books, websites and films which may help you with further independent research and presentations. It may also be helpful when further information is required for internal assessments and extended essays in history. You may wish to share the contents of this area with your school or local librarian.

Internal assessment

All IB History diploma students are required to write a historical investigation which is internally assessed. The investigation is an opportunity for you to dig more deeply into a subject that interests you. This gives you a list of possible areas for research.

CHAPTER 1

Native Americans and civil rights in the Americas

This chapter looks at the fate of the indigenous inhabitants of the Americas after the European conquest that began in the sixteenth century. It investigates the reasons for the inequality they have suffered and how and to what extent they have attained civil rights. You need to consider the following questions throughout this chapter:

✪ How and to what extent did the indigenous population of Latin America achieve equality after 1945?

✪ How and to what extent did Native Americans achieve equality in the USA after 1945?

✪ How and to what extent did First Peoples achieve equality in Canada after 1945?

1 The indigenous population in Latin America

▶ **Key question:** *How and to what extent did the indigenous population of Latin America achieve equality after 1945?*

Background: the Latin American indigenous population before 1945

← What was the situation of the indigenous population before 1945?

From the sixteenth century, the history of **Latin America** was dominated by tense interactions between conquerors (Spanish and Portuguese) and conquered (the **indigenous** population). The culturally arrogant conquerors created a hierarchical society based upon their notions of 'race' (see Source A, page 10). At the bottom was the 'inferior' indigenous population, which remained subjugated, despite frequent rebellions.

The newly independent republics in the nineteenth century

The Latin American colonies gained independence in the nineteenth century. The new national governments were not particularly interested in indigenous land rights and culture, and invariably oppressed and exploited both the indigenous population and **mestizos**. By 1900, the indigenous populations had lost a large proportion of their land, and were forced to pay special taxes and provide unpaid labour services in nations such as Bolivia, Colombia, Ecuador, Guatemala, Mexico and Peru.

🔑 **KEY TERM**

Latin America The countries in Central and South America that gained their independence from Spain and Portugal in the nineteenth century.

Indigenous Original/native inhabitants.

Mestizos Offspring of Europeans and native peoples.

Study Source A. Why might some people find it offensive to be described as of 'the Indian race'?

An extract from *The History of Latin America* by Marshall Eakin, published by Palgrave, New York, USA, 2007, page 136.

Race is a social construct that has no genetic basis, since every culture defines what we call 'race' in different ways. Contemporary notions of race arise out of nineteenth century social science that attempted to define races scientifically. Scientists today, especially those working in genetics, almost universally reject the notion of biologically defined categories of race. They tell us, in effect, that there are no clear biological or genetic boundaries that separate the human species sufficiently to define racial groups. What we tend to call race, is, in fact, our own culture's reading of physical appearance, in particular, skin tones. And these readings are highly subjective and variable.

KEY TERM

Mexican Revolution
A revolt against the dictatorship of Porfirio Díaz began in 1910 then developed into a struggle between several different Mexican groups that lasted until about 1920.

Aztecs Central Mexican people conquered by Spain in the sixteenth century.

The indigenous population in Latin America 1900–45

In countries such as Colombia, Ecuador, Mexico and Venezuela, large mestizo populations were incorporated into society and politics, but darker skinned peoples remained at the bottom of the Latin American hierarchy. The large indigenous populations of Guatemala, Ecuador, Peru and Bolivia were impoverished and discriminated against. Resistance proved useless. However, by the 1920s, countries with large indigenous and mestizo populations such as Paraguay, Honduras, Nicaragua, El Salvador and Mexico were glorifying population diversity as a national characteristic. After the **Mexican Revolution** (1910–20), it suited the new Mexican government to try to create a sense of national identity by depicting the Spanish as evil conquerors and the **Aztecs** as their noble victims, as in Diego Rivera's propagandist murals (see Source B).

SOURCE B

What is the attitude of the artist in Source B to the Spanish conquerors and the conquered indigenous population?

Detail from a Diego Rivera mural depicting Mexican history in the *Palacio Nacional* in Mexico City, painted between 1929 and 1935.

The *indigenismo* movement, which was particularly fashionable in Guatemala, Ecuador, Bolivia and Peru, saw indigenous culture as the source of the best national values, revered the communal character of the **Inca** state, and urged revitalization of indigenous communities through land redistribution and the incorporation of indigenous people as equal citizens in the nation's progress. However, despite all this glorification of the indigenous past, Mexican President Cárdenas (1934–40) typified the attitude of successive Mexican governments when he said the goal was to 'Mexicanize' the 'Indians', not to 'Indianize' Mexico. By 1945, Mexico was a proudly mestizo nation but the indigenous peasants remained impoverished and regarded as socially inferior.

The indigenous population after 1945

The proportion of indigenous people varied from state to state in the twentieth century. They constituted over half of the population in Guatemala, Peru and Bolivia, one-third in Ecuador, and around one-tenth in Mexico. Mestizos constituted the majority in Colombia, Ecuador, El Salvador,

> **KEY TERM**
>
> **Indigenismo** Latin American movement that revered indigenous culture as a source of what was best in national values.
>
> **Inca** Indigenous Peruvian; the Inca Empire stretched from Ecuador to Chile before the Spanish conquest.

← Why and with what results did indigenous activism increase after 1945?

Judging from Source C, what difficulties can statistics present to the historian?

SOURCE C

Comparative statistics from the Instituto Indigenista Interamericano (III) and the World Bank, showing numbers and percentages of indigenous peoples of national population in Latin America in 1994–5.

Country	Indigenous population		Part of the total population in per cent	
	III	World Bank	III	World Bank
Argentina	350,000	360,000	1.00	1.10
Bolivia	4,500,000	4,150,000	63.00	56.80
Brazil	300,000	225,000	0.20	0.20
Chile	800,000	550,000	6.00	4.20
Colombia	600,000	300,000	2.00	0.90
Costa Rica	30,000	26,000	1.00	0.90
Ecuador	4,100,000	3,100,000	40.00	29.50
El Salvador	400,000	1,000	7.00	0.02
Guatemala	5,800,000	3,900,000	66.00	43.80
Honduras	600,000	110,000	12.04	2.10
Mexico	7,800,000	12,000,000	9.00	14.20
Nicaragua	160,000	48,000	5.00	14.25
Panama	140,000	99,000	5.05	4.10
Paraguay	100,000	80,000	3.00	1.90
Peru	8,400,000	9,100,000	40.00	40.80
Uruguay	0	–	0	–
Venezuela	400,000	150,000	2.00	0.80
Total of LA & the Caribbean	34,225,000	34,426,000	7.72	12.76

Sources: World Bank, *Regional and Sectorial Studies: Indigenous Peoples & Poverty in Latin America*, Washington, DC, September 1994, and Instituto Indigenista Interamericano (III), *América Indígena* Vol. LV, No. 3, Mexico, 1995.

Honduras, Mexico, Nicaragua, Panama, Paraguay and Venezuela, while the population was of predominantly European descent in countries such as Argentina, Chile, Costa Rica and Uruguay.

Reasons for increased Indian activism and unity

In 1945, countries with large indigenous populations were significantly poorer than those without. The large indigenous populations of Mexico, Guatemala, Peru, Ecuador and Bolivia were impoverished (around 90 per cent of cultivable land was owned a small minority that was white or mestizo) and greatly discriminated against (most were not allowed to vote). So, it is not surprising that after 1945 they increasingly agitated for economic

Map showing Latin American nations with large percentages of indigenous populations in 2000

and political equality and respect for their culture. Increased indigenous activism was also due to the politicization of the peasants, indigenous organizations, liberation theology, economic problems, globalization and sympathetic governments.

The politicization of the peasants

In 1945, the indigenous peasantry was generally illiterate, focused on scraping a living, and politically inactive. However, some started to become politicized. For example, in the remote regions of the **Andes**, the **radical left** contributed to the politicization of indigenous peasants. Other contributory factors in Peru included:

- **labour union** politicization of occasional labourers in the mines of Cerro de Pasco and the steel refineries of La Oroya
- exposure to city life when doing temporary work in the Peruvian capital, Lima
- contact with friends and family who had gone to work on the coast and remained there
- increased literacy and access to political information.

Indigenous organizations

Historian Guillermo de la Peña (1998) wrote of the 'proliferation and persistence' of indigenous organizations in the 1960s and 1970s, despite the many authoritarian governments. Organizations such as the Colombian Regional Council of the Cauca Indians (CRIC), established in 1971, raised ethnic consciousness, as did the international organizations that they joined, such as the South American Indian Council (CISA), established in 1980. These organizations emphasized 'Indianism', arguing that the physical survival of Indians required their cultural survival and that they were entitled to autonomy. These organizations gained national and international publicity and made it difficult for governments and politicians to ignore the indigenous population.

Liberation theology

In 1962, the Second Vatican Council concluded that the Catholic Church needed to do more to help the poor and the Catholic Bishops' conference at Medellín, Colombia (1968) agreed. Followers of **liberation theology** organized the poor into Christian Base Communities (CEBs), which combined religious study with agitation for measures that would help the poor, such as land redistribution, water rights and better wages. From the 1960s to the 1980s, a considerable minority of Catholic clergy fought for their impoverished flocks' rights, and helped to mobilize the indigenous population. For example, in Guatemala in the early 1970s, the Catholic Church collaborated with idealistic students in literacy projects for the indigenous peasants. Some Catholic priests gave lessons in the Guatemalan Constitution, Article 1 of which declared that all Guatemalans were equal regardless of race or religion. However, many Catholics were uneasy about

 **KEY TERM**

Andes South American mountain range running through Colombia, Venezuela, Ecuador, Peru, Bolivia, Argentina and Chile.

Radical left Communists, militant labour unionists.

Labour union An organization of workers seeking improved pay and working conditions.

Liberation theology Latin American Catholic clergy movement, inspiring parishioners to work for change in this life, rather than waiting for their reward in heaven.

the pronouncements of liberation theologians. For example, El Salvador's Archbishop Óscar Romero (1917–80) said, 'When all peaceful means have been exhausted, the Church considers insurrection moral and justified.'

In 1980, Pope John Paul II visited Brazil, forbade the clergy from holding political office and condemned violence as a means of social change – and the liberation theology movement declined.

SOURCE D

An extract from the final document of the third conference of Latin American bishops at Puebla, Mexico, 1979, attended by Pope John Paul II. Quoted in *A History of Latin America: Independence to the Present, Volume 2*, eighth edition by Benjamin Keen and Keith Haynes, published by Houghton Mifflin, Boston, USA, 2009, page 307.

We identify as the most devastating and humiliating scourge, the situation of inhuman poverty in which millions of Latin Americans live, with starvation wages, unemployment and underemployment, malnutrition, infant mortality, lack of adequate housing, health problems, and labor unrest.

? Give reasons for and against the usefulness of Source D in any assessment of the situation of the indigenous populations of Latin America in 1979.

Economic problems

Economic problems triggered self-help movements among the indigenous populations. For example, **coca** grower unions in Bolivia campaigned for the right to earn a living from growing coca (see page 161).

Globalization

From the 1980s, **globalization** accelerated developments in Latin American culture and society. Technology and the mass media, along with migration from rural areas to cities, exposed the indigenous population to foreign ideas on individualism and civil rights.

Sympathetic governments

Some governments recognized that racial divisions, discrimination and inequality hampered national progress. Others simply sought indigenous support. The resultant government demonstrations of sympathy generated activism. For example, the socialistic military regime of General Velasco Alvarado (1968–75) in Peru gave the **Quechua** language equal status with Spanish and redistributed land to indigenous communities. This bequeathed a legacy of militancy and a heightened cultural and racial self-awareness among the Andean indigenous population.

In 1989, Convention 169 of the **International Labour Organization (ILO)** required governments to ensure the equality of indigenous peoples. Many Latin American governments ratified that convention, and several amended their **constitution** to recognize indigenous rights in 'multi-ethnic' and 'pluri-cultural' states. Even when governments were slow to recognize such rights in practice, as in Bolivia, government commitment to such rights provided a quasi-legal justification for increased indigenous assertiveness.

🔑 KEY TERM

Coca Leaf that can be used as a mild sedative or processed into cocaine. Coca tea is a traditional drink for most Andean natives.

Globalization Increasing internationalization of national economies, finance, trade and communications.

Quechua Member/language of an indigenous ethic group in Peru, Bolivia, Colombia, Ecuador and Chile.

International Labour Organization (ILO) An agency of the United Nations which seeks the promotion of social justice and internationally recognized human and labour rights.

Constitution The rules and system by which a country's government works.

From the 1990s, a series of progressive **left-wing** governments were elected in countries such as Argentina, Bolivia, Brazil, Chile, Ecuador, Paraguay, Uruguay and Venezuela. The governments of this **Pink Tide** focused on economic and social inequality and often worked to help indigenous peoples. For example, in Venezuela, Hugo Chavez introduced a new constitution that allocated three seats to the elected representatives of the indigenous peoples.

Methods for obtaining equality

The methods by which Latin American indigenous populations tried to gain equality included rebellions, organizations, publicity, protests and voting.

Rebellions and violence

Rebellions were a long-established but frequently unsuccessful means of protest, a notable exception being Bolivia in 1952 (see pages 157–9). Rebellions against the military governments of Guatemala (see pages 21–2) and Nicaragua gained little. Violence was often counter-productive, as in Peru.

In 1960, the indigenous **Aymara** and Quechua constituted around half of Peru's population. Most lived in poverty in the Andean highlands and were regarded as greatly inferior by the relatively prosperous coastal inhabitants. President Fernando Belaúnde Terry (1963–8) promised **agrarian reform** but did little. The indigenous peasant population therefore began to seize cultivated land, arguing that they had paid for it with their labour over the generations. In late 1963, the government sent in the military. Around 8000 peasants were killed, 3500 imprisoned and 19,000 forced to leave their homes.

Landlessness, unemployment and underemployment remained endemic in the highlands. A splinter group of the Peruvian **Communist** Party set up the **guerrilla** organization *Sendero Luminoso* (Shining Path) that from 1980 encouraged the peasantry to invade, occupy and rob élite-owned land. Shining Path waged guerrilla war on the 'establishment', including tax collectors and wealthy merchants. In 1982, the government responded with indiscriminate attacks on villages. From 1980 to 1988, an estimated and mostly innocent 15,000 peasants were killed, roughly half by the military and half by Shining Path. Eventually, Shining Path's violence totally alienated the peasantry.

Organizations

Organizations were usually more effective than rebellions. In the 1960s, the Brazilian government worked to convert the Amazon rainforest into farmland and cattle ranches. Indigenous peoples were killed or evicted. What the government described as 'integration', the indigenous population described as extermination. In 1973, some influential figures in the Catholic Church established the Indigenous Mission Council (CIMI), which organized meetings of indigenous chiefs in 1974, 1975 and 1976. At these meetings,

 **KEY TERM**

Left wing Those sympathetic to the ideas of socialism, under which system the national economy is controlled by the government to prevent extremes in wealth or poverty.

Pink Tide The left-wing governments elected in many Latin American countries from the end of the twentieth century.

Aymara Member and language of an indigenous ethnic group in Peru, Bolivia, Argentina and Chile.

Agrarian reform The Latin American indigenous population owned a disproportionately small amount of land. Sometimes governments redistributed the land to remedy this inequality.

Communist Believer in the economic system under which capitalism and the private ownership of property are rejected and the land and industry are controlled by the state in order to attain economic equality.

Guerrillas Groups of fighters who use tactics such as sabotage, raids and assassination, usually against governments.

massacres such as that perpetrated by ranchers in 1976 in the Brazilian state of Matto Grosso were denounced. CEBs (see page 13) brought people together to discuss legal tactics and form unions.

Unionization encouraged the Peruvian government to work to end forced labour and to redistribute land but, despite the 1964 Agrarian Law, the land tenure situation changed very little and the government became increasingly repressive. However, even when activists faced setbacks, their continuous pressure usually contributed to eventual improvement.

Publicity and protests

The effectiveness of publicity and protests was demonstrated in Bolivia, where the daughter of an impoverished highlands family with only six years of formal education, Domitila Barrios de Chúngara (1937–2012), drew worldwide attention to the plight of workers. In 1965, the average lifespan of a Bolivian tin miner was 35 years. If he died or was unable to work because of an industrial accident, his wife received no aid. Domitila led the Housewives' Committee of Siglo XX, established in 1961 to co-ordinate protest. She joined in labour movements, strikes and demonstrations aimed at improving working conditions for miners and creating jobs for women. Frequently arrested, she was mistreated and tortured in jail. After she attended the United Nations (UN) International Women's Year Tribunal in Mexico in 1975, she wrote *Let Me Speak!*, published in 1978 (see Source E). Her activism contributed to greater Bolivian government attention to workers' problems.

? How far would you trust the testimony of the activist Domitila Barrios de Chúngara in Source E about the dictator General Banzer?

SOURCE E

An extract from *Let Me Speak!* by Domitila Barrios de Chúngara, published by Monthly Review Press, New York, USA, 1978, page 187. She refers to the clash between a group of labour organizers and representatives of Bolivian dictator General Hugo Banzer (1971–8). Banzer's men had destroyed Siglo XX's radio transmitter in retaliation for a strike.

We women, like the workers, repudiate this attempt against our culture and our people … We won't stand for this treatment. And we demand you immediately return our property, which has cost us so much to get … General Banzer has taken office in a country where no one elected him. He came in through the force of arms, he killed a whole lot of people and among them are children and our comrades. He machine gunned the university; he repressed and goes on repressing a lot of people. Our resources are being turned over to foreigners, especially to Brazil. Now I ask you, which measure has been in favor of the working class?

Protests and publicity helped to internationalize the struggle for equality, which generated further publicity, as when Guatemalan indigenous leader Rigoberta Menchú won the 1992 Nobel Peace Prize and when the UN declared 1993 the International Year of the Indigenous Peoples of the World. In 2007, the third Continental Summit of Indigenous Nations and Peoples was held in Guatemala, and Guatemalan Mayans learned a great deal about effective protest from contacts with more militant Bolivian and Ecuadoran indigenous movements.

Enfranchisement

The vote was perhaps the most important method for gaining equality. Many indigenous people were illiterate and therefore disenfranchised in Peru until 1979 and in Ecuador until 1980. However, once they had the vote, more sympathetic politicians (including indigenous ones) could be elected, as in Bolivia in 2005 and Ecuador in 2006.

Continuing indigenous inequality

Racism, greed, cultural clashes, internal divisions, unsympathetic governments and financial issues made it difficult to end the long-standing poverty, deprivation and social inequality of the indigenous population.

← **Why has equality not been achieved?**

Racism

As the twentieth century progressed, official disapproval of racism increased. However, according to the historians Benjamin Keen and Keith Haynes (2009), the indigenous peoples remained 'the principal victims of racist exploitation and violence', which according to one estimate led to a decrease in Brazil's indigenous population from one million to 180,000 during the twentieth century. Around 1000 of the 9000 **Yanomamis** living in Brazil and 12,000 in Venezuela have been murdered since 1975, mostly by gold miners. Similar killings of Amerindians have been reported in Colombia, Mexico and Guatemala.

 **KEY TERM**

Yanomamis Amerindian tribe living in the Amazonian rainforest.

SOURCE F

An extract from *A History of Latin America: Independence to the Present, Volume 2*, eighth edition by Benjamin Keen and Keith Haynes, published by Houghton Mifflin, Boston, USA, 2009, page 303.

'The Indian problem,' writes Mexican sociologist Pablo González Casanova, 'is essentially one of internal colonialism. The Indian communities are Mexico's internal colonies … Here we find prejudice, discrimination, colonial forms of exploitation, dictatorial forms, and the separation of a different population, with a different race and culture.' Some Mexican social scientists claimed that Mexicans have long been blind to their own racism and discrimination. One cited a paragraph written in 1985 by a leading historian, Enrique Krauze: 'Mexico constructed a tradition of natural liberty and equality that was rooted in the culture of the people and freed us very early from slavery, servitude, and racism.' These revisionist scholars assigned much of the blame for this blindness to an indigenous policy that dated from the time of independence.

According to Source F, what is the position of revisionist Mexican scholars on 'the Indian problem' in Mexico?

Culture clashes and divisions

Divisions within the indigenous communities have been important, as in Bolivia where the Aymara and Quechua found it difficult to co-operate in campaigning for equality. Divisions within national communities made campaigns for indigenous rights problematic when some indigenous customs (arranged marriages, public beatings and the prohibition of land sales by individuals) were considered undesirable and unacceptable even by some indigenous people. Furthermore, many indigenous people lived outside their community in cities, where the implementation of their laws would clash with the other legal system.

Unsympathetic governments

Some governments were unsympathetic. For example, the dictatorial Somoza regime in Nicaragua killed thousands of indigenous peasantry, who were mobilized by Sandinista guerrillas. However, after the Somoza regime collapsed in 1979, the new Sandinista government sought the speedy assimilation of indigenous peoples into society. As a result, **Miskitos** rebelled and 15,000 fled into neighbouring Honduras.

Some of the Latin American governments most opposed to social reform were steadfastly supported by the USA, which valued their anti-Communism during the **Cold War**. In 1999, US President Bill Clinton visited Guatemala and apologized for US support for murderous right-wing Guatemalan governments (see pages 21–3).

Divergent interest groups

Even sympathetic governments struggled to balance the interests of the indigenous population and national prosperity, as in Peru, where Quechua Alejandro Toledo, elected president in 2001, displeased other Quechua when he allowed the privatization of oil and gas discovered in the Amazon region. In 2009, during the presidency of Alan García Pérez, police clashed with indigenous activists over the exploration. Thirty people died. Many cities erupted in violent demonstrations by students and labour unions against a free trade pact with the USA that gave rights to foreign companies in the Peruvian rainforest without the consultation with the indigenous peoples mandated by the ILO Convention 169 (see pages 14–15) and ratified by Peru. The indigenous protesters said they had the right to determine the future of their ancestral homelands. President García said the natural resources were vital to Peru's development and belonged to all Peruvians.

How do Mexico and Guatemala illustrate the problems faced by the indigenous populations of Latin America after 1945?

→ Case studies of indigenous populations in Latin America

Case study: Mexico and mestizo domination

In the late nineteenth century, police turned Indians away from Mexico City's centre on state occasions, so that foreigners would not see them. The indigenous population had long suffered such discrimination and

KEY TERM

Miskitos Indigenous population resident on the Nicaraguan and Honduran coasts.

Cold War The state of extreme tension between the capitalist USA and Communist USSR and their allies 1945–91.

humiliation, along with deprivation, at the hands of mestizos and whites. From the late 1930s, Mexican governments tried to protect indigenous languages and cultures. *Caciques* and village councils had some of their traditional authority restored, and native children were often educated in bilingual schools. However, the indigenous population remained impoverished and dissatisfied and turned to organizations, especially in the 1970s.

COCEI

In 1974, the indigenous peasantry and students established the Coalition of Workers, Peasants and Students (COCEI) in Oaxaca, which had a long tradition of indigenous rebellion over land rights. COCEI demanded the restoration of land, electoral democracy, the defence of **Zapotec** culture and economic self-government. COCEI candidates in municipal elections were fraudulently deprived of victory in 1974, 1977 and in 1980, when COCEI formed a **popular front** with the Communist Party. After great protests and publicity, the COCEI candidate, Leopoldo de Gyves, became mayor of Juchitán. He helped to revive Zapotec culture and made speeches in the native language until the state government overthrew him in 1982.

> **Feet and race**
> The Mexican government found it hard to distinguish the indigenous population from mestizos. According to the 1943 census, those wearing shoes were mestizos, those without were indigenous people. This criterion was only finally deleted in the 1980 census.

UCEZ

In western Mexico in 1979, the Unión de Comuneros Emiliano Zapata (UCEZ) was established to defend indigenous property and communal cultural traditions. Supported by some members of the Catholic clergy and leftist political parties, UCEZ provided legal aid and organized mass meetings to articulate and publicize grievances. It refused to participate in electoral politics but was popular and effective. For example, it forced the resignation of the corrupt delegates of the Ministry of Agrarian Reform in Michoacán.

The Chiapas rebellion

Alan Sandstrom studied indigenous villages in the 1990s. He noted that the indigenous population remained disproportionately poor, were considered 'backward' by 'many' urbanized Mexicans, and reflected Mexican racial prejudice in that even they favoured children with lighter hair and skin. Continuing discontent was demonstrated in Chiapas, a predominantly rural state with a large indigenous population and one of the lowest literacy rates in Mexico, and where the great landowners still owned around 40 per cent of the land. Although Chiapas produced a large proportion of Mexico's electricity supply, 70 per cent of the local population went without.

KEY TERM

Caciques Local leaders of indigenous groups.

Zapotec Indigenous people in Mexico's Oaxaca province.

Popular front Alliance of several leftist parties.

In January 1994, around 12,000 guerrillas led by a council of 24 **Mayan** commanders and calling themselves the Zapatista Army of National Liberation (EZLN) took control of three cities in Chiapas and demanded self-rule for indigenous communities. A counter-offensive of 14,000 Mexican army troops was launched, using aerial bombing of villages, executions without trial and torture of suspects. Hundreds of guerrillas were wounded and 145 died. The EZLN was quickly forced out of the cities, but the uprising continued for several years, during which time landless *campesinos* occupied nearly 100,000 acres of farmland (prompting over 100 wealthy landowners to stage a hunger strike in Mexico City). The number of civilian deaths caused considerable national unease and a 100,000-strong protest march in Mexico City forced the government to halt the military operation.

The Chiapas rebellion demonstrated the importance of assistance from outside the indigenous population, as shown in the roles of Bishop Samuel Ruiz, who vociferously defended the poor Mayan *campesinos* in his diocese of San Cristóbal de las Casas in Chiapas, and Subcomandante Marcos.

Subcomandante Marcos

White, pipe-smoking Subcomandante Marcos was a guerrilla leader in the Chiapas rebellion, which he attributed to '500 years of poverty and exploitation'. In Marcos, who many think is a former university professor, Mexico's Mayans acquired a spokesman of international renown who expertly manipulated the media to gain national and international attention for their plight. Such was his charisma that hundreds of women proposed marriage to him.

SOURCE G

Masked, white guerrilla leader Subcomandante Marcos, champion of the indigenous poor in the Mexican province of Chiapas, talking on the microphone, photographed in 2001.

Research Subcomandante Marcos, shown in Source G. Suggest reasons why he wears the mask.

In 2000, newly elected president Vicente Fox, keen to grant indigenous communities greater self-government, withdrew the military from Chiapas, and ordered the release of jailed rebels. Chiapas remained restless and in spring 2001, Subcomandante Marcos led an EZLN march to Mexico City in order to demand indigenous autonomy and control of their resources. *En route*, they were greeted by thousands of supporters and received petitions (see Source H). The Mexican Congress was unhelpful and indigenous communities remained at the mercy of paramilitaries paid by the great landowners and conservative politicians. Despite their organizations, protests and guerrilla activities, 'Indians continue to have second-class status' in Mexico, according to historian Burton Kirkwood (2005).

SOURCE H

An extract from 'The Declaration of the Indigenous Peoples of Morelos', given to the Zapatista Army of National Liberation marchers in 2001. Quoted in *A History of Latin America: Independence to the Present, Volume 2*, eighth edition by Benjamin Keen and Keith Haynes, published by Houghton Mifflin, Boston, USA, 2009, page 303.

*What do we want and demand? To be treated with respect as indigenous peoples. That we should not be jailed for defending our land ... An end to industrial and commercial megaprojects in communal ... land. An end to the destruction of our forests, waters, and natural resources. An end to the **neoliberal** modernization that is causing the disappearance of the indigenous peoples. That we be taken into account when decisions are made. We want to be part of development, not a simple rung on which others step for their development.*

> In what ways does the declaration in Source H suggest indigenous inequality and how far would you trust its assessment of the indigenous situation in Mexico? **?**

> **⚸ KEY TERM**
>
> **Neoliberal** Proponent of an economic system that promotes free trade and private business rather than government intervention to deal with inequality.

Case study: the Guatemalan indigenous population and genocide

In 1945, Guatemala was one of the poorest Latin American nations; two per cent of the population controlled 74 per cent of the arable land. The indigenous Mayan majority was mostly illiterate, with a life expectancy of less than 40, and the highest infant mortality rate in the Americas (over 50 per cent). The election of Juan José Arévalo in 1944 led to 10 years of democracy. The vagrancy law under which most of the indigenous population were forced to work on the estates of the white and mestizo élite was abolished, land was redistributed, authority devolved to village committees and racial discrimination criminalized.

Agrarian reform

Under Arévalo's successor, Jacobo Árbenz, an agrarian reform law (1952) was passed because the peasantry had been mobilized by the Guatemalan National Peasant Confederation (CNCG), which had nearly 250,000 members and had contributed to a great increase in indigenous peasant uprisings. As a result of the agrarian reform, over 100,000 peasant families received land, credit and technical aid from new state agencies by 1954. Middle-class anxiety about 'the rise of the Indians against civilization' and

Oligarchy Government by a privileged few.

Scorched-earth campaign Destruction of crops so the population lacks food.

Genocide Deliberate destruction of an ethnic group.

the impact of land redistribution on the influential US-owned United Fruit Company were important factors in the US-supported overthrow of Árbenz in 1954 and the reversal of the land reform. Once power was returned to the traditional **oligarchy**, peasant unions became illegal.

Repression

Democracy ended in 1954 and under a series of white and mestizo military dictatorships and a civil war that lasted nearly four decades (1960–96), Guatemala's indigenous population struggled to survive. Over 200,000 died.

Although ethnic tensions and clashes over land were more important, the persecution of the mostly indigenous peasantry was justified as part of 'fighting Communism'. That prompted increased US aid to the Guatemalan government. In 1967, the Guatemalan military, deployed by Defence Minister Colonel Rafael Arriaga Bosque and assisted by the US military, launched its first **scorched-earth campaign**, in which around 8000 civilians were killed in order to defeat around 300 guerrillas. The US embassy described Arriaga Bosque as one of Guatemala's 'most effective and enlightened leaders'.

Organizations

The indigenous population of Guatemala was never passive in the face of government hostility. The powerful Committee of Peasant Unity (CUC) developed out of a variety of groups such as peasant leagues, Mayan cultural associations and CEBs (see page 13). By 1980, it organized 150,000 workers in strikes that halted cotton and sugar export production and gained wage increases. In the 1980s, Mayan guerrilla groups wrought considerable damage on the Guatemalan economy.

Genocide?

Increased guerrilla activity prompted the governments of Lucas García (1978–82) and the Pentecostal lay minister General Efraín Ríos Montt (1982–3) to try to pacify 'Indian barbarism' in the countryside. Ríos Montt declared that his presidency was the 'will of God' and told Guatemala's indigenous population, 'If you are with us, we will feed you; if not, we will kill you.' In his scorched earth policy against the indigenous majority, the Guatemalan military systematically eliminated entire indigenous communities, supposedly in order to eliminate the guerrillas. By 1983, the army controlled the countryside. Although the violence peaked between 1981 and 1983, the civil war continued until 1996, when the Guatemalan government and the coalition representing four guerrilla groups signed a peace agreement.

In 1997, a UN commission concluded that Mayans were killed because they were Mayan, not because the army believed that they were the support base of the guerrillas, and that this was **genocide**. The commission found that 200,000 Mayans had been killed, tens of thousands tortured, and even more made homeless and landless as hundreds of Mayan villages were eliminated. 40,000 people 'disappeared' and around 200,000 Guatemalans fled to

Chiapas in Mexico. The Catholic Church estimated that more than one million people (15 per cent of the population) had been displaced, some temporarily, some permanently.

SOURCE I

Guatemalan photographer Daniel Hernández-Salazar's photograph for the Catholic Church's 1998 report on the genocide in Guatemala entitled, 'So That All Shall Know'. Combined with the image of a naked man, the bones were those of a victim of the civil war.

What message is the photographer trying to get across in the image in Source I?

SOURCE J

An extract from a declassified cable dated 21 October 1982, sent by the US embassy in Guatemala to the US Secretary of State. Printed in *The Guatemala Reader* edited by Greg Grandin et al., published by Duke University Press, Durham, USA, 2011, pages 382–3.

Why might the US embassy's analysis in Source J have been incorrect?

The Embassy has analyzed reports made in the U.S. by Amnesty International, the Washington Office on Latin America and the Network in Solidarity with the People of Guatemala and the Guatemalan Human Rights Commission. We conclude that a concerted disinformation campaign is being waged in the US against the Guatemalan government by groups supporting the Communist insurgency in Guatemala. This has enlisted the support of conscientious human rights and church organizations which may not fully appreciate that they are being utilized. This is a campaign in which guerrilla mayhem and violations of human rights are ignored … The campaign's object is simple: to deny the Guatemalan army the weapons and equipment needed from the US to defeat the guerrillas … .

Survival and revival

Despite the genocide, the indigenous population survived and revived. Indigenous peoples still constituted roughly half of the population and became far more organized and vocal, encouraged by the 1992 Nobel Peace Prize awarded to indigenous Guatemalan activist Rigoberta Menchú for raising awareness of indigenous rights. In 1993, thousands of indigenous Guatemalans marched in the nation's capital, contributing to a renaissance of Mayan culture. The 1996 peace agreements committed the Guatemalan government to recognize the identity and rights of the indigenous populations, but the government did not live up to all of its promises and disillusioned activists talked of creating an indigenous Guatemalan nation.

? Does it matter to someone studying the treatment of indigenous Guatemalans whether Rigoberta Menchú included some events she never witnessed and greatly exaggerated others?

I, Rigoberta Menchú

Nobel Peace Prize winner Rigoberta Menchú's Mayan family were first mobilized by a Catholic Action group, then by CUC (see page 22), and finally by guerrillas (see page 22). As a 23 year old, she wrote a very dramatic account of the persecution of Guatemalan Indians, *My Name is Rigoberta Menchú and This is How My Consciousness was Raised* (1983), which was translated into many languages. Some questioned its accuracy, but it turned world attention to the persecution of indigenous people, especially the Guatemalan genocide.

Rigoberta Menchú said, 'My story is the story of all poor Guatemalans. My personal experience is the experience of a whole people.' In 1999, US anthropologist David Stoll's response to her book, *Rigoberta Menchú and the Story of All Poor Guatemalans*, argued that she included events she never witnessed and greatly exaggerated others. Stoll was criticized by other anthropologists who pointed out that many of the indigenous population did die, and her book did reflect the hardship and terrors faced by them.

The twenty-first century

In 2005, the government announced programmes to publicize Mayan culture, yet simultaneously the military was violently evicting rural Mayans from farms that they had been occupying for three years. More than half of Guatemalans lived in chronic poverty, one-fifth in extreme poverty. Land distribution remained highly inequitable. The average Mayan life expectancy was 45 years, compared to 61 for other Guatemalans. The indigenous infant mortality rate remained twice that of the non-indigenous population and three-quarters of Mayan children suffered from malnutrition. Only one-tenth of the indigenous population was literate. According to the historian Thomas Pearcy (2006), there is still 'ethnic hatred' in Guatemala.

SOURCE K

Rigoberta Menchú (centre) in a bus station during a 30-hour tour of different neighbourhoods of Guatemala City in November 2011.

What is the significance of Rigoberta Menchú's clothing in Source K?

Indigenous populations in Latin America: conclusions

Have the indigenous populations attained equality?

Writing in 2010, historian Teresa Meade wrote that with the aid of radical church groups, reformist political parties and domestic and international agencies, 'a new agenda is in motion' in Latin America, calling for greater equality and redress for centuries of abuse of indigenous peoples. Writing in 2000, historian John Kicza gave a similarly hopeful assessment of the situation of the indigenous population of Latin America (see Source L). However, while their situation has certainly improved since 1945, there is still a long way to go before the indigenous population attains full equality. Ultimately, as the historian Guillermo de la Peña noted in 1998, they are 'still the most underprivileged sector in Latin American society'.

SOURCE L

An extract from *The Indian in Latin American History: Resistance, Resilience and Acculturation*, edited by John Kicza, published by SR Books, Wilmington, USA, 1999, page xviii.

The native peoples of the Americas have displayed remarkable cultural resilience in the face of demographic catastrophes; loss of land and local political autonomy; recurrent infusions of outside technologies, animals, foods, and procedures over the centuries; and disrespectful treatment of their values and ways of life by the governments and citizens of those nations into which they have been merged. To the extent possible, Indian peoples have been selective about what aspects of the outside world they incorporate into their cultures. The indigenous communities have not been without resources. They have used their

According to Source L, what problems have native peoples of the Americas faced, and how and with what success have they handled them? How far would you agree with the assertions in Source L?

internal unity … to incorporate the changes forced upon them on the best terms that they could muster. Nor were they cowed or passive before the impositions of colonial and national governments. Both individual Indians and Indian corporations commonly initiated petitions and lawsuits to demand remedies for perceived injustices. Local rebellions by native peoples were endemic in large parts of Latin America over the centuries; some indigenous communities had well-earned reputations for insurrection. Occasionally, these rebellions became widespread and threatened major regions and even national governments. Through a combination of selective adaptation and peaceful (or sometimes violent) resistance, the native peoples of Latin America… have been making their own histories for 500 years.

Latin American Indians have been so successful in drawing upon their own resources and capacities that today their numbers are growing and they constitute a majority of the population in countries such as Guatemala and Bolivia and a substantial plurality in Mexico, Ecuador, and Peru. Even in countries where they do not make up a large part of the population – Brazil, Colombia, and Chile, for example – native peoples have been able to assert their rights and claims and make the national societies come to grips with the issues of native autonomy and control over land and other resources.

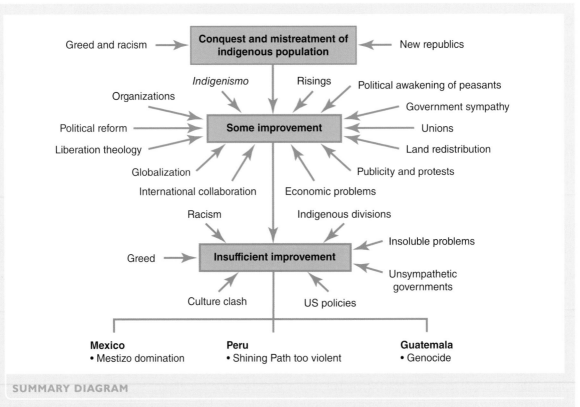

The indigenous population in Latin America

2 Native Americans in the USA

▶ *Key question: How and to what extent did Native Americans achieve equality in the USA after 1945?*

Background: Native Americans in the USA before 1945

What was the situation of Native Americans before 1945?

During the seventeenth century, Europeans created settlements on North America's east coast. They treated Native Americans as inferior and took their lands. The 13 American colonies declared independence from Britain in a Declaration of Independence (1776) that stated 'all men are created equal'. However, those that the Declaration called 'merciless Indian Savages' were not given citizenship in the new United States of America.

Native Americans in the nineteenth-century USA

In the nineteenth century, white Americans moved westward and through a combination of force and treaties took possession of Indian lands. Native American tribes were either decimated or militarily defeated and placed on **reservations** on land whites did not want. Many Native American children were taken away from their parents and 'civilized' in federal-funded boarding schools in the 1880s.

Native Americans in the USA 1900–45

Successive US governments were either uninterested in or actively hostile to the defeated Native Americans. They were finally granted citizenship in 1924, but this had few practical advantages. Their death rate exceeded their birth rate and a 1928 **federal government** report detailed disease, discontent and great poverty, all exacerbated after 1929 by the **Great Depression**. They suffered terrible racism. For example, from 1931 the state of Vermont sterilized disproportionate numbers of the Abenaki tribe because they were supposedly 'immoral', 'criminal' or 'suspected feeble-minded' (as late as 1973–6, according to the General Accounting Office of Congress, 3406 women were sterilized without their permission).

The Roosevelt years 1933–45

The increasingly desperate Native American situation aroused some white sympathy. **Democrat** President Franklin D. Roosevelt's Commissioner for Indian Affairs, John Collier, assisted the preservation of Indian culture through educational programmes and sponsored the Indian Reorganization Act (1934), which restored some tribal control over reservation land and facilitated federal loans to struggling tribes. Collier persuaded **Congress** that Native American schoolchildren should not be forced to attend Christian church services and that tribes should be allowed to practise their traditional religion. Collier got Congress to stop trying to halt the use of peyote, a

🔑 **KEY TERM**

Reservation An area of land set aside for Native American tribes in the nineteenth century.

Federal government The USA is a federal state, where political power is divided between the federal government (consisting of the President, Congress and the Supreme Court, all located in Washington, DC) and the states.

Great Depression Worldwide economic depression which began in 1929 and lasted for around 10 years.

Democrat The Democratic Party favours government intervention on behalf of the less fortunate.

Congress Legislative branch of US government, consisting of the Senate and the House of Representatives.

substance obtained from a cactus that produced hallucinatory visions. The **Bureau of Indian Affairs (BIA)** employed more Native Americans, and tribes acquired more land, better medical services, larger federal grants and renewed pride in their culture.

Why and with what results did Native American activism increase after 1945?

Native Americans in the USA 1945–60

The impact of the Second World War

In the Second World War, around 75,000 Native Americans left the reservations to serve in the armed forces and work in defence industries. They returned with increased rights consciousness. For example, they criticized the white-dominated BIA for dictatorial meddling, such as banning alcohol (until 1953).

The Truman years 1945–53

Initially, Democrat President Truman continued Roosevelt's sympathetic policies and Congress created the Indian Claims Commission, which aimed to compensate Native Americans for previous unjust land loss. From 1946 to 1968, the commission distributed around $400 million, which contributed to tribal economic development. Ironically, according to Native American historian Donald Fixico (2004), although intended to 'solve' the 'Indian problem', the commission 'mobilized and solidified Native people while making them keenly aware of the government's long history of unfulfilled obligations'.

In 1950, Truman appointed Dillon Myer as commissioner. Myer intervened in tribal affairs in a dictatorial fashion. For example, he sold **Pueblo** tribal land without their consent. He tried to break up reservations and scatter the people. His relocation programme aimed to get Native Americans jobs in the cities, but many ended up on welfare and one-third returned to their reservations. Native Americans felt Myer was trying to destroy their civilization and asked that jobs be brought to reservations.

The Eisenhower years 1953–61

Native American historian Angie Debo (1995) described the presidency of **Republican** Dwight D. Eisenhower (1953–61) as 'back to the bad old days'.

Termination of reservations

Congress disliked tribal self-government and in 1953 increased the state governments' jurisdiction over reservations. In order to try to stop taxpayers having to subsidize Native Americans, and to release reservation lands for white economic development, Congress 'terminated' some reservations, especially where the Natives were few, poor, and on land that might prove valuable to white men. For example, scattered bands of poor, illiterate Utah Paiutes were 'terminated' because it was believed there was oil and uranium on their land.

Lack of progress

Indians made less progress than African Americans in the Eisenhower years because:

- African Americans had more contact with whites and used white traditions such as national organization and litigation (see Chapter 2).
- Native Americans were fewer, less urbanized, and culturally disoriented.
- Separate tribes and geographical segregation worked against effective national organizations and made Native Americans easier prey for an administration that preached the virtues of self-help and minimal federal intervention.

The Cold War retarded Native American progress because it generated pressure for conformity and consensus, and a desire to promote assimilation to US culture. Viewing reservations as divisive and racist, some white liberals sought integration for Native Americans and encouraged Eisenhower's 'termination' programme.

Increased Native American assertiveness 1960–80

← **How and why were Native Americans more assertive in 1960–80?**

Continued Native American problems

Reservation poverty, unemployment, poor housing and education were an embarrassment to the world's richest nation. Half of the 700,000 Native American population lived short, hard lives on the reservations, where unemployment ranged from 20 to 80 per cent and life expectancy in 1968 was 44 years (the national average was 64). Native Americans had exceptionally high rates of suicide and alcoholism. Their continuing deprivation was championed by presidential candidate Robert Kennedy, who publicized appalling poverty on Native American reservations in Oklahoma and New York State in 1968.

Native Americans gravitated to the cities but poor education ensured low-paying jobs, poor housing, poor schools and a high crime rate.

National Congress of American Indians

Impressed by the progress of the National Association for the Advancement of Colored People (NAACP) (see pages 55–6), Native Americans established the first pan-Indian movement, the National Congress of American Indians (NCAI), in 1944. The NCAI was invigorated by Eisenhower's termination policy, helped to bring about its end in 1958, then persuaded President Kennedy (1961–3) to promise more jobs on reservations. The NCAI copied NAACP's litigation strategy, suing state and federal governments over discrimination in employment and schooling and for breaking treaties. The NCAI did not seek integration into US society but worked for the survival of the separate Native American cultural identity.

Rights revolution
Increasingly assertive
movements for equal rights
for minorities and women in
the 1960s.

Direct action Physical
protest, such as occupation
of land.

Uncle Tom Uncle Tom in
Harriet Beecher Stowe's
novel *Uncle Tom's Cabin*
(1852) was perceived as
excessively deferential to
whites by twentieth-century
African Americans, who
described obsequious
contemporaries as Uncle
Toms.

USSR Union of Soviet
Socialist Republics, the name
given to Russia from 1922,
also known as the Soviet
Union.

Sit-ins African American
protesters sat in and refused
to move from white-only
restaurants in the mid-
twentieth century.

Supreme Court The
judicial branch of the federal
government, which rules on
the constitutionality of actions
and laws.

Ghettos Areas in cities
inhabited mostly or solely by
(usually poor) members of a
particular ethnicity or
nationality.

During the 1960s' **rights revolution** Natives gained in self-confidence and became more assertive, using **direct action** to attain their goals, and asking to be called Native Americans rather than Indians. They became increasingly critical of the BIA, and NCAI leaders who co-operated with it were despised as 'apples' (red on the outside but white on the inside) or 'Uncle Tomahawks' (a variant on the African American '**Uncle Tom**').

National Indian Youth Council

In 1961, 500 tribal and urban Native American leaders attended a national conference of Native political organizations in Chicago. This inspired some young, college-educated Native Americans to organize the National Indian Youth Council (NIYC).

Treaty rights

Over the centuries, the US government made and then broke several hundred treaties with Native Americans. In 1969, Vine Deloria Jr wrote a bestseller, *Custer Died for Your Sins: An Indian Manifesto*, in which he quoted President Lyndon Johnson talking about US 'commitments' and President Richard Nixon decrying the failure of the **USSR** to respect treaties: 'Indian people laugh themselves sick when they hear these statements.' Native Americans began to draw attention to broken treaties.

Native Americans directed their protests against all levels of government. An old Washington state treaty took Native American land but left them exclusive fishing areas. State courts closed river areas to Native American fishermen in 1964. Inspired by African American **sit-ins** (see page 73), the NIYC staged a 'fish-in' to remind white Americans of Native American treaty rights. In 1968 the **Supreme Court** ruled in favour of Native rights under the treaty, but said that the state could 'regulate all fishing' so long as it did not discriminate against the Native Americans. Washington state authorities ignored the ruling and continued to arrest Indian fishermen. Protests, raids and arrests continued into the 1970s.

Red Power and American Indian Movement

Inspired by the separatist Black Power movement (see pages 108–16), a Red Power movement developed. 'We do not want to be pushed into the mainstream of American life', said the NIYC president. NCAI's director defined Red Power as 'the political and economic power to run our own lives in our own way'. Red Power militants used a variety of methods to achieve their aims, including monitoring police racism, establishing survival schools, gaining publicity through occupations, protest marches and writing, and litigation. Most militant of all was the American Indian Movement (AIM).

AIM in the ghettos

AIM developed in one of the few Native American big-city **ghettos**, in Minneapolis–St Paul, in 1968. When young AIM members monitored police racism, the Native American population in the local jails dropped by 60 per cent. With 40 **chapters** across the USA and Canada, AIM worked to improve ghetto housing, education and employment, and attracted members from the reservations. AIM stressed positive imagery, and attacked white use of names such as the 'Washington Redskins' football team: 'Even the name Indian is not ours. It was given to us by some dumb honky [white] who got lost and thought he'd landed in India.' AIM was important in one of the most famous examples of Indian activism, at Wounded Knee (see page 32), after which it established **survival schools**. Schools such as Heart of the Earth Survival School, established by AIM in Minneapolis in 1972, instructed urban children in Native languages and culture.

Occupation

Occupation was an effective way to gain publicity.

IAT and the occupation of Alcatraz, November 1969 to June 1971

Alcatraz Island was an unused federal prison in San Francisco Bay. Inspired by the loss of San Francisco's Indian Center, 14 members of the Indians of All Tribes (IAT) occupied the island in 1969 and made headlines. Within a month, over 600 Native Americans from over 50 different tribes occupied Alcatraz. After the federal government cut off telephones, electricity and water, most left. Federal forces then invaded the island and physically evicted the remainder.

SOURCE M

An extract from the Proclamation of the 'Indians of All Tribes' from Alcatraz in 1969, quoted at http://foundsf.org/index.php?title= ALCATRAZ_Proclamation

We feel that this so-called Alcatraz Island is more than suitable for an Indian reservation, as determined by the white man's own standards. By this we mean that this place resembles most Indian reservations in that:

1. *It is isolated from modern facilities, and without adequate means of transportation.*
2. *It has no fresh running water.*
3. *The sanitation facilities are inadequate …*
5. *There is no industry and so unemployment is very great.*
6. *There are no health care facilities.*
7. *The soil is rocky and non-productive and the land does not support game.*
8. *There are no educational facilities.*
9. *The population has always exceeded the land base.*
10. *The population has always been held as prisoners and dependent upon others.*

… We will work to de-pollute the air and waters in the Bay Area… [and to] restore fish and animal life.

KEY TERM

Chapters Local branches of a national organization.

Survival schools Under Title IV of the Indian Education Act (1972), Native Americans could control their children's education.

How effective is this proclamation in Source M? Give reasons for your answer.

AIM, the Trail of Broken Treaties and the occupation of the BIA 1972

In 1972, AIM activists marched from San Francisco to Washington, DC along what they called 'The Trail of Broken Treaties', in order to publicize the need for compensation for multiple US government violations of nineteenth-century treaties with Native Americans. The protesters occupied the BIA building in Washington. The Nixon administration took notice (see page 33).

AIM and the occupation of Wounded Knee 1973

In 1890, **Sioux** people were massacred at the village of Wounded Knee on the Pine Ridge Reservation. In 1973, Wounded Knee was occupied by around 300 Sioux people in order to publicize the reservation's problems. It had over 50 per cent unemployment and exceptionally high suicide and alcoholism rates. Life expectancy was only 46 years. The trigger event for the occupation of Wounded Knee was the killing of Wesley Bad Heart Bull by a white man whose indictment for manslaughter could have led to his release within a decade. When the murdered man's mother protested, she was arrested on a charge that could have led to 30 years' incarceration.

The occupation force demanded free elections of tribal leaders, an investigation of the BIA, and the review of all treaties. Many of the protesters were members of AIM, brought in, according to a female participant, 'because our men were scared. It was mostly the women that went forward and spoke out'. Several hostages were held at gunpoint and heavily armed federal forces quickly besieged Wounded Knee. Two Natives were killed. After 71 days, peace was agreed and the federal government promised an investigatory commission. Although the commission said the 1868 treaty was superseded by the federal government's power to take land, the occupation paid off. The federal government became more sensitive to Native American concerns.

Writers

Writers such as Vine Deloria Jr (*Custer Died for Your Sins*, 1969) and Dee Brown (*Bury My Heart at Wounded Knee*, 1971) raised national awareness of the mistreatment of Native Americans.

SOURCE N

An extract from the Mohawk newspaper *Akwesasne Notes* by Vine Deloria Jr (1968), quoted in *A People's History of the United States* by Howard Zinn, published by Longman, Harlow, UK, 1996, page 517.

Every now and then I am impressed with the thinking of the non-Indian. I was in Cleveland last year and got to talking with a non-Indian about American history. He said that he was really sorry about what has happened to Indians, but that there was a good reason for it. The continent had to be developed and he felt that Indians had stood in the way, and thus had had to be removed. 'After all,' he remarked, 'what did you do with the land when you had it?' I didn't

KEY TERM

Sioux Native American tribe, mostly resident in the Great Plains.

Mohawk Native American, resident on the US and Canadian east coasts.

According to Source N, what is the typical non-Indian view of the history of the American Indian? How does the writer ridicule that view?

understand him until later when I discovered that the Cuyahoga River running through Cleveland is inflammable. So many combustible pollutants are dumped into the river that the inhabitants have to take special precautions during the summer to avoid setting it on fire. After reviewing the argument of my non-Indian friend I decided that he was probably correct. Whites had made better use of the land. How many Indians could have thought of creating an inflammable river?

Litigation

Native American lawyers gained some successes in the law courts, as shown over mineral rights. Traditionally, the federal government leased mineral rights on reservations to private companies and Native Americans gained little. In 1973, the Northern **Cheyenne** of Montana won a federal court victory enabling them to renegotiate mineral contracts. Sometimes, victories took time. In 2005, the Peabody Coal Company had to stop mining on **Navajo and Hopi** reservation lands after 50 years of protests, controversy and litigation.

The federal government and Native Americans 1960–80

Increased Native American assertiveness made the federal government more helpful.

President Lyndon Johnson (1963–9) and Native Americans

Native Americans were among the greatest beneficiaries of Johnson's **War on Poverty**, although some of them disliked the resulting **welfare dependency** culture. Johnson appointed a Native American to head the BIA in 1966, and his 1968 Civil Rights Act contained an 'Indian Bill of Rights', designed to protect Native Americans from both white and tribal dictatorship. It faciliated access to better health services, housing, education, welfare and poverty benefits, and employment (Native Americans had to rely heavily on federal job creation schemes as the limited pool of skilled workers, poor communications and distance from markets made reservations unattractive to private industry). However, some Native Americans resented the interference in tribal affairs.

President Richard Nixon (1969–74) and the Self-Determination Act

In 1975, Congress passed Nixon's Indian Self-Determination Act, which restored the special legal status of Native American tribes. It gave them most of the powers exercised by state governments, some control over federal programmes on their lands, and increased control over education.

KEY TERM

Cheyenne Native American tribe in the western USA.

Navajo and Hopi Native Americans of Arizona, Utah and New Mexico.

War on Poverty President Johnson's programmes to help the poor, e.g. Social Security Act (1965).

Welfare dependency Reliance on federal aid.

← How did the federal government respond to increased Native American assertiveness?

Look at Source O. Other than a natural increase in population, what might explain the dramatic increase in persons describing themselves as 'Indians' to census-takers?

SOURCE O

US Indian population – census details.

1960 – 523,591

1970 – 792,730

1980 – 1.37 million

1990 – 1.8 million

Court decisions

In response to Native American litigation, the Supreme Court recognized the 'unique and limited' sovereignty of Native American tribes in *US v. Wheeler* (1978). Court decisions in 1979 resulted in the restoration of 1800 acres (730 ha) to **Narrangansetts** in Rhode Island and $100 million compensation to the Sioux for 'dishonourable dealing' in the acquisition of the Black Hills in South Dakota (the Sioux rejected the money and demanded the land instead).

Ironically, as historian Paula Marks (1998) noted, 'All of this governmental activity to address Indian problems and concerns actually fed activism rather than defused it.'

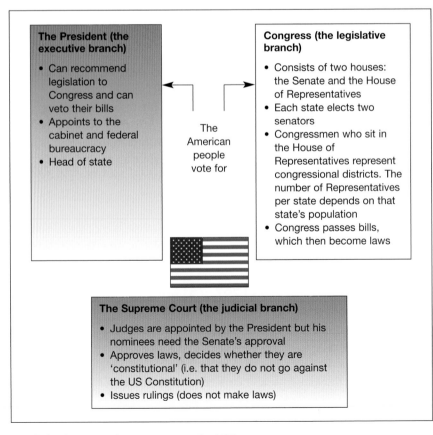

The President (the executive branch)

- Can recommend legislation to Congress and can veto their bills
- Appoints to the cabinet and federal bureaucracy
- Head of state

The American people vote for

Congress (the legislative branch)

- Consists of two houses: the Senate and the House of Representatives
- Each state elects two senators
- Congressmen who sit in the House of Representatives represent congressional districts. The number of Representatives per state depends on that state's population
- Congress passes bills, which then become laws

The Supreme Court (the judicial branch)

- Judges are appointed by the President but his nominees need the Senate's approval
- Approves laws, decides whether they are 'constitutional' (i.e. that they do not go against the US Constitution)
- Issues rulings (does not make laws)

The federal system of government in the USA

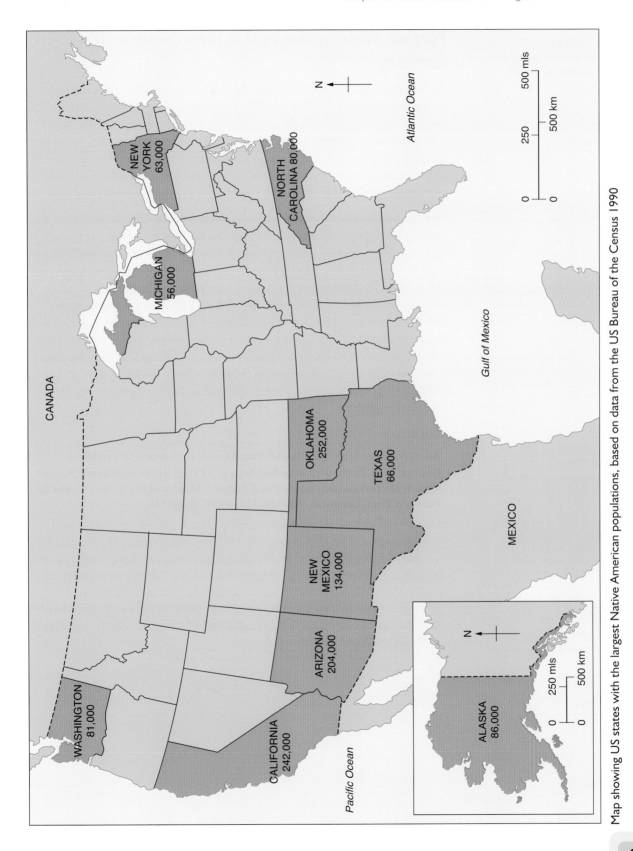

WASHINGTON 81,000

CALIFORNIA 242,000

ARIZONA 204,000

NEW MEXICO 134,000

OKLAHOMA 252,000

TEXAS 66,000

MICHIGAN 56,000

NEW YORK 63,000

NORTH CAROLINA 80,000

CANADA

MEXICO

Gulf of Mexico

Atlantic Ocean

Pacific Ocean

N

500 mls
250
0

500 km
0

ALASKA 86,000

N

250 mls
0

500 km
0

Map showing US states with the largest Native American populations, based on data from the US Bureau of the Census 1990

→ Native Americans in the late twentieth century

By the end of the twentieth century the USA contained 2.5 million Native Americans (one per cent of the national population), a quarter of whom lived on reservations. With greater pride in their ethnicity and protection from the federal government, their lives had improved since 1945. However, although their income had improved by a third during the 1990s, it was still only half the national average. Their disease, poverty, unemployment, suicide and alcoholism rates remained the highest of all ethnic groups.

Problems with self-government remained (see Source P). Native Americans continued to clash with state and federal authorities over land rights and customs. The American Indian Religious Freedom Act (1978) was 'effectively gutted' (Donald Fixico, 2004) by the increasingly conservative Supreme Court, which in 1990 refused to review a decision restricting the use of peyote. Under the unsympathetic Republican President Ronald Reagan (1981–9), self-determination was interpreted as justification for a decrease in federal financial aid. In contrast, under the Democrat President Bill Clinton (1993–2001), the 1996 Native American Housing and Self-Determination Act (NAHASDA) gave block grants to allow tribes to build their own housing and thereby attract unsuccessful urban Native Americans back to the reservations.

SOURCE P

What point is Source P making? Is it effective?

An extract from an open letter from Native Americans to President George H.W. Bush, who attacked Iraq in 1991 in order to liberate Kuwait from Iraqi occupation, quoted in *A People's History of the United States* by Howard Zinn, Longman, Harlow, UK, 1996, page 615.

Dear President Bush. Please send your assistance in freeing our small nation from occupation. This foreign force occupied our lands to steal our rich resources. They used biological warfare and deceit, killing thousands of elders, children and women in the process. As they overwhelmed our land, they deposed leaders and people of our own government, and in its place, they installed their own government systems that yet today control our daily lives in many ways. As in your own words, the occupation and overthrow of one small nation … is one too many. Sincerely, An American Indian.

Key debate

Vine Deloria Jr and Clifford Lytle (1984) argued that the 1975 Indian Self-Determination and Education Act and American Indian Policy Review Commission Act promised more than they delivered, mostly due to insufficient funding. Others were more positive. Stephen Cornell (1988) said Native Americans gained more influence over federal actions and over their own financial and organizational resources. Donald Parman (1994) argued that the educational provisions were successful, especially in the growth of community colleges, and that the 1975 legislation paved the way for other helpful laws such as the Indian Health Care Improvement Act (1976).

Some historians see Native Americans as victims (often passive) of federal and state government policies, but Donald Fixico (2004) argued that while these policies 'undoubtedly' changed Native lives, the changes 'rarely' reflected policymakers' desires: termination failed, relocation did not manage to cut ties to the reservations, and Reagan's interpretation of self-determination led to increased Native assertiveness and sovereignty, as demonstrated by the construction of more gambling casinos on reservation land. These currently earn tribes over $1 billion annually, but are unpopular with state governments, because they have a competitive advantage over state-regulated gambling.

← **Do Native Americans have meaningful self-determination?**

TOK Is it ever possible for indigenous cultures of the Americas to receive the same amount of respect as members of the majority/ruling population? (Social Sciences, Emotion.)

Colonial era	Conquest, racism, inferiority	✗
19th century	Military defeat, reservations, boarding schools	✗
1900–50	Citizenship	—
	Poverty	✗
	Indian New Deal	✓
1950–2000	Termination	✗
	Organizations, activism, militancy, made federal government increasingly sensitive to needs, but	✓
	still worst off of all ethnic minorities	✗

SUMMARY DIAGRAM

Native Americans in the USA

3 First Peoples in Canada

> ▶ **Key question:** How and to what extent did First Peoples achieve equality in Canada after 1945?

Background: First Peoples before 1945

From the seventeenth century, **First Nations** peoples struggled in the face of European settlers who took their land, pressure to adopt 'Canadian culture', and governments and law courts based on alien European concepts. From the 1870s, many First Nations peoples signed treaties with the federal government that established **reserves** on which they were to live and farm.

The Indian Act 1876

The **Indian Act** of 1876 gave white officials ultimate authority over the First Nations peoples. Responsibility for their education was given to the Churches, which practised forced cultural assimilation in residential schools that took children away from their parents and the reserves, prepared them for traditionally low-paid occupations, and punished them for speaking their own language or practising their own religion.

Resistance

In the late nineteenth century there were roughly 10,000 **Inuits**, 10,000 **Métis** and 120,000 other First Nations people. Some refused to seek permission from **Indian Agents** to sell their produce or leave their reserves and ignored bans on cultural practices such as **Sun Dances** and **potlatches**. The Métis rebelled over land loss in 1870 and 1885, but the government quashed them and did nothing to alleviate the poverty and discrimination from which they continued to suffer in the twentieth century.

First Nations people 1900–45

The League of Indians in Canada was established in 1919 because:

- Indian Acts of 1905 and 1911 enabled the Canadian government to expropriate or exchange reserve lands so as to 'encourage' indigenous people off their communal land and further assimilation
- the **Department of Indian Affairs** was unsympathetic
- other Canadians were hostile or indifferent
- shared experiences in the First World War increased pan-Indian consciousness.

Afflicted by internal divisions, police surveillance, accusations of Communism, harassment by the Department of Indian Affairs and leadership problems, the league nevertheless inspired more militant successors.

KEY TERM

First Nations Indigenous peoples in Canada. More recently, members of the various nations refer to themselves by their tribal or national identity.

Reserves Areas officially designated as living space for Canada's indigenous population.

Indian Act The 1876 Indian Act said how reserves and tribes should operate and who should be recognized as 'Indian'. It was amended on many occasions.

Inuit Indigenous people in Canada, formerly known as Eskimos.

Métis Of mixed European and First Nations or Inuit blood.

Indian Agents Canadian government representatives with ultimate authority over reserves.

Sun Dances Religious ceremonies of prairie First Nations peoples.

Potlatches Ceremonial exchange of gifts by coastal First Nations peoples of British Columbia.

Department of Indian Affairs Canadian government department set up under the 1880 Indian Act to regulate First Nations peoples.

The forgotten people

In 1934, an Albertan provincial commission investigated the Métis' shocking living conditions and concluded they suffered intense discrimination and were facing extinction. Around 90 per cent had tuberculosis, and paralysis, blindness and syphilis were rampant. According to historians Alvin Finkel and Margaret Conrad (1993), they became 'the forgotten people, invisible even in the census until 1981', when they were recognized for the first time as an ethnic group.

Canada's indigenous population 1945–70

In 1945, the average lifespan of impoverished Natives was half that of other Canadians, infant mortality rates remained at over four times the national average, and many died from excessive alcohol drunk to numb the sense of social, cultural and economic despair. On the reserves they suffered from poor nutrition and inadequate housing. Off the reserves, they were discriminated against in employment, housing and schools, where they were streamed into non-academic courses. Many Native children remained in the hated residential schools.

← **Why and to what extent did the position of First Nations people improve 1945–70?**

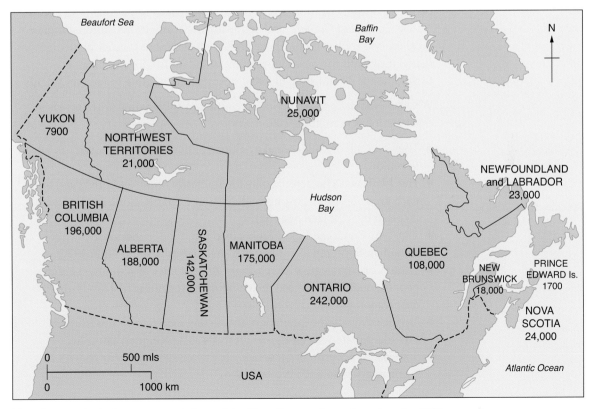

Map showing the indigenous populations of the Canadian provinces (based on the 2006 census)

However, there were some hopeful signs. The **Aboriginal** population had begun a numerical recovery after 1930. Some organizational experience had been gained. When many Church-educated Indians became advocates of Native rights, the Churches adopted less aggressively assimilationist policies. In 1945, responsibility for Native health was transferred from the Department of Indian Affairs to the Department of National Health and Welfare, which contributed to some improvement in Indian health. Although a special parliamentary committee report on the Indian Act (1948) 'demonstrated continued Euro-Canadian disregard for the traditions of Canada's first peoples' (Finkel and Conrad, 1993), the revised Indian Act of 1951 ended the ban on potlatches and Sun Dances. The 1956 Citizenship Act granted formal citizenship to Inuit and **status Indians**, who were given the vote in provincial then federal elections in 1960. Elected **band** councils were given more decision-making powers although the Department of Indian Affairs could overrule their decisions.

Increased militancy

Native progress was traditionally hampered by poor education, geographical dispersal and internal divisions, especially between status Indians who benefited from the Indian Act, and the Métis and non-status Indians who did not. In 1961 the National Indian Council (NIC) was created to improve Native unity and lives but disagreements between status Indians, non-status people and Métis led non-status Indians and Métis to establish their own Native Council of Canada, and status Indians formed the National Indian Brotherhood (NIB) (1968). These bodies proved more successful in negotiating with the new Department of Indian Affairs and Northern Development (established in 1966) over matters relating to land and rights.

Why did Native people respond to continued subjugation with increased organization and militancy after 1960?

- They had the organizational traditions of the League of Indians on which to build.
- The 1960s was characterized by the militancy of the less privileged and each group's actions inspired others. Some First Nations peoples were inspired by AIM (see page 30).
- The 1961 Canadian Bill of Rights inspired rights-consciousness (the Canadian Supreme Court began to hear cases based on it in 1970).
- Other Canadians grew increasingly affluent after 1945 and First Nations people sought to decrease the disparity by regaining lost lands and the observation of treaty rights.
- The discovery and exploitation of new raw materials in the North of Canada threatened Aboriginal lifestyles and prompted activism.
- Sometimes government insensitivity encouraged activism, as with the Trudeau government's White Paper.

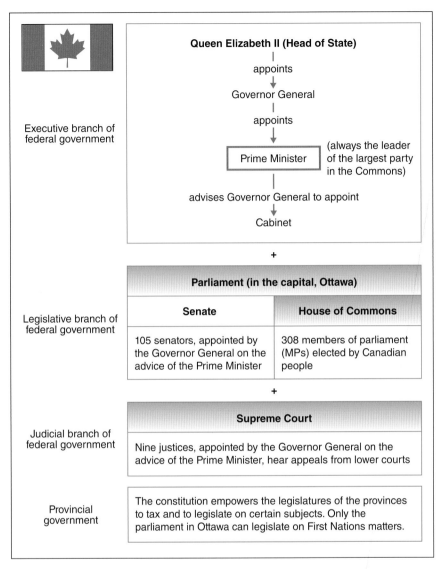

The federal system of government in Canada

The Trudeau government's White Paper

In the Trudeau government's 1969 White Paper (see Source Q, page 42), Minister of Indian Affairs Jean Chretien proposed that:

- the Indian Act be abolished
- the Department of Indian Affairs be dismantled and responsibility for Aboriginal people devolved to the provinces
- Aboriginal land claims be rejected
- First Nations people lose their special status and be assimilated into the general Canadian population with 'other ethnic minorities' status.

Produced without any real consultation with the indigenous population, the White Paper prioritized individual rights over traditional Native collective rights. NIB led the attack on the White Paper, pointing out that Natives wanted self-government and the reassertion of their culture not assimilation. They claimed that the White Paper policy would constitute 'cultural genocide'. Surprised by this outraged reaction, the Trudeau government dropped the White Paper, but ignored the demand for self-government.

Trudeau established an Indian Claims Commission in 1969 to settle land claims but the government was so slow to deal with them that the Natives looked to the courts for redress.

SOURCE Q

An extract from *A History of the Canadian Peoples* by J.M. Bumsted, published by Oxford University Press, Toronto, Canada, 2007, page 418.

The White Paper was consistent with federal policy towards all minorities, including French Canadians, at the end of the 1960s. It called for the enhancement of the individual rather than the collective rights of Native Peoples: 'The Government believes that its policies must lead to the full, free, and non-discriminatory participation of the Aboriginal people in Canadian society. Such a goal requires a break with the past. It requires that the Aboriginal people's role of dependence be replaced by a role of equal status, opportunity, and responsibility, a role they can share with all other Canadians' (Statement of the Government of Canada on Indian Policy, 1969:5). An assimilationist document, the White Paper insisted that treaties between the Crown and Aboriginals had involved only 'limited and minimal promises' that had been greatly exceeded in terms of the 'economic, educational, health, and welfare needs of the Indian people' by subsequent government performance (Statement of the Government of Canada on Indian Policy 1969:5). Allowing Aboriginal people full access to Canadian social services (many of which were administered provincially) would mark an advance over existing paternalism.

Ottawa seemed surprised that Native people responded so negatively to the White Paper, conveniently ignoring its implications for the concepts of treaty and Aboriginal rights. Prime Minister Trudeau defended the policy as an enlightened one, noting that 'the time is now to decide whether the Indians will be a race apart in Canada or whether they will be Canadians of full status.' He added, 'It's inconceivable, I think, that in a given society one section of the society have a treaty with the other section of the society. We must all be equal under the law' (Indian-Eskimo Association of Canada, 1970: Appendix 8).

?
Using Source Q and your own knowledge, give arguments for and against Trudeau's assimilationist position on Canadian Indians.

Harold Cardinal 1945–2005

A member of the Sucker Creek Reserve band, Harold Cardinal became president of Alberta's Indian Association in 1968. Natives considered his bestselling response (see Source R) to the 1969 White Paper to be the first effective statement of their grievances.

SOURCE R

Extracts from *The Unjust Society: The Tragedy of Canada's Indians* by Harold Cardinal (1969), quoted and described in *A History of the Canadian Peoples* by J.M. Bumsted, published by Oxford University Press, Toronto, Canada, 2007, pages 417–18.

Cardinal described the White Paper as a 'thinly disguised programme of extermination through assimilation', adding that the federal government, 'instead of acknowledging its legal and moral responsibilities to the Indians of Canada and honouring the treaties that the Indians signed in good faith, now proposes to wash its hands of Indians entirely, passing the buck to the provincial governments.'

Cardinal … [observed] that while 'Canadian urbanites have walked blisters on their feet and fat off their rumps to raise money for underdeveloped countries outside Canada', Canadians generally did not 'give a damn' about the plight of their own Native people. He also attacked 'Uncle Tomahawks' among his own people who continually apologized for being Aboriginal… Cardinal was also a critic of Canada's 'two founding peoples' [English and French] concept, pointing out that it did not recognize 'the role played by the Indian even before the founding of the nation state known as Canada'. He insisted that the First Nations were not separatists; they merely wanted their treaty and Aboriginal rights recognized so that they could take their place 'with the other cultural identities of Canada'.

> What were Harold Cardinal's grievances in Source R, and how justified were they?

Continued problems 1970–2000

> **What difficulties did the indigenous population face in the late twentieth century?**

Despite their increased activism and greater visibility in Canadian society, which had resulted in higher government expenditure, Natives still suffered problems in the 1970s. Those who lived in the cities were rarely fully assimilated. Uneducated and discriminated against in housing and employment, they lived in urban ghettos with poor housing, poverty and frequent drunkenness. Natives and Métis ran Friendship Centres and addiction programmes in order to help urban dwellers. However, band leaders generally felt it better to live on the reserves, even though infant mortality and overall death rates remained high, conditions were frequently characteristic of nations far less developed than Canada, and there were usually great economic problems.

Industry versus the indigenous population

White-owned industries frequently impacted on Natives, who were particularly angry when industrial developments near reserves depleted the wildlife and poisoned the waters on which they depended, but did not offer them jobs (companies preferred to employ trained personnel from outside). For example, in 1970 severe mercury poisoning was found in First Nations people in the province of Ontario, due to water pollution by Dryden Chemicals Company. This contributed to the eventual establishment of the Indian Health Transfer Policy, which prepared the way for First Nations people to take control of their own health services.

Control of education

The residential school system was gradually phased out from the 1960s, and pressure from NIB and provincial associations forced the government to increase Native responsibility for their education. From 1973, it became common for Native children to attend local schools controlled by band councils, particularly at elementary level. However, the national government did not build high schools near to reserves, so many children had to spend several hours daily travelling to and from school, or live in towns.

Legal inequality

Nova Scotia and Manitoba initiated Royal Commissions to investigate discrimination against Aboriginals in the criminal justice system.

Donald Marshall

In 1986, Nova Scotia set up a Royal Commission to examine the wrongful 11-year imprisonment of Donald Marshall, a **Mi'kmaq**, for a murder he did not commit. Its report concluded that he had been the victim of repeated instances of incompetence and cover-up, partly due to his being Aboriginal.

Helen Betty Osborne

The Manitoba Public Inquiry into the Administration of Justice and Aboriginal People was sparked by the murder of Helen Betty Osborne in The Pas, a town in Manitoba, in 1971. Boarding in The Pas while attending high school, she was abducted by four white youths. When she refused to have sex with them they stabbed her over 50 times. Although the murder was common knowledge among the white population, and one of the youths even bragged about the incident, no one would give names to the Royal Canadian Mounted Police (RCMP). After 14 years, one was convicted. The provincial attorney general said that the RCMP would have acted with greater urgency if the victim had been white. The RCMP blamed the conspiracy of silence among the white community. The inquiry concluded that racism was behind the miscarriage of justice.

Land disputes

From the first arrival of Europeans in Canada, the great issue with the Natives was control and use of land. This remained a focal point of contention throughout the twentieth century.

Successes

After the Trudeau government established the Indian Claims Commission in 1969, a series of landmark court decisions, many by the Canadian Supreme Court, reaffirmed the principle of Aboriginal rights. In 1973, the Canadian Supreme Court ruled in the Calder case that the Nisga'a band of British Columbia had **Aboriginal title** to their land that had never been and could not be extinguished (see Source S), although it was 1999 before British Columbia finally created a reserve.

SOURCE S

From the ruling of Mr Justice Wilfred Judson of the Supreme Court of Canada in the Calder case (1973), quoted in *A History of the Canadian Peoples* by J.M. Bumsted, published by Oxford University Press, Toronto, Canada, 2007, page 516.

The fact is that when the settlers came the Indians were there, organized in societies and occupying the land as their forefathers had done for centuries. This is what Indian title means. What they are asserting in this action is that they had a right to continue to live on their lands as their forefathers had lived, and that these rights have never been lawfully extinguished. What emerges from the evidence is that the Nishgas in fact are and were from time immemorial a distinctive cultural entity with concept of ownership indigenous to their culture and capable of articulation under the common law.

> What is Source S's justification for 'Indian title'? ?

Another landmark development in the history of land disputes took place in the Mackenzie Valley, where the Trudeau government supported proposed oil and gas pipeline projects, but appointed Justice Thomas Berger to study the issue. Berger listened to the indigenous population, concluded that pipelines would damage the environment and the lifestyle of the Natives, and recommended in 1977 that the construction be halted for a decade. Trudeau agreed. Berger brought the Aboriginal perspective on proposed industrial developments to public attention in such a way that in future it would prove impossible for politicians to ignore Aboriginal peoples.

The 1982 Constitution Act

'Existing Aboriginal rights' and treaty rights were recognized in the 1982 Constitution Act, but individual cases had to be decided by the courts. In the resultant flood of litigation, in which the Supreme Court never defined 'existing Aboriginal rights', Natives sometimes obtained quite favourable rulings. The Inuit of the east Arctic got 350,000 km² (135,000 square miles) of land in 1992 and in 1999 the eastern Arctic became a separately administered territory called Nunavit ('the people's land' in Inuktitut) where 17,500 of the 22,000 population were Inuit. Many considered Nunavit a bold experiment in Native self-government. Others said Nunavit was not really run by the Inuit, but was more like a traditional colony, as the territory contained federal agencies and co-management boards.

Land disputes: problems

- Resolution of land claims did not always bring economic advancement. In the 1980s, a federal study of Inuit and Cree of north Quebec found them living in poverty, despite financial compensation from the provincial governments for the surrender of land claims in 1975.
- Sometimes the courts were unsympathetic. In 1991, Chief Justice Allan McEachern rejected Aboriginal rights to exclusive land ownership and self-government, mostly because he rejected the oral history on which their claims were based (in 1997 the court overruled him).

- The courts frequently disagreed. In 1993, Donald Marshall (see page 44) was arrested again and charged under the Fisheries Act for catching eels during the closed season in Nova Scotia. Although his lawyers argued that he was exempt from the fishery regulations because of treaties between the Crown and the Mi'kmaq dating from 1760–1, Marshall was found guilty. That decision was upheld by the Nova Scotia Supreme Court, but rejected by the Supreme Court of Canada in 1999, which ruled that he had a treaty right to a 'moderate livelihood' from the natural resources of his region. This ruling led to tension, bitterness and violence in some maritime communities when non-Native fishermen and fisheries and oceans officials tried to stop Mi'kmaq lobster fishers claiming their 'treaty right'.
- The federal government was slow to settle any land claims but especially those by non-treaty Indians who lacked reserves or treaty Indians who claimed more territory than the government allotted them. In 1990, there were over 500 claims outstanding, but only three or four were settled per year. Frustration over land claims bogged down in bureaucracy and in the courts led some to greater militancy.

Land disputes and militancy

Some Natives gained inspiration from AIM in the USA (see page 30). The federal government had done little to protect the Aboriginals when the British Columbian government had ignored treaties and seized lands for industrial and urban expansion. In the 1980s, several British Columbian bands clashed with loggers despoiling traditional Aboriginal lands. In 1991, the government of British Columbia responded to increased Native militancy by agreeing to negotiate land issues.

The most sensational confrontation occurred in Quebec in 1990, when provincial police clashed with Mohawk Warriors over the development of a golf course on sacred Mohawk land at a reserve near Oka. In the ensuing violence, one policeman died and provincial Premier Robert Bourassa called in the Canadian army. Not all Mohawks liked the Warriors, who ran gambling casinos and smuggling operations, but there was unanimity over this land. The federal government criticized the Warriors as terrorists but their activism forced the government to buy the lands and give them to the Mohawks. Violence paid off.

Provinces vs the federal government: the 1982 charter

The Constitution Act of 1982 incorporated a Charter of Rights and Freedoms that prohibited discrimination over gender and colour. However, Native lobbies failed to get an amendment guaranteeing self-government, because British Columbia, Alberta, Saskatchewan and Quebec traditionally favoured the rights of developers over the rights of the Aboriginals, feared losing the right to control provincial resources, and opposed the charter.

Elijh Harper and the Constitution Act

At Meech Lake in 1987, the provinces agreed to Quebec's demands for modification of the 1982 Constitution in order to preserve provincial rights. Aboriginals criticized this Meech Lake Accord as sacrificing Native self-government for provincial rights. The first **treaty Indian** to be elected to the Legislative Assembly of Manitoba, Cree leader Elijah Harper, gained national publicity in 1990 when he exploited procedural methods to stop Manitoba passing the accord, which lapsed, killed off by Aboriginal peoples and the misgivings of several provinces.

The Charlottetown Accord

After the failure of the Meech Lake Accord, the provincial governments and some Native leaders produced the Charlottetown Accord in 1992, which called for 'the recognition of the inherent right of self-government' that would preserve Native 'languages, cultures, economies, identities, institutions, and traditions' and gave the Métis the opportunity to access to some Aboriginal programmes and services. However, opposition grew. The *Parti Québécois* leader, Jacques Parizeau, said that under the accord, Aboriginal peoples would end up controlling most of Canada. Many Natives were critical, saying the accord did nothing to speed up land claim negotiations. Some status Indians asked why, as sovereign peoples, the accord said that they had to negotiate with the federal and provincial governments. The Charlottetown Accord was therefore rejected.

The residential schools

During the 1990s, the First Nations were increasingly perceived as a very important Canadian political problem in relation to land rights, self-government and compensation for earlier mistreatment.

The federal government and the Churches were slow to respond to complaints about mistreatment in the residential schools, so in the 1990s ex-pupils took them to court. In 1998, the Canadian government announced its Aboriginal Action Plan to deal with past injustices, as part of which the federal government acknowledged its role in the residential schools, apologized, and offered $350 million in compensation. However, no agreement resulted. Legal fees over these Aboriginal suits bankrupted many Churches (see Source T), dioceses and religious orders.

> **KEY TERM**
>
> **Treaty Indian** Status Indian.

SOURCE T

An extract from the 'United Church Apology to First Nations Peoples Regarding Residential Schools', read by the Right Reverend Bill Phipps (1998), quoted in *A History of the Canadian Peoples* by J.M. Bumsted, published by Oxford University Press, Toronto, Canada, page 522.

On behalf of the United Church of Canada I apologize for the pain and suffering that our church's involvement in the Indian Residential School system has caused. We are aware of some of the damage that this cruel and ill-conceived system of assimilation has perpetrated on Canada's First Nations people. For this

What can you infer from Source T about the differing viewpoints on the United Church's involvement in the residential schools system?

we are truly and most humbly sorry ... We know that many within our church will still not understand why each of us must bear the scar, the blame for this horrendous period in Canadian history. But the truth is we are the bearers of many blessings from our ancestors, and therefore we must also bear their burdens.

The Royal Commission report of 1996

In 1991, Prime Minister Brian Mulroney created the Royal Commission on Aboriginal Peoples. Its 1996 report proposed self-government for First Nations people, said that the Canadian government should negotiate 'nation to nation' with a First Nations government, recommended a $2 billion grant to the governments of the First Nations, and 'set out a 20-year agenda for change'. Inspired by the commission, the federal government announced the Aboriginal Right to Self-Government Policy in 1995, which recognized the right of the indigenous population to decide on a suitable form of self-government. As a result of the commission, the Indian Health Transfer Policy granted self-determination in health and several accords were signed between First Nations people and federal and provincial governments. However, long-standing tensions over land ownership, land use and Native political rights continued into the twenty-first century.

Was the Aboriginal population equal after 2000?

→ The indigenous population in the twenty-first century

The strength of the Native lobby, led by the Assembly of the First Nations (formerly NIB), had forced reconsideration of the rights of Natives, but Natives remained aggrieved and their problems continued:

- The indigenous population's living conditions remained unsatisfactory. In 2005, Health Canada investigated *Escherichia coli* and skin disease among the Kashechewan First Nation, and found that local operators who ran the water treatment plants were unqualified (chlorine was not being used in the water treatment) and that the skin disorders were due to living in unhygienic conditions.
- First Nations people suffered higher rates of poverty, unemployment, incarceration, suicide, substance abuse and health problems than other Canadian citizens.
- The life of expectancy of the 500,000 Natives was 8.1 years shorter for males and 5.5 years shorter for females.
- Natives remained below the national average in educational attainment.
- While two-thirds of status Indians lived on over 2600 reserves, the remainder lived mostly in larger southern cities such as Winnipeg, Manitoba, where disaffection led to increasing numbers of gangs.
- Self-government gave chiefs councils wide-ranging and self-regulatory powers that some people criticized as excessive, likely to fragment Canada, and poorly exercised.

- Many Aboriginals demanded more powers and financial compensation for centuries of mistreatment. A 2005 meeting of first ministers and Aboriginal leaders in Kelowna, British Columbia, led to Prime Minister Paul Martin's announcement that $5 billion of federal funds would be committed to Aboriginals over five years in order to try to decrease the gap in living standards between them and other Canadians, but Martin's Liberal government fell and the new Conservative government dumped the Kelowna Accord.

On the other hand, there were positive signs. During the twentieth century, the Aboriginal population increased 10-fold, suggesting improved healthcare and a better standard of living. National Aboriginal Day, first celebrated in 1996, recognized the cultures and contributions of the First Nations, Inuit and Métis peoples, although few provinces regarded it as a statutory holiday. In 2008, Prime Minister Stephen Harper apologized for the residential school system. Following Trudeau's establishment of the Indian Claims Commission, a series of landmark court decisions, many from the Supreme Court, established the Aboriginal right to hold lands and to negotiate over them with the government.

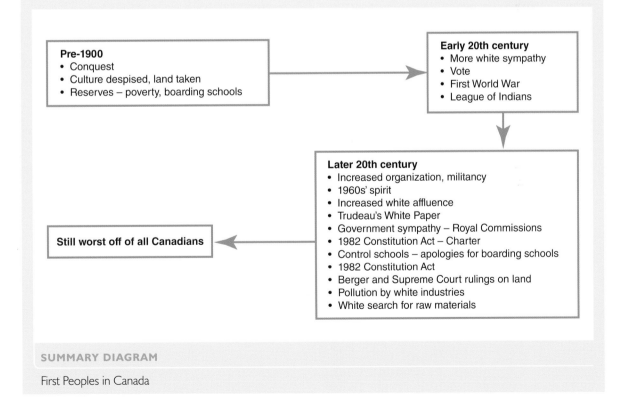

SUMMARY DIAGRAM

First Peoples in Canada

Chapter summary

Native Americans and civil rights in the Americas

The Spanish and Portuguese conquest deprived Latin America's indigenous population of land and respect. There was no improvement under the new Latin American republics, even when in the early twentieth century republics such as Mexico glorified their indigenous heritage in order to create a national identity. Countries with indigenous majorities such as Bolivia, Ecuador, Guatemala and Peru were among the poorest in Latin America and within Latin American countries the indigenous population was invariably the most impoverished.

The Latin American indigenous population became more vociferous in the later twentieth century, when unions, improved communications, organizations, globalization, liberation theology and sympathetic governments all helped to put their rights on the national political agenda. Methods for obtaining equality included rebellion, protests and publicity, and most importantly, the franchise. Still, equality proved impossible to achieve, owing to racism, greed, cultural clashes, internal divisions, unsympathetic governments and the financial cost of ending long-standing indigenous poverty. Peru's Shining Path illustrated how violence failed to bring about improvement. Mexico demonstrated how mestizos dominated the indigenous population, and Guatemala unsuccessfully attempted genocide of the indigenous majority.

Overall, despite some cause for optimism, the indigenous populations of Latin America had not attained equality by 2000.

In what became the USA, the Native American population was deprived of land and despised under the colonial regime and the new republic. Native Americans were put on reservations and their children frequently 'civilized' in boarding schools. Their situation was desperate by the early twentieth century, but under Roosevelt the indigenous population gained some federal government respect for their culture and some control over their reservations.

After 1945, Native American activism increased as a result of the Second World War, the Indian Claims Commission and the African American example. New and more militant Indian organizations such as NIYC and AIM were established. They publicized continuing indigenous problems in occupations, litigation and writings. The federal government responded with greater aid and support for self-determination, although clashes over land use and possession and cultural practices continued.

The conquered First Peoples in Canada also suffered from land loss, white cultural arrogance, segregation on reserves and boarding schools. The First Peoples entered the twentieth century in great poverty and deprivation, but from the 1960s became increasingly organized and militant, inspired by previous organizational experience, African Americans, AIM, the Canadian Bill of Rights, the increased affluence of other Canadians, the exploitation of raw materials on their lands and Prime Minister Trudeau's assimilationist proposals in the 1969 White Paper. In the late twentieth century, First Peoples continued to suffer from poverty, discrimination and the impact of white-owned industries on their environment, but indigenous organizations pressured the government into granting greater self-determination and investigations of legal inequality and land disputes. Although the First Peoples did not gain all they wanted, their rights were very much on the federal and state agendas, and their situation had improved since the start of the twentieth century.

✓ Examination advice

How to answer 'analyse' questions

When answering questions with the command term <u>analyse</u> you should try to identify the key elements and their relative importance.

Example

<u>Analyse</u> the effectiveness of a Native American organization in one country in the region after the 1960s.

1 To answer this question successfully, you need to discuss what constituted success or effectiveness and what constituted failure for one Native American organization. Your focus should be on one country only. You could write about a group in the USA, Canada or a Latin American country such as Bolivia. In questions such as these, you need to set the terms and then answer the question using these parameters. For example, if you were to write about the American Indian Movement (AIM) in the USA, you could discuss how effective the group was politically and/or socially. You should also define for whom the group was effective. In other words, was AIM effective for Native Americans or the US population or both?

2 Take several minutes and write down the goals, successes and failures of the AIM. This will help you with your essay when you need to analyse how effective the group was. An example is given below.

Goals
- *Improve housing, education, employment.*
- *Bring attention to problems Native Americans faced.*
- *Receive compensation for US treaty violations.*

Successes
- *Fewer jailed when Minneapolis–St Paul police monitored.*
- *1972: Trail of Broken Treaties March from San Francisco to Washington, DC, gained attention.*
- *1973: Wounded Knee incident gained attention – Nixon administration responded.*
- *1975: Indian Self-Determination Act. Some control regained on reservations.*

Failures
- *Continued poverty, high disease rates.*
- *Governmental attention was not sustained.*

3 In your introduction, briefly explain what the AIM tried to achieve and to what extent the group was effective. Order the successes from most important to least important. Be sure to provide the historical context, as well. An example of a good introductory paragraph is given below.

> In the wake of the rise of student and women's groups in the 1960s, Native American groups such as the American Indian Movement (AIM) also sought to bring attention to the serious problems faced by the original inhabitants of North America. AIM carried out a number of actions meant to raise awareness for both Native Americans and the rest of US society. These included a march on Washington, DC, as well as the seizure of the small town of Wounded Knee on the Pine Ridge Reservation in 1973. While these actions did lead to the restoration of some rights for Native Americans through Congressional action, significant and long-term achievements were lacking.

4 For each of the key points you raise in your introduction, you should be able to write one or two long paragraphs. Here, you should provide your supporting evidence. Be sure to make a judgement about each item's effectiveness.
5 In the final paragraph, you should tie your essay together stating your conclusions. Do not raise any new points here.
6 Now try writing a complete answer to the question following the advice above.

Examination practice

Below are two exam-style questions for you to practise on this topic.

1 In what ways and with what effects did the political struggle of the Native Americans change in the 1960s and 1970s? Support your answer with examples of two countries in the region.
(For guidance on how to answer 'In what ways and with what effects' questions, see pages 194–5.)

2 Compare and contrast the success of Bolivian indigenous movements (see pages 154–68) with Canadian First Nations organizations.
(For guidance on how to answer 'compare and contrast' questions, see pages 235–8.)

CHAPTER 2

African Americans and the Civil Rights Movement

This chapter traces the history of African American oppression through slavery and then segregation. It looks at the long- and short-term origins of the Civil Rights Movement and the debates as to when exactly that movement began. It explores what tactics African Americans used to try to gain equality and which were the most effective. The relative importance of the reasons for improvement is also discussed. You need to consider the following questions throughout this chapter:

✪ What were the long-term causes of the Civil Rights Movement?

✪ What was the main reason for the mass activism that began in 1955?

✪ When did the Civil Rights Movement begin?

✪ How and why was *de jure* segregation ended?

① African Americans to 1945

▶ **Key question:** *What were the long-term causes of the Civil Rights Movement?*

The **Civil Rights Movement** originated long before the famous period in which Martin Luther King Jr led African American protests against discrimination.

African Americans before 1900

In the seventeenth century, Europeans conquered and colonized North America. They considered importing and enslaving Africans acceptable because they needed cheap and plentiful labour and because Africans, with their non-Christian culture, were perceived as uncivilized.

African Americans in the Constitution

The Constitution of the newly independent United States of America said black slaves were 'worth' only three-fifths of a white person. The vast majority of slaves were in the Southern states (see the map on page 69). The Constitution gave states great power over education, transportation, voting and law enforcement, making jurisdictional clashes with the federal government likely.

← How 'free' were slaves after emancipation?

 **KEY TERM**

Civil Rights Movement Movement for legal, social, political and economic equality for African Americans.

The Civil War 1861–5 and Reconstruction

Relations between blacks and whites were usually tense. Blacks resented enslavement, while whites feared revolt, the loss of unpaid labour, competition from freed slaves, and threats to white domination and racial purity. There were also tensions between Northern and Southern whites over slavery when the USA expanded westward: Northerners who no longer owned slaves clashed with Southerners over whether slavery should be allowed within the new territories. Republican presidential candidate Abraham Lincoln (1809–65) opposed the extension of slavery to the western territories, so his election prompted the Southern states to secede from the Union of the United States and to establish the Confederate States of America. Lincoln was determined not to allow the South to leave the Union, and in the Civil War (1861–5) Lincoln's North defeated the **Confederacy**. It was primarily military necessity that made Lincoln begin the process of ending slavery with the 1862 Emancipation Proclamation.

After the defeat of the South, the black population was given theoretical equality in three very important constitutional amendments. The 13th **Amendment** (1865) abolished slavery, the 14th Amendment (1868) said black people were citizens, and the 15th Amendment (1870) said black males should be allowed to vote. During the **Reconstruction** of the South (1865–77), black people voted and had more access to education, but their sudden release from slavery meant most struggled economically.

Segregation

The federal government soon tired of the South's 'race' problem and left the region to its own devices. Southern whites quickly restored their supremacy over state governments, and in the late nineteenth century introduced **Jim Crow** laws that discriminated against black people, legally enforcing their segregation from whites in schools, houses and public facilities such as transportation and education. In *Plessy v. Ferguson* (1896), the Supreme Court ruled that 'separate but equal' facilities were not against the 14th Amendment. The black population was certainly in separate facilities, but they were not equal.

Segregation in the South was enshrined in state law (*de jure* **segregation**). Segregation in the North, evidenced in schools, housing and some public facilities, was segregation in fact rather than in law (*de facto* **segregation**). Even in the North, African Americans had little protection from the law and **lynching** was not uncommon.

→ African Americans 1900–45

In the first half of the twentieth century, the origins of the Civil Rights Movement were to be found in black inequality, individual activists, greater black consciousness, the labour movement, the New Deal, the National Association for the Advancement of Colored People (NAACP) and two world wars.

KEY TERM

Confederacy The 11 Southern states that left the Union became the Confederate States of America.

Amendment The US Congress could amend the Constitution if 75 per cent of the states approved.

Reconstruction When the 11 ex-Confederate states were rebuilt, reformed and restored to the Union.

Jim Crow A popular 1830s comic, black-faced, minstrel character developed by white performing artists. Post-Reconstruction Southern state laws that legalized segregation were called 'Jim Crow laws'.

De jure segregation The legal segregation of the races, set down in laws in the South until 1964.

De facto segregation Segregation of the races in fact rather than in the law.

Lynching Unlawful killing (usually by hanging).

What factors and tactics brought about improvement to the conditions of African Americans?

Individual activists

African Americans did not always passively accept their inferior political, social, economic and legal status, but in the early twentieth century they disagreed over tactics for improvement. Many black Southerners went North after 1910 in search of a better life in the **Great Migration**. A few began to organize protests, although the historian Adam Fairclough (2001) described them as 'sporadic and uncoordinated'. Black Southern educationalist Booker T. Washington (1856–1915) advocated **accommodationism**, which concentrated on economic improvement, while black Northern academic W.E.B. Du Bois (1868–1963) waged a propaganda war against the *status quo* and helped to establish the NAACP in 1909 (see below).

Greater black consciousness

In the first half of the twentieth century, black consciousness greatly increased, through labour unions, newspapers such as the *Baltimore Afro-American*, the flowering of black culture in New York City's Harlem ghetto (the Harlem Renaissance) and organizations. The two most significant organizations in the first half of the twentieth century were the integrationist NAACP, with its predominantly middle-class membership and litigation tactic (see below), and flamboyant West Indian-born Marcus Garvey's Universal Negro Improvement Association (UNIA), which favoured armed self-defence and the separation of the races. UNIA was the first black mass movement in the USA, boasting around half a million members by 1925.

The labour movement

In 1925, left-wing African American A. Philip Randolph set up and led an all-black labour union, the Brotherhood of Sleeping Car Porters. Membership reached 15,000 by the 1940s, giving Randolph a great deal of influence. He successfully put pressure on President Franklin D. Roosevelt (1933–45) to decrease discrimination in federal employment during the Second World War (see page 56).

The New Deal

Following the Wall Street crash (1929), the USA was plunged into the Great Depression. In 1933, President Roosevelt introduced his New Deal, a hitherto unprecedented programme of government intervention to stimulate the economy and help the poor. As the majority of African Americans were poor, many benefited, even though New Deal officials frequently practised discrimination. The programme helped to awaken African Americans to the power and potential of federal government aid, and black voters began to turn from the 'Great Emancipator' Abraham Lincoln's Republican Party to Roosevelt's Democratic Party.

NAACP

NAACP's litigation tactic aimed to bring about a slow but steady erosion of the Jim Crow laws. NAACP-initiated cases brought about a Supreme Court

KEY TERM

Great migration Early twentieth-century northward movement of black Southerners.

Accommodationism Booker T. Washington's philosophy, which advocated initial black concentration on economic improvement rather than on social, political and legal equality.

Grandfather clause
Southern state laws allowed the illiterate to vote if they could prove an ancestor had voted before Reconstruction, which no African American could do.

Primaries Elections to choose a party's candidate for elective office.

Poll tax Tax levied on would-be voters that made it harder for blacks (who were usually poor) to vote.

ruling that ended the **grandfather clause** (1915). In the 1930s, the organization focused on obtaining a ruling that unequal expenditure on black and white education was against the 14th Amendment. Star black lawyer Thurgood Marshall argued successfully for equal salaries for black teachers in Maryland and Virginia in 1935–40. He focused first on equality in graduate schools, where fewer whites would be affected, and there would be fewer complaints. In *Missouri ex rel Gaines v. Canada* (1938), the Supreme Court decreed that all races had the right to the same quality of graduate education. As a result of NAACP's Texas campaign against all-white **primaries**, the Supreme Court declared the exclusion of African Americans from the primaries unconstitutional under the 15th Amendment in *Smith v. Allwright* in 1944. The NAACP also lobbied Congress for anti-lynching legislation (the House of Representatives passed the bill in 1937 and 1940 but the Senate rejected it) and arranged protests, for example, against segregated lunch counters in Topeka, Kansas.

US involvement in two world wars

When the USA fought in two world wars (1917–18 and 1941–45), black soldiers noticed the disparity between US government rhetoric about freedom and democracy and their own reality. The Second World War in particular raised black consciousness and promoted black activism:

- In 1941, Adam Clayton Powell led a bus boycott in Harlem, which led to the employment of more black bus drivers.
- In 1941, A. Philip Randolph threatened to bring Washington to a standstill unless there was equality in the segregated armed forces and in the workplace, so President Roosevelt reluctantly established the Commission on Fair Employment Practices (FEPC), which promoted equality in the defence industries in which two million black people were employed.
- In 1942, Christian socialist James Farmer set up the Congress of Racial Equality (CORE), which organized sit-ins (see page 73) at *de facto* segregated Chicago restaurants and demanded the desegregation of interstate transport.
- In New Orleans in 1943, a bus driver ordered a black soldier to sit at the back of the bus, in accordance with state and city laws. All 24 black passengers ended up in jail for demonstrating solidarity with him.
- NAACP membership rose during the war from 50,000 to 450,000. For example, in 1942, Rosa Parks (see pages 62–5) joined the NAACP, which she said 'was about empowerment through the ballot box. With a vote would come economic improvements.' She 'failed' the literacy test in 1943 but successfully registered to vote in 1945, although paying the $16.50 **poll tax** was expensive for a part-time seamstress. She resented her brother being drafted by a democracy in which he could not vote.

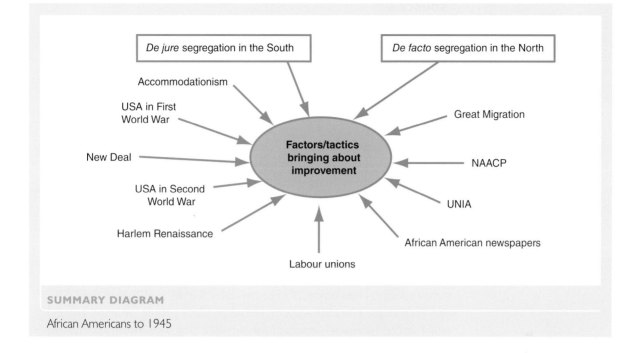

SUMMARY DIAGRAM

African Americans to 1945

2 Short-term causes of the Civil Rights Movement 1945–55

> ▶ *Key question: What was the main reason for the mass activism that began in 1955?*

Underlying the Civil Rights Movement was the long-standing inequality of the Southern black population, but it could be argued that the trigger for the mass activism that began in 1955 was the sympathy demonstrated by President Truman and the Supreme Court.

A sympathetic president: Harry Truman 1945–53

> How did Truman help African Americans?

Although a self-confessed racist, President Truman did more for African Americans than any president since Lincoln.

Attacks on black soldiers

Like many contemporaries, Truman was horrified by attacks on black servicemen returning from the Second World War. The worst attacks were in the Deep South and Truman gave US citizens a moral lead, saying that legal equality was the black man's basic right, 'because he is a human being and a natural born American'.

Look at Source A and at Source H on page 69. Suggest why returning black soldiers received particularly bad treatment in Mississippi and South Carolina.

SOURCE A

Extracts from two letters written by President Truman in 1948, quoted in _Truman_ by David McCullough, published by Simon & Schuster, New York, USA, 1992, pages 721–2.

My very stomach turned over when I learned that Negro soldiers, just back from overseas, were being dumped out of army trucks in Mississippi and beaten. Whatever my inclinations as a native of Missouri might have been, as President I know this is bad. I shall fight to end evils like this ... I am not asking for social equality, because no such things exist, but I am asking for equality of opportunity for all human beings ... When a mayor and a City Marshal can take a Negro Sergeant off a bus in South Carolina, beat him up and put out one of his eyes, and nothing is done about it by the State Authorities, something is radically wrong with the system.

'To Secure These Rights'

In 1946, Truman established a liberal civil rights committee to investigate racist violence. Their report, 'To Secure These Rights' (1947), said the USA could not claim to lead the free world while black people were not equal. It called on the federal government for anti-lynching legislation, abolition of the poll tax, voting rights laws, a permanent FEPC, and an end to discrimination in interstate travel and in the armed forces.

In his 1947 and 1948 State of the Union addresses, Truman urged Congress to pass the civil rights legislation suggested by the committee. In 1948, under the threat of mass protest organized by A. Philip Randolph, he set an example by issuing executive orders to end discrimination in the armed forces and to guarantee fair employment in the civil service. He set up the Fair Employment Board (1948) to try to give minorities equal treatment in federal hiring, and established a Committee on Government Contract Compliance (CGCC) that threatened to withhold federal government contracts from employers who discriminated against black workers. He made some significant appointments, such as an African American governor of the US Virgin Islands. Most importantly of all, he put the full moral weight of the presidency behind the struggle for civil rights. Truman's lead encouraged further black activism.

> ### Sympathetic state and city governments
> By 1952, 11 states and 20 cities had fair employment laws, 19 states had legislation against some form of racial discrimination, and only five states retained the poll tax.

NAACP and a sympathetic Supreme Court 1945–55

How and why did the Supreme Court catalyse change?

NAACP's legal challenges to segregation, especially in education (see page 56), were vital in eroding Jim Crow laws and inspiring further black activism.

Supreme Court rulings 1950

In response to the work of NAACP lawyers against 'separate but equal' in the law courts, the Supreme Court made three civil rights decisions in 1950 that almost overturned *Plessy v. Ferguson* (see page 54). It held that:

- Segregation on railway dining cars was illegal under the Interstate Commerce Act (*Henderson v. US*).
- A black student could not be physically separated from white students in the University of Oklahoma (*McLaurin v. Oklahoma State Regents*).
- A separate black Texan law school was not equal to the University of Texas Law School to which the black petitioner had therefore to be admitted (*Sweatt v. Painter*).

Brown v. Board of Education (1954)

Kansas was one of 17 states that had legally segregated schools. Oliver Brown, a Church minister in Topeka, Kansas, could not send his daughter to a whites-only school five blocks away. In order to get to the all-black school 20 blocks away, she had to walk across railroad tracks. He decided to challenge the segregated school system. The NAACP supported Brown's litigation, believing there was a good chance of success as Kansas was not a Southern state.

Thurgood Marshall argued before the Supreme Court that segregation was against the 14th Amendment. In *Brown v. The Board of Education, Topeka, Kansas* (1954), Chief Justice Earl Warren and the Supreme Court adjudged that even if facilities were equal (they never were), separate education was psychologically harmful to black children.

Results and significance of Brown

The *Brown* ruling was highly significant:

- A great triumph for the NAACP's long legal campaign against segregated education, *Brown* seemed to remove all constitutional sanctions for racial segregation by overturning *Plessy v. Ferguson*.
- The victory was not total: the Supreme Court gave no date by which desegregation had to be achieved and said nothing about *de facto* segregation.
- The NAACP returned to the Supreme Court and obtained the *Brown II* (1955) ruling that integration be accomplished 'with all deliberate speed', but there was still no date for compliance. Warren believed that schools and administrators needed time to adjust. The white reaction suggests that he was right.

SOURCE B

Williams school in Ruleville, Sunflower County, Mississippi, in 1950: 'separate' but clearly not 'equal'.

🔑 **KEY TERM**

Ku Klux Klan Violent, white supremacist organization.

- White Citizens Councils were quickly formed throughout the South to defend segregation. By 1956, they boasted around a quarter of a million members. The Councils challenged desegregation plans in the law courts and Southern politicians, all of whom were white, were supportive. The **Ku Klux Klan** was revitalized once more.
- Acceptance of the *Brown* ruling varied. In the peripheral and urban South desegregation was introduced quite quickly: 70 per cent of school districts in Washington, DC and in the border states of Delaware, Kentucky, Maryland, Missouri, Oklahoma and West Virginia desegregated schools within a year. However, in the Deep South, in Georgia, South Carolina, Alabama, Mississippi and Louisiana, schools remained segregated. Some school boards maintained white-only schools by manipulating entry criteria. From 1956 to 1959, there was a 'massive resistance' campaign in Virginia: whites closed some schools rather than desegregate. Virginia labour unions financed segregated schools when the public schools were closed.
- *Brown* inspired further activism. Rosa Parks recalled, 'You can't imagine the rejoicing among black people, and some white people.'

Emmett Till

In 1955, 14-year-old Chicagoan Emmett Till visited his Southern relations. Either unsure or defiant of Southern conventions, he wolf-whistled at a white woman. Several days later, his mutilated body was dragged out of a Mississippi river. For the first time white men were charged with murdering a black male in Mississippi. Their defence argued that Till was really alive and well in Chicago and that this was all an NAACP plot! After the all-white jury's verdict was 'not guilty' (journalist William Bradford Huie paid the killers of Emmett Till to describe how and why they murdered him), more black people became civil rights activists.

SOURCE C

An extract from an article in *Look* magazine by journalist William Bradford Huie, published in 1956. He paid Emmett Till's killers to describe how and why they murdered him. Quoted at www.pbs.org/wgbh/amex/till/sfeature/sf_look_confession.html

Milam: 'Well, what else could we do? He was hopeless. I'm no bully; I never hurt a nigger in my life. I like niggers – in their place – I know how to work 'em. But I just decided it was time a few people got put on notice. As long as I live and can do anything about it, niggers are gonna stay in their place. Niggers ain't gonna vote where I live. If they did, they'd control the government. They ain't gonna go to school with my kids. And when a nigger gets close to mentioning sex with a white woman, he's tired o' livin'. I'm likely to kill him. Me and my folks fought for this country, and we got some rights. I stood there in that shed and listened to that nigger throw that poison at me, and I just made up my mind. 'Chicago boy,' I said, 'I'm tired of 'em sending your kind down here to stir up trouble. Goddam you, I'm going to make an example of you – just so everybody can know how me and my folks stand.'

Judging from Source C, what motivated the murder of Emmett Till?

SOURCE D

The coffin of Emmett Till.

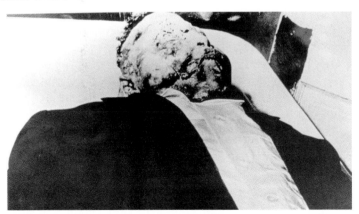

Look at Source D. Why do you suppose Emmett Till's mother wanted an open coffin funeral service?

The Montgomery bus boycott 1956

Many see the Montgomery bus boycott as the real start of the Civil Rights Movement.

The arrest of Rosa Parks

In December 1955, Mrs Rosa Parks returned home by bus after a hard day's work as a seamstress in a department store in Montgomery, Alabama. The bus soon filled up. A white man was left standing. The bus driver ordered four black passengers to move. Mrs Parks refused. She was arrested and charged with a violation of the Montgomery city bus segregation ordinance that forbade black passengers sitting parallel with whites.

Rosa Parks and the NAACP

Many writers portray 42-year-old Rosa Parks as a tired old lady who had been exhausted by the day at work and could not take any more, but her defiance was premeditated. She had joined the NAACP in 1943 and became Montgomery branch secretary, working very closely with the branch leader E.D. Nixon, a railroad porter inspired by and close to A. Philip Randolph (see page 55). The branch had been looking to challenge Montgomery's bus segregation laws. They had contemplated using Claudette Colvin, arrested in March 1955 for refusing to give up a seat to a white passenger, but Colvin was a pregnant, unmarried teenager accused of assault. As Parks said, the white press would have depicted her as 'a bad girl'. As the challenge would cost the NAACP half a million dollars, Nixon decided that 'respectable' Rosa Parks was a safer test case.

The mobilization of Montgomery's black community

Weeks before the Rosa Parks incident, a black mother had boarded a Montgomery bus, two babies in her arms. She placed the babies on the front 'white' seats in order to free her hands to pay her fare. The driver yelled, 'Take the black dirty brats off the seats', then hit the accelerator. The babies fell into the aisle. Many of the Montgomery black community had had enough.

After Rosa Parks' arrest, the NAACP and the black teachers and students of Alabama State College mobilized for a bus boycott in protest. Students copied and distributed propaganda leaflets to elicit total support from the black community. Believing that Church involvement would increase working-class black participation and decrease the possibility of disorder, NAACP worked with local Church leaders, especially Dr Martin Luther King Jr. The 26-year old Baptist minister had already rejected an offer to lead the local NAACP branch, but he let his church be used as a meeting place to plan the boycott. The church would provide organization, location, inspiration and some financial aid.

The boycott

Boycotts hit white pockets and were a traditional and effective mass weapon. Black passengers boycotted streetcars throughout the South between 1900 and 1906 and used their economic power (most bus passengers were black) to gain bus seating on a **first-come, first-served** basis in Baton Rouge, Louisiana, in 1953. These Baton Rouge tactics were now adopted in Montgomery. Montgomery's black community successfully boycotted buses on the day of Rosa Parks' trial, demanding first-come, first-served, courteous drivers and the employment of black drivers. No one as yet demanded an end to segregation on the buses. When the city commissioners rejected the proposed changes, the one-day boycott became a year-long one.

The Choice of Leader: Martin Luther King Jr

The community agreed that King would be a good leader of the boycott. Some historians say he was a compromise candidate, others that there was no better alternative: the national NAACP did not want to get involved and also lacked the influence of the Church, while Alabama State College employees risked dismissal. King therefore headed the new umbrella organization, the Montgomery Improvement Association (MIA).

Black unanimity

A successful long-term boycott required unanimity and sacrifice among Montgomery's 50,000 black population. For the most part, it was achieved. On one occasion during the boycott, an African American used the bus. As he got off, an elderly black woman with a stick raced toward the bus. 'You don't have to rush, auntie', said the white driver. 'I'll wait for you.' 'In the first place, I ain't your auntie', she said. 'In the second place, I ain't rushing to get on your bus. I'm jus' trying to catch up with that [man] who just got off, so I can hit him with this here stick.'

SOURCE E

An extract from an interview with Rosa Parks in 1997 on http://teacher. scholastic.com/rosa/interview.htm#brave

[Q] What was it like walking all those miles when the bus boycott was going on?

[A] We were fortunate enough to have a carpool organized to pick people up and give them rides. Of course, many people walked and sometimes I did too. I was willing to walk rather than go back to the buses under those unfair conditions.

Black vs white

The Montgomery White Citizens Council organized the opposition. Its membership doubled from 6000 in February 1956 to 12,000 by March. The council was dominated by leading city officials who ordered harassment of blacks. In January 1956, King was arrested for the first time for driving at 30 mph (48 km/h) in a 25 mph (40 km/h) zone. His house was bombed. His family urged him to quit. He said later he was tempted but felt called by God to continue. King's speeches were inspirational and even appealed to some whites (see Source F, page 64). He stressed this was 'non-violent protest', but it was not **passive resistance**, it was 'active non-violent resistance to evil'.

KEY TERM

First-come, first-served
Southern buses were divided into black and white sections. Sometimes black people would be standing while the white section was empty. They therefore sought seating on a first-come, first-served basis.

Passive resistance
Non-violent refusal to comply with a particular policy.

Using Source E and your own knowledge, suggest reasons why the black community in Montgomery was able to sustain the bus boycott for one year.

SOURCE F

An extract from a Martin Luther King Jr speech to the MIA, December 1955, quoted in *The Papers of Martin Luther King Jr., III*, edited by Clayborne Carson, published by University of California Press, Berkeley, USA, 1997, page 73.

If we are wrong, the Supreme Court of this nation is wrong. If we are wrong, the Constitution of the United States is wrong. If we are wrong, Jesus of Nazareth was merely a … dreamer.

When Montgomery whites used the state of Alabama's law against boycotts against the black community, their mass indictments attracted national media coverage, inspiring Northerners to make collections for the MIA. King was the first boycott leader to be tried. Found guilty, he chose a fine rather than 368 days in jail.

This white hostility made the MIA up the stakes. After litigation partly funded by the NAACP, a federal district court said segregation on buses was unconstitutional, citing *Brown*. Montgomery city commissioners appealed to the Supreme Court but it backed the federal district court in *Browder v. Gayle* (1956). When desegregated buses began operating (December 1956), the boycott was called off.

Results and significance of the Montgomery bus boycott

- Rosa Parks is the best remembered female participant in the Civil Rights Movement, but it could be argued that her defiance and the boycott were very much a product of the whole black community of Montgomery. As she said, 'Every day in the early 1950s we were looking for ways to challenge Jim Crow laws.'
- The boycott did not just come out of the blue: a boycott had long been discussed and planned by the Montgomery NAACP and the Women's Political Council at Alabama State College. Bus boycotts were not new. Montgomery blacks used tactics used at Baton Rouge in 1953. However, there had never been a boycott as long, well organized, well supported and well publicized as the Montgomery one.
- It demonstrated the power of a whole black community using direct but non-violent action. Montgomery whites could not believe local blacks had started and sustained the movement: 'We know the niggers are not that smart'. 'Our leaders', responded Claudette Colvin, 'is just we ourselves'. This was what was new. Here was an alternative to NAACP's litigation tactic.
- It demonstrated the importance of the Churches in the fight for equality.
- It showed the importance and potential of black economic power. Black shoppers could not get downtown without the buses, so businesses lost $1 million. White businessmen began to work against segregation.
- It demonstrated how white extremism frequently helped to increase black unity and determination.

- It revealed the hatred and determined racism of many white Southerners, but also the idealism of a handful of Southern whites like Reverend Robert Graetz, minister at a black Lutheran church in Montgomery, who supported the boycott. His house was bombed.
- It brought King, with all his inspirational rhetorical gifts, to the forefront of the movement. In 1957 he helped to establish a new organization, the Southern Christian Leadership Conference (SCLC) (see pages 72–3). This proved particularly important as the NAACP had been persecuted in the Deep South since *Brown*, although it also aroused jealousy among other black leaders and organizations. King claimed the Montgomery bus boycott signalled the emergence of 'the New Negro', although Roy Wilkins bitterly disagreed (see Source G, page 66).
- It showed the continuing effectiveness of the NAACP strategy of working through the law courts (it took the *Browder* decision to finally get the buses desegregated) and the importance of dedicated individuals such as Rosa Parks.
- In Montgomery itself, the boycott was a limited victory. Apart from the buses, the city remained segregated. Some whites retaliated violently, but when the Ku Klux Klan responded to *Browder v. Gayle* by sending 40 carloads of robed and hooded members through Montgomery's black community, the residents did not retreat behind closed doors as usual, but came out and waved at the motorcade, showing how black morale had been boosted.
- It inspired similar successful bus boycotts in 20 Southern cities, individuals such as Melba Pattillo (see page 68), more Northern white support and more co-operation between Northern and Southern blacks.

Martin Luther King Jr and controversy in 1955

As soon as he gained fame during the Montgomery Bus Boycott, King became involved in great controversies. First, a friend noted that:

King's colleagues felt that he was taking too many bows and enjoying them … he was forgetting that victory … had been the result of collective thought and collective action.

King felt the need to reassure people:

I just happened to be here … If M.L. King had never been born this movement would have taken place … there comes a time when time itself is ready for change. That time has come in Montgomery, and I had nothing to do with it.

One local activist agreed: it was 'a protest of the people … not a one-man show … the leaders couldn't stop it if they wanted to'.

Second, when King claimed the boycott signalled the emergence of 'the new Negro', NAACP leader Roy Wilkins disagreed (see Source G, page 66).

? Study the content of Source G and give reasons that help to explain Wilkins' viewpoint. Do you think there was a 'New Negro'?

SOURCE G

NAACP leader Roy Wilkins, talking in 1956 about the 'New Negro', quoted in *Sweet Land of Liberty* by Robert Cook, published by Longman, Harlow, UK, 1998, page 39.

The Negro of 1956 who stands on his own two feet is not a new Negro; he is the grandson or the great grandson of the men who hated slavery. By his own hands, through his own struggles, in his own organized groups – of churches, fraternal societies, the NAACP and others – he has fought his way to the place where he now stands.

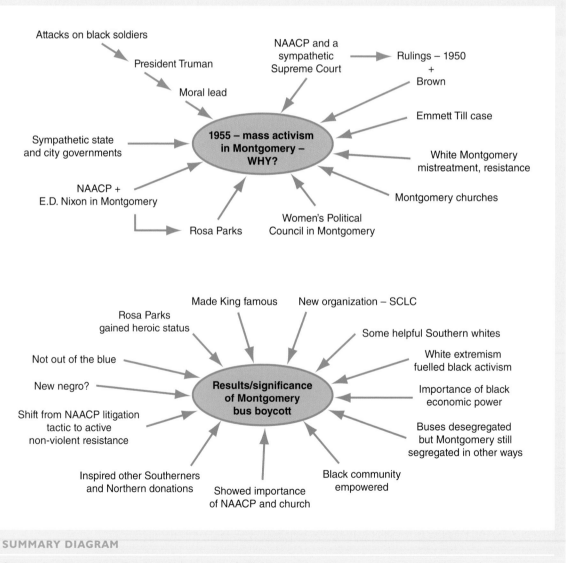

SUMMARY DIAGRAM

Short-term causes of the Civil Rights Movement 1945–55

③ Key debate

▶ **Key question:** *When did the Civil Rights Movement begin?*

Was the Second World War a great turning point?

Historians disagree over the extent and impact of black militancy during the Second World War. In the 1970s, historian Harvard Sitkoff contended that new black militancy during the war (see page 56) led to violence in 47 cities in 1943, but in 1997, he emphasized that patriotism led blacks to decrease the direct action that had grown up in the 1930s. While Sitkoff later saw no direct line of continuity between wartime civil rights activism and 1960s' activism, historian Mark Newman (2004) disagreed, pointing out that the foundations for the 1960s were laid during the Second World War. Historian Dr Stephen Tuck (2001) described the Second World War as 'absolutely key' in transforming the black situation (see pages 57–8).

Did the Civil Rights Movement begin before 1955?

After Martin Luther King Jr's death in 1968, most historians took the classic phase of civil rights activity to be the years of King's ascendancy, from 1955 to 1965. However, subsequent studies of local community action emphasized that the Civil Rights Movement had its origins in the 1930s and 1940s, owing much to the impact of the New Deal, the Second World War and the continuing work of NAACP. Historian Adam Fairclough's study of Louisiana (1995) emphasized the importance of pre-King labour unions, schools, teachers, businessmen and organizations such as NAACP. Studies of individual states by historians such as John Kirk (Arkansas, 1996) and John Dittmer (Mississippi, 1994) confirmed that at the very least there was a 'civil rights struggle' if not a 'civil rights movement' long before 1955. However, Fairclough admitted the 'earlier challenges did not seem to have the force of post-1955 protests': the 'undercurrent of discontent' was 'unstructured and ineffective; the countless instances of individual defiance did not add up to collective resistance'. For example, when A. Philip Randolph called for a one-day boycott of segregated transport in 1943, Southern blacks ignored him.

E.D. Nixon's biographer, John White, confirmed that the 'classic' period had its roots in preceding decades. Probably the main, if subsequently unheralded, force behind the Montgomery bus boycott, Nixon was inspired by and participated in Randolph's black labour movement in the 1920s and NAACP activities in the 1930s and 1940s. Nixon's actions in 1955–6 clearly did not 'come out of the blue'.

While many historians date the start of the Civil Rights Movement to the 1950s, they disagree over the crucial events. Sociologist Aldon Morris (1984) dated it to the Baton Rouge bus boycott (1953). Harvard Sitkoff (1993) saw the *Brown* decision (1954) as the start of the struggle, but law Professor Michael Klarman (1992) concluded that *Brown* 'was a relatively unimportant motivating factor for the Civil Rights Movement', and that its real significance was to generate a vicious white backlash. Historian David Garrow (1994) disagreed, saying that *Brown* inspired the Montgomery bus boycott. Studies of Georgia and Louisiana suggest *Brown* did not generate civil rights activism immediately, although many activists attested its inspirational importance. While Garrow thought the Montgomery bus boycott signalled the start of the Civil Rights Movement, historian Mark Newman (2004) said it 'did not spark a mass movement', and cited SCLC's early ineffectiveness as proof. Charles Payne (1998) argued that the sit-ins (see pages 73–4) 'were a definitive break with the past, the beginning of a period of sustained mass activism'. William Chafe (1980) saw the Greensboro sit-ins as spontaneous, owing little to existing civil rights organizations, and as a great turning point, while Morris (1984) linked them to a pre-existing network of churches, colleges and civil rights groups.

T O K

Given that history is a continuum, is it ever possible to determine definitively when a process 'began'? (History, Logic, Language.)

④ The end of segregation in the South 1955–65

▶ **Key question:** *How and why was* de jure *segregation ended?*

De jure segregation in the South was ended with the Civil Rights Act of 1964 and the Voting Rights Act of 1965. Organizations such as NAACP and individuals such as Martin Luther King Jr played a vital part in this, as did the federal government and changing white opinion.

What were the causes and consequences of the Little Rock Crisis?

→ ## NAACP and Little Rock 1957

Causes of the crisis

The city of Little Rock planned full compliance with *Brown* by 1963. Central High School was to be the first integrated school and nine black students reported there in September 1957. Struggling to get re-elected, Arkansas Governor Orval Faubus decided to exploit white racism to ensure victory. He declared it his duty to prevent the disorder that would arise from integration and ordered the Arkansas **National Guard** to surround the school and to keep black students out.

KEY TERM

National Guard State-based US armed forces reserves.

Melba Pattillo

One of the nine students, Melba Pattillo, wrote about her experiences years later. She had volunteered to be a guinea-pig when asked by the NAACP and church leaders. Her father was against it, saying it endangered her and his job. A white man violently assaulted her crying, 'I'll show you niggers the

SOURCE H

A map showing racial tensions in the USA.

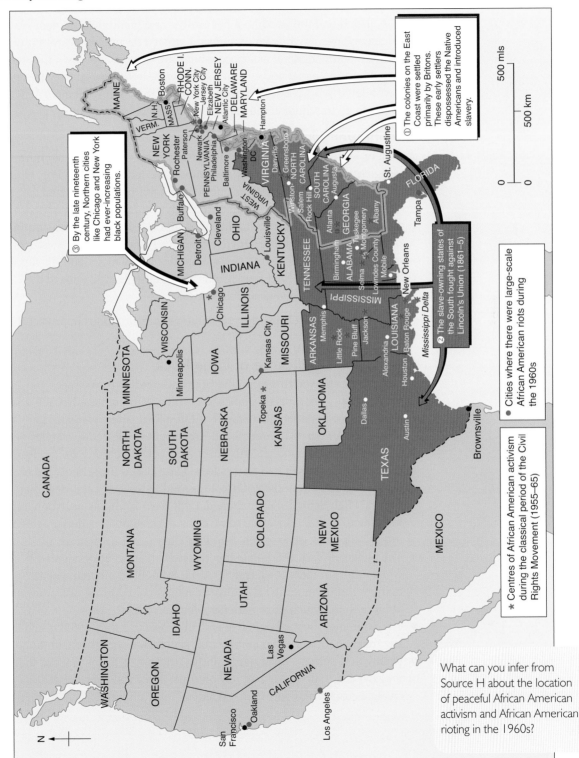

① The colonies on the East Coast were settled primarily by Britons. These early settlers dispossessed the Native Americans and introduced slavery.

③ By the late nineteenth century, Northern cities like Chicago and New York had ever-increasing black populations.

② The slave-owning states of the South fought against Lincoln's Union (1861–5)

• Cities where there were large-scale African American riots during the 1960s

∗ Centres of African American activism during the classical period of the Civil Rights Movement (1955–65)

500 mls

500 km

0

0

What can you infer from Source H about the location of peaceful African American activism and African American rioting in the 1960s?

69

Supreme Court cannot run my life.' Others cried 'Two, four, six, eight, we ain't gonna integrate', 'Keep away from our school', 'Go back to the jungle', 'Lynch the niggers'. Pattillo was inspired by the 'self-assured air' of Thurgood Marshall, and had the backing of her mother and grandmother, many blacks and a few whites. A white boy, whom she trusted despite the warnings of her family, befriended her at school, where she was pushed down the stairs and had burning paper and chemicals thrown at her. Subsequently though, she wondered 'what possessed my parents and the adults of the NAACP to allow us to go to school in the face of such violence'.

Eisenhower's intervention

President Eisenhower (1953–61) said before the crisis that he could never envisage sending in federal troops to enforce the federal court ruling, which doubtless encouraged Faubus. Eisenhower did not believe in federal government activism, but was forced to intervene. Little Rock's mayor told him the mob was out of hand and begged him to act, and the Constitution and federal law seemed threatened. Eisenhower said he had an 'inescapable' responsibility for enforcing the law against 'disorderly mobs' and 'demagogic extremists', and that Soviet propaganda about Little Rock damaged the USA's international 'prestige and influence'.

So, to Southern cries of 'invasion', Eisenhower sent in troops to protect the black children.

Results and significance of Little Rock

- Little Rock showed that Supreme Court rulings like *Brown* met tremendous grassroots resistance in practice. Although the NAACP tried to push desegregation along faster at Little Rock, there was still no dramatic immediate improvement. Faubus got re-elected four times.
- Neither local nor national authorities were keen to enforce *Brown*. Faubus did what Eisenhower had always feared and closed the schools rather than integrate. Eisenhower did not respond. It was not until 1960 that Central High School was integrated. Little Rock's schools were only fully integrated in 1972. However, some cities, such as Atlanta, desegregated to avoid Little Rock-style violence and publicity.
- The image of black children being harassed and spat at by aggressive white adults in Little Rock (see Source I) influenced moderate white opinion throughout the USA. On-site television reporting was pioneered at Little Rock, which drew national television crews.
- The Supreme Court ploughed ahead. In *Cooper v. Aaron* (1958) it said any law that sought to keep public schools segregated was unconstitutional.
- Finally, and perhaps most significantly, African Americans realized that they needed to do more than rely on court decisions. They needed to create a crisis that would demand federal intervention.

SOURCE I

Elizabeth Eckford, one of the 'Little Rock nine', trying to enter Central High School in Little Rock, Arkansas in 1957.

What can you infer from Source I about race relations in Little Rock?

?

SOURCE J

President Eisenhower's defence of Southerners to Chief Justice Earl Warren, quoted in *Eisenhower* by Stephen Ambrose, published by Simon & Schuster, London, UK, 2003, page 380.

All they are concerned about is to see that those sweet little girls are not required to sit in schools alongside some big overgrown Negroes.

Read Source J. Confusingly, some books quote Eisenhower as saying 'bucks' rather than 'Negroes'. Why do other books use 'Negroes'? If Eisenhower actually said 'bucks' should that be reprinted in books such as this one?

?

Eisenhower's Civil Rights Acts

← **Why were the acts passed and how important were they?**

Eisenhower told his speechwriter that although he might call for equality, that did not mean that blacks and whites had 'to mingle socially or that a Negro could court my daughter'. He explained his unease about *Brown* by referring to the 'great emotional strains' and the likely violence against blacks that would arise from the desegregation of schools. As a Republican, he was ideologically averse to large-scale federal government intervention in any great issue, which was why he made no comment on the fate of Emmett Till or the Montgomery bus boycott, and why he was reluctant to use federal power to enforce *Brown* until Little Rock forced his hand. Nevertheless, he called for an end to racial discrimination, worked against it in federal employment and hiring, and was behind the first Civil Rights Acts since the Civil War era.

The 1957 Civil Rights Act

Hoping to win black votes in the 1956 elections, the Eisenhower administration drew up a civil rights bill that aimed to ensure all citizens could exercise the right to vote (only 20 per cent of Southern blacks were registered to vote). In his State of the Union address in January 1957, Eisenhower praised the bill, expressing 'shock' that only 7000 of Mississippi's 900,000 blacks were allowed to vote, and that registrars were setting impossible questions (such as 'How many bubbles are there in a bar of soap?') for those trying to register.

KEY TERM

Filibuster Use of tactic to delay congressional voting on a bill.

Justice Department Branch of the federal government in Washington, DC with special responsibility for enforcing the law and administering justice.

Democratic senators worked to weaken the bill, believing it would damage national and party unity. They claimed it sought to use federal power 'to force a co-mingling of white and Negro children'. Eisenhower then cravenly claimed he did not really know what was in the bill ('there were certain phrases I did not completely understand') and did not fight to keep it intact. Senator Strom Thurmond of South Carolina **filibustered** for 24 hours to try to kill the bill. It passed as a much-weakened act that did little to help blacks exercise the vote (any public official indicted for obstructing a black voter would be tried by an all-white jury). However, it established a Civil Rights Division in the **Justice Department** to prosecute violations of civil rights and a federal Civil Rights Commission to monitor race relations. As the first such act since Reconstruction, it pleased some black leaders. Others felt it was a nauseating sham.

The 1960 Civil Rights Act

In late 1958, Eisenhower introduced another bill because he was concerned about a recent spate of bombings of black schools and churches. While Eisenhower considered the bill to be moderate, Southern Democrats again diluted its provisions. It finally became law because both parties sought black votes in the presidential election year. The act made it a federal crime to obstruct court-ordered school desegregation and established penalties for obstructing black voting.

These Civil Rights Acts of 1957 and 1960 added few black voters to the electoral rolls (70 per cent of Southern blacks remained disenfranchised in 1960), but constituted an acknowledgement of federal responsibilities and encouraged civil rights activists to work for more legislation.

What tactics did black organizations use, and with what success?

→ Organizations

Whereas the NAACP had focused on litigation, organizations established after the Montgomery bus boycott emphasized different tactics.

SCLC 1957–60

The SCLC was established because King felt that a specifically Southern and Christian organization was needed at a time when the NAACP, a national organization, was persecuted in the South because of *Brown*, and CORE lacked dynamism. King hoped that a Church-based organization would be less likely to be persecuted. He also felt that new tactics were needed. Although the NAACP's legal challenges had demolished 'separate but equal' in the law courts, *de jure* segregation continued in the South. CORE had attempted direct non-violent action to effect change in the past (see page 56), but had failed to mobilize large numbers of people and to make headlines. However, the Montgomery bus boycott had shown that now such tactics could be successful.

Drawing attention to abuses was King's favourite tactic, and the easiest method was to organize a march. His 1957 march in Washington, DC attracted around 20,000 people, but even King admitted that the SCLC achieved little else in its first three years of existence. Poorly organized and without a salaried staff or mass support, SCLC's Crusade for Citizenship, a grassroots campaign designed to encourage blacks to vote, failed.

NAACP leader Roy Wilkins disliked King and SCLC (see pages 65–6). 'Jealousy among black leaders is so thick it can be cut with a knife', said the African American *Pittsburgh Courier*. Wilkins was jealous of King and the SCLC, and they disagreed over tactics. Wilkins and the NAACP favoured litigation; King preferred mass action. A new organization, SNCC, preferred empowerment of local communities.

Sit-ins and the birth of the SNCC 1960

In 1960, four black college students spontaneously ignored a request to leave the all-white Woolworth's cafeteria in Greensboro, North Carolina. Other students took up and retained the seats, day after day, forcing the lunch counter to close. These 'sit-ins' across the South were joined by 70,000 students, better educated than their parents and more impatient with the slow progress towards equality. Responsibility for this mass action can be attributed to the original four, or the students who joined them, or the other black protesters who had pioneered the same technique in Chicago in the Second World War and in Oklahoma and Kansas in 1957–8, or the press, which covered Greensboro extensively.

When a Greensboro SCLC member contacted him, King quickly arrived to encourage the students and assure them of full SCLC support, saying, 'What is new in your fight is the fact that it was initiated, fed, and sustained by students.' Atlanta students persuaded King to join them in sit-ins. Although critics such as disgruntled SCLC employee Ella Baker implied that King always had to be in the forefront, King's leadership was characterized by a willingness to be led by others when their methods were effective.

The significance of the sit-ins

The sit-ins confirmed that the focus of black activism had switched from legal challenges to direct action. They helped to erode Jim Crow. Loss of business made Woolworth's desegregate all its lunch counters by the end of 1961 and 150 cities soon desegregated various public places. Black students had been mobilized, although when they set up the Student Non-Violent Co-ordinating Committee (SNCC, pronounced SNICK), inter-organizational strife increased. SNCC accused SCLC of keeping donations intended for SNCC, NAACP lawyer Thurgood Marshall refused to represent 'a bunch of crazy colored students', while King's public acknowledgement of NAACP/

SOURCE K

A sit-in at a Woolworth's lunch counter in Jackson, Mississippi, in May 1963.

SCLC divisions infuriated Roy Wilkins. Blacks desperately needed a single leader who could unite all activists. King never managed to fulfil that role, for which others such as the prickly Wilkins were probably far more to blame than he was.

Encouraged by Ella Baker, the students felt their actions had rendered King's cautious programme and 'top-down' leadership obsolete. SNCC worked to empower ordinary African Americans and from 1961 to 1964, mobilized many in places like Danville (Virginia), Lowndes County (Alabama), Albany (Georgia), Pine Bluff (Arkansas) and the Mississippi Delta.

CORE and the Freedom Rides 1961

CORE's 'Freedom Rides' electrified the Civil Rights Movement. A small, integrated group (see Source L) travelled the South testing Supreme Court rulings against segregation on interstate transport (*Morgan v. Virginia*, 1946) and on interstate bus facilities (*Boynton v. Virginia*, 1960). CORE had used the tactic in 1947 without success. Now CORE's director James Farmer explained that:

We planned the Freedom Ride with the specific intention of creating a crisis. We were counting on the bigots in the South to do our work for us. We figured that the government would have to respond if we created a situation that was headline news all over the world, and affected the nation's image abroad.

As expected, racists attacked black passengers. In Alabama, they used clubs and chains and burned the buses. SNCC sent in reinforcement riders.

The Freedom Rides publicized white racism and lawlessness in the South and led Attorney General Robert Kennedy and the Interstate Commerce Commission to try to enforce the Supreme Court rulings on desegregated interstate travel in November 1961, demonstrating yet again the importance of exposing Southern white lawlessness and provoking federal intervention. However, black divisions remained. CORE insisted SCLC announce that CORE had originated the Freedom Ride!

SOURCE L

Extracts from transcripts of interviews with Freedom Riders (no date given), quoted on www.outreach.olemiss.edu/Freedom_Riders/Resources/

1. Charles Person, African American:

I grew up in Atlanta … at a time when America needed scientists … My [test] scores and my [grades] were good enough to get me accepted at MIT [Massachusetts Institute of Technology], but Georgia Tech was also the number one engineering school in the South, so I applied to Georgia Tech, and of course rejected my application. So I could not understand, here we were competing with the Russians, because the Russians had launched Sputnik, and we say we needed scientists, yet I was being denied an opportunity to go to a school which I was eminently qualified to go to, so that gave me the impetus to get involved in all the civil rights activities that were happening on campus … So this was a great time, the energy on campus with all the kids being involved in all those kind of activities, it just snowballed. Once I got involved, it was infectious.

2. Sandra Nixon, African American:

I grew up in New Orleans … I was … in college at Southern University in New Orleans and met some … members of the Congress on Racial Equality. After listening to them talking about the social injustices that were going on in the city of New Orleans, I decided to become a member of … CORE.

3. Joan Trumpower Mulholland, white

I was born in Washington DC … My involvement came about from my religious conviction, and the contradiction between life in America with what was being taught in Sunday School. I was at Duke University in Durham [North Carolina], which was the second city to have sit-ins, and the Presbyterian chaplain arranged for the students … to come over and talk with us about what the sit-ins were about and the philosophical and religious underpinnings … At the end, they invited us to join them on sit-ins in the next week or so, and that started a snowball effect.

4. Albert Gordon, white:

Why some of us have been ready to do things, and others not? In my own past, I was born in Europe, and I did see the Nazis, and most of my family was killed by the Nazis during World War II in the concentration camp, because I was Jewish … So those things can explain in part my social conscience, but by no means all together … When I saw the young people first in the first sit-ins and the courage that they had to have, and then saw a couple of years later the bus in Anniston, and Jim Peck being so brutally beaten, I thought I just had to do something, and simply volunteered and proceeded.

What can you infer about the Freedom Riders as a group and about their motives from Source L?

The Albany Movement 1961–2

In late 1961, SNCC organized black students from Albany State College, Georgia, in sit-ins in Albany's bus station, which had ignored the Interstate Commerce Commission's order to desegregate. Hundreds were arrested. White businesses were boycotted but the city authorities still refused to desegregate, despite pressure from Attorney General Kennedy.

Older leaders of the 'Albany Movement' invited King to join them, which angered SNCC leaders who stressed that the Albany Movement was 'by and for local Negroes'. King led a march and came to a promising agreement with the city authorities, but after he left, the authorities reneged on the agreement.

How and why had the Albany Movement failed?

The Albany Movement petered out in a series of decreasingly supported protests. King considered Albany a major defeat. Although the interstate terminal facilities were desegregated, and more black voters were allowed to register, the city closed the parks, sold the swimming pool, integrated the library only after removing all the seats, and refused to desegregate the schools.

The Albany Movement had failed to generate helpful publicity (when blacks became violent, the local police chief was careful not to respond in kind). Black divisions had been damaging: some were paid informants of the white city leadership, local black leaders resented 'outsiders', and the NAACP, SNCC and SCLC failed to co-operate.

On the other hand, the entire black community of Albany had been mobilized and local leaders claimed that fear of white power had greatly decreased. SNCC demonstrated that its 'jail not bail' strategy could fill the jails with protesters and bring the courts and jails to a standstill. King learned that SCLC intervention in an area without a strong SCLC presence was inadvisable and that it was probably more effective to focus on one particular aspect of segregation. He said that as blacks had little political power, it was unwise to concentrate on talks with the white authorities; it made more sense to boycott white businesses so businessmen would advocate negotiations. All these lessons suggested tactics for Birmingham, Alabama.

Birmingham, April to May 1963

In 1963, King concentrated on segregation and unequal opportunities in Birmingham, Alabama. King chose Birmingham for several reasons:

- Faced with competing civil rights organizations and the increasing attractiveness of black nationalism (see Chapter 3), the SCLC had to demonstrate that it could be dynamic and successful.
- The SNCC and NAACP were relatively inactive in Birmingham, where the local black leader was affiliated to the SCLC and King's own brother was a pastor.

- White divisions looked promising. While white businessman felt racism held the city back, white extremists had recently castrated a Negro, prohibited the sale of a book that featured black and white rabbits, and campaigned to stop 'Negro music' being played on white radio stations.
- King described Birmingham as 'by far' the USA's 'worst big city' for racism. It was likely to produce the kind of violent white opposition that won national sympathy. Birmingham's Public Safety Commissioner 'Bull' Connor was a hot-tempered, determined segregationist who had ensured that Freedom Riders under attack from a racist Birmingham mob were unprotected by his police, to whom he gave the day off for Mother's Day. Bull and Birmingham would show the media segregation at its worst. 'To cure injustices', said King, 'you must expose them before the light of human conscience and the bar of public opinion'.
- King was impatient with the Kennedy administration's inactivity: 'The key to everything is federal commitment', he said. He hoped Connor would elicit a response from Kennedy.

Events in Birmingham

In Birmingham, King was leading rather than led. He made miscalculations. The SCLC failed to recruit enough local demonstrators, because many felt that the recent electoral defeat and imminent retirement of Connor made action unnecessary. King admitted that there was 'tremendous resistance' in the black community to his planned demonstrations. The SCLC had to use demonstrators in crowded areas to give the impression of mass action and to encourage onlookers to participate.

Then, as expected, Connor attracted national attention. His police and their dogs turned on black demonstrators. King defied an injunction and marched, knowing his arrest would gain national attention and perhaps inspire others. Kept in solitary confinement and not allowed private meetings with his lawyer, he wrote the inspirational 'Letter from Birmingham Jail' in which he eloquently defended direct action. His wife Coretta's phone call to President Kennedy obtained his release.

It remained difficult to mobilize sufficient demonstrators. 'You know, we've got to get something going', said King. 'The press is leaving.' Despite considerable local opposition and King's doubts about the morality of the policy (the black nationalist Malcolm X said, 'Real men don't put their children on the firing line'), the SCLC enlisted black school children, some as young as six. This proved successful. Soon, 500 young marchers were in custody and Birmingham was creating headlines again. Connor's high-pressure water hoses tore clothes off students' backs and SCLC succeeded in its aim of 'filling the jails'. A leading SCLC official 'thanked' Bull Connor for his violent response, without which there would have been no publicity.

An agreement was reached to improve the situation of Birmingham blacks, but the Klan tried to sabotage it, bombing King's brother's house and King's motel room. Blacks began to riot, a policeman was stabbed, and

Birmingham degenerated into chaos, which President Kennedy said was 'damaging the reputation' of Birmingham and the USA. Robert Kennedy feared this could trigger off national violence, and urged his brother to protect the Birmingham agreement: 'If King loses, worse leaders are going to take his place.'

Results and significance of Birmingham

Birmingham was the first time King really led the movement. He had correctly assessed how Connor would react and how the media would depict his reactions. 'There never was any more skilful manipulation of the news media than there was in Birmingham', said a leading SCLC staffer. King had shown that he could lead from the front and force desegregation, if through rather artificially engineered violence. He recognized that non-violent demonstrations 'make people inflict violence on you, so you precipitate violence'. However, he excused it: 'We are merely bringing to the surface the tension that has always been at the heart of the problem.' Critics accused him of hypocrisy. One said, 'He marches for peace on one day, and then the very next day threatens actions we think are coldly calculated to bring violent responses from otherwise peaceful neighborhoods.'

While little changed in Birmingham itself, SCLC's campaign immediately inspired protests throughout the South and showed the USA and the world Southern segregation at its worst. The Kennedy administration admitted that Birmingham was crucial in persuading President Kennedy to push the bill that eventually became the 1964 Civil Rights Act. 'We are on the threshold of a significant breakthrough', said King, 'and the greatest weapon is the mass demonstration'.

The March on Washington, August 1963

Marches were a favourite tactic of civil rights activists, and the nation's capital was a favourite location. Masterminded by A. Philip Randolph, the March on Washington of August 1963 aimed to encourage passage of the civil rights bill and executive action to increase black employment. Initially, NAACP leader Roy Wilkins was not supportive, which worried King, who felt the march would maintain black morale and advertise the effectiveness of non-violent protest. He feared that non-violence was decreasingly popular among blacks, many of whom were embittered by the slow pace of change.

The march proved a great success. The predominantly middle-class crowd was around a quarter of a million, roughly 25 per cent of whom were white. King's memorable speech (see Source M) made a powerful appeal to white USA, with its references to the Declaration of Independence and the Bible, and emphasis on the Old Testament God who freed his enslaved people. This was King the leader at his best, involved in an action the morality of which could not be doubted, and the effectiveness of which he immeasurably increased by helping to persuade Wilkins to participate and by making a superb speech.

SOURCE M

An extract from Martin Luther King's 'I Have a Dream' speech, 1963, quoted on http://mlk-kpp01.stanford.edu/index.php/about/encyclopedia/documentsentry/doc_august_28_1963_i_have_a_dream/

I have a dream. It is a dream deeply rooted in the American dream. I have a dream that one-day this nation will rise up and live out the true meaning of its creed – we hold these truths to be self-evident, that all men are created equal …

I have a dream that my four little children will one-day live in a nation where they will not be judged by the color of their skin but by the content of their character. I have a dream today! …

Let freedom ring … When we allow freedom to ring, when we let it ring from every village and every hamlet, from every state and every city, we will be able to speed up that day when all of God's children – black men and white men, Jews and Gentiles, Protestants and Catholics – will be able to join hands and sing in the words of the old Negro spiritual, 'Free at last, free at last; thank God Almighty, we are free at last.'

> **?** Using the extract in Source M and your own research into the speech, give reasons why this speech has become so famous.

The significance of the march

The March on Washington was the first time the major civil rights leaders collaborated on a national undertaking (the unity did not last). It impressed television audiences across the world. Historians disagree over the extent to which its emotional impact helped the passage of civil rights legislation: while many contemporaries were thrilled by the march, the *New York Times* described Congress as unmoved by it, and Malcolm X was unimpressed (see Source N).

SOURCE N

Extracts from Malcolm X on the March on Washington (1. Told to an *Amsterdam News* reporter, 1963. 2. Speech, 4 December 1963, quoted on http://politics.lilithezine.com/Malcolm-X-December-4-1963.html. 3. From *The Autobiography of Malcolm X*, published by Penguin, London, UK, 1965, pages 278–81).

1. *The Negroes spent a lot of money, had a good time, and enjoyed a real circus or carnival type atmosphere.*

2. *Now that the show is over, the black masses are still without land, without jobs, and without houses. Their Christian churches are still being bombed, their innocent little girls murdered. So what did the March on Washington accomplish? Nothing.*

3. *How was a one-day 'integrated' picnic going to counter-influence those representatives of prejudice rooted deep in the psyche of the American white man for 400 years?*

> **?** Read Source N. Why and how fairly did Malcolm X criticize the March on Washington?

SNCC and Mississippi

The SNCC's finest hour was the Black Freedom Movement in Mississippi, where in 1960, only 5.2 per cent of black adults could vote (the Southern average was over 30 per cent). White voter registrars set impossible questions and opened offices at inconvenient hours to stop black voter registration. Although half of Mississippians were black, there had been no elected black official since 1877. With black people politically powerless, Mississippi whites spent three times more on white students and 70 per cent of Mississippi's black population were illiterate. With only six black doctors in Mississippi, black babies were twice as likely to die as white babies. Half a million black Mississippians had migrated north to escape to a better life. King's close associate Andrew Young confessed that the SCLC 'knew better than to try to take on Mississippi'. In 1961, NAACP activists, increasingly victimized, called for help from the SNCC, knowing that SNCC's white volunteers would attract media attention to Mississippi's racist horrors.

SNCC activities and achievements in Mississippi

Unprotected by the federal government and in fear of white extremists, SNCC worked at the local community level, establishing Freedom Schools to educate would-be voters and get them registered. It was the local, poorer black people such as sharecropper Fannie Lou Hamer, not the black middle class, who responded when the SNCC organized the 'Freedom Vote' (a mock election for disenfranchised blacks) in 1963, and promoted another voter registration drive (the Mississippi Summer Project, or **Freedom Summer**), in 1964. Predominantly white Northern volunteers poured into Mississippi to help. All of the USA took notice of 'Mississippi Freedom Summer' after three young activists (two were white) were murdered by segregationists.

SNCC also helped to organize the Mississippi Freedom Democratic Party (MFDP) delegation to the Democratic **National Convention** in Atlantic City in 1964. The MFDP delegates pointed out that while half of Mississippi's population was black, the Mississippi delegation for the Democratic Party was 'lily-white'. Although the MFDP delegation was not welcomed in Atlantic City, MFDP successfully politicized many poor black Mississippians (especially women), developed new grassroots leaders, and brought black Mississippi suffering to national attention.

Disillusioned with the lack of federal protection, the SNCC became far more militant, which contributed to the disintegration of the civil rights coalition.

The 1964 Civil Rights Act

During 1963, the Kennedy administration finally introduced a civil rights bill to Congress, where it remained stuck when Kennedy was assassinated and Vice President Lyndon Johnson became president.

Johnson's motivation

Johnson was determined to get Kennedy's civil rights bill through Congress. He envisioned a 'Great Society' for America, with 'an end to poverty and racial injustice'. He believed that discrimination was morally wrong, and described how, when his black cook drove to Texas, she could not use the whites-only facilities in a petrol station:

When they had to go to the bathroom, they would … pull off on a side road, and Zephyr Wright, the cook of the vice-president of the United States, would squat in the road to pee. That's wrong. And there ought to be something to change that.

Johnson remained convinced that reform would help the economic, political and spiritual reintegration of the South within the nation. He felt duty-bound to see the late president's bill through, his sense of obligation increased by the tragic circumstances of Kennedy's death. When Johnson told Roy Wilkins he was 'free at last' from his Texas constituency and as president could help blacks, Wilkins considered him 'absolutely sincere'.

How and why the bill passed

The civil rights bill faced considerable opposition in Congress, including the longest filibuster in Senate history, but finally became an act because:

- Black activists had drawn the attention of the nation and its legislators to injustices. 'The real hero of this struggle is the American Negro', said Johnson.
- NAACP, trade unionists and the Churches had lobbied Congress incessantly.
- Kennedy had won over the Republican **minority leader** Everett Dirksen before his death.
- The nation was saddened by Kennedy's death. Passing his bill seemed an appropriate tribute. Johnson made emotive appeals to Kennedy's memory and to national traditions and ideals.
- Important congressional leaders such as Hubert Humphrey worked hard on the bill.
- A Johnson aide gave the credit for the passage of the bill to the president himself, who devoted a staggering amount of his time, energy and political capital to breaking the Senate filibuster and ensuring the passage of the act.
- Johnson won over a few Southerners by appealing to their self-interest, as when he emphasized how the bill would help to get blacks and **Hispanics** working (see pages 148–9).
- The bill had increasing national support: by January 1964, 68 per cent of US citizens favoured it. After Birmingham, national religious organizations increasingly supported the measure. Congress could not afford to ignore this marked swing in public opinion.

 **KEY TERM**

Minority leader Leader of the party with fewer members in Congress.

Hispanics Spanish-speaking people in the USA, usually of Latin American origin.

The significance of the Civil Rights Act of 1964

The 1964 Civil Rights Act gave the federal government the legal tools to end *de jure* segregation in the South, prohibited discrimination in public places, furthered school desegregation and established an Equal Employment Commission.

However, the act did little to facilitate black voting, and little to improve race relations. Many black people felt the act had not gone far enough. They still suffered from poverty and discrimination. The weeks following the passage of the act saw riots in the black ghettos of many East Coast cities and there were signs of a Northern working-class white backlash in the popularity of Alabama's racist Governor George Wallace in presidential primaries. Johnson was hurt and angry. He knew 'we [Democrats] just delivered the South to the Republican Party for a long time to come'. He felt he had done a great deal and at great cost to help black people and now rioters embarrassed him and the party.

Selma 1965

Despite the 1964 Civil Rights Act, little changed in Selma, Alabama, where about half of the 29,000 population was black and had segregated schools, buses, churches, restaurants, playgrounds, public toilets and drinking fountains. They used a different library and swimming pool. They could only have certain jobs and houses. White neighbourhoods had paved streets, black ones had dirt roads. The average white family income was four times that of black families. The local newspapers kept the black and white news separate. Despite an SNCC campaign, only 23 blacks were registered to vote. Lawsuits initiated by Robert Kennedy's Justice Department were still bogged down in the courts.

King announced Selma 'has become a symbol of bitter-end resistance to the Civil Rights Movement in the Deep South'. It promised exploitable divisions within the white community. Selma's Sheriff Jim Clark could be trusted to react as brutally as Bull Connor, which would result in national publicity and revitalize the SCLC and the whole Civil Rights Movement. While some local black activists feared the SCLC would 'come into town and leave too soon' or ignore them, others said that as the SNCC had lost its dynamism there it was an ideal opportunity for the SCLC. Concentration on Selma was the most specific thing the SCLC had done for a year, a year in which King said he and the others had 'failed to assert the leadership the movement needed'.

King led would-be voters to register at Selma County Court building, but despite a federal judge's ruling, there were no registrations. Several incidents made headlines. A trooper shot a black youth who was trying to shield his mother from a beating. Whites threw venomous snakes at blacks trying to register. Keen for the media to show brutality, King held back men who tried to stop Clark clubbing a black woman. He publicly admitted in a letter to the *New York Times* that he wanted to be arrested to publicize the fact that Selma blacks were not allowed to register to vote: 'This is Selma, Alabama. There are more Negroes in jail with me than there are on the voting rolls.'

However, when Selma did not prove as explosive as King had hoped, the SCLC and SNCC organized a march from Selma to Montgomery (Alabama's capital) to publicize the need for a Voting Rights Act. Eighty Alabama whites joined the march. Television viewers saw state troopers attack the marchers with clubs and used tear gas, and this 'Bloody Sunday' aroused nationwide criticism of Selma's whites. President Johnson asked King to call off the next march, but King felt that constituted a betrayal of his followers. Without informing the SNCC, King got the marchers to approach the state troopers then retreat. SNCC felt betrayed and accused him of cowardice.

How significant was Selma?

Historian Stephen Oates (1994) described Selma as 'the movement's finest hour'. King thought the nationwide criticism of 'Bloody Sunday' was 'a shining moment in the conscience of man' (there were sympathetic interracial marches in cities such as Chicago, Detroit, New York and Boston). Johnson had the voting rights bill ready before Selma, but Selma and 'Bloody Sunday' constituted a dramatic reminder that there were US citizens who could not vote and could be attacked without redress. Selma sped up the passage of the Voting Rights Act (August 1965), in support of which Johnson made a persuasive speech before Congress that was one of his best (see page 149). King said the speech brought tears to his eyes. On the other hand, although the NAACP had been very supportive in the law courts, the SNCC publicly criticized the SCLC as perpetually leaving behind 'a string of embittered cities' such as St Augustine (1964) and Selma, which were worse off than when the SCLC had first got there. The SNCC said the SCLC just used people in those cities to make a point. Disgruntled St Augustine activists claimed King and SCLC had 'screwed' them. One said, 'I don't want him back here now.' Selma's activists felt betrayed by SCLC's withdrawal. The SCLC had raised a great deal of money because Selma was in the headlines, then left and spent the money in the North (see page 91). SNCC gleefully quoted an arrogant SCLC representative who said, 'They need us more than we need them. We can bring the press in with us and they can't.' The SNCC also accused the SCLC of 'leader worship' of King. Black divisions were clearly worsening.

The Voting Rights Act 1965

The Voting Rights Act ended literacy tests and poll taxes (see page 56). It had a dramatic effect on the South. By late 1966, only four of the old Confederate states had fewer than 50 per cent of their eligible blacks registered. By 1968, even Mississippi was up to 59 per cent. In 1980, the proportion of registered black voters was only seven per cent less than the proportion of whites. The numbers of African Americans elected to office in the South increased six-fold from 1965 to 1969, then doubled from 1969 to 1980. The enlarged black vote went a little way towards countering the Democratic Party's loss of Southern white voters.

A legislative revolution 1964–5

Johnson engineered a legislative revolution with the Civil Rights Act, the Voting Rights Act, an Elementary and Secondary Education Act (1965) that provided federal funding to poorer states such as Mississippi and helped to increase the percentage of black students with a high school diploma (40 per cent in 1960 and 60 per cent in 1970), and a Higher Education Act (1965) that gave significant aid to poor black colleges and contributed to a four-fold increase in black college students within a decade. Although his healthcare reform in 1965 was not specifically aimed at African Americans, it helped to halve the black infant mortality rate.

How had Johnson managed it? It was a 'unique set of circumstances', according to biographer Irving Bernstein (1996). Owing to his 24 years in Congress, for many of which he was Democratic Party leader, Johnson had unprecedented experience in getting legislation through the Democrat-dominated Congress. Congressmen knew their constituents were unusually receptive at this time to righting national wrongs, partly because they felt it would somehow atone for Kennedy's death. Most important of all, Johnson was exceptionally persuasive and determined, and had a lifelong commitment to helping the poor.

However, for Johnson as for King, the best times were over (see Chapter 3).

Events	Achievements
NAACP and Little Rock 1957	Publicized failure to comply with *Brown*; forced federal intervention
Eisenhower's Civil Rights Acts 1957, 1960	Feeble, but set precedents
SCLC 1957–60	20,000 marched on Washington, but little else
Sit-ins 1960	Many places desegregated; SNCC established; grassroots work
CORE's Freedom Rides 1961	Desegregated interstate travel
Albany Movement 1961–2	Bad publicity; some desegregation
Birmingham 1963	Good publicity, great contribution to 1964 Civil Rights Act
March on Washington 1963	Inspirational publicity, contribution to 1964 Civil Rights Act
SNCC and Mississippi 1961–4	Empowerment of local communities; good publicity
Civil Rights Act 1964	Ended *de jure* segregation in South
Selma 1965	Good publicity; vital to passage of 1965 Voting Right Act
Voting Rights Act 1965	Filled gaps in 1964 act; enabled blacks to vote

SUMMARY DIAGRAM

The end of segregation in the South 1955–65

Chapter summary

African Americans and the Civil Rights Movement

When Europeans colonized North America, they introduced slavery. It continued in the Southern states until the Civil War (1861–5), after which freed slaves were given theoretical equality in the civil rights amendments of 1865–70. However, the federal government soon lost interest in their welfare, and Southern white supremacy was restored with the introduction of *de jure* segregation. Many Southern blacks migrated North, although even there *de facto* segregation reaffirmed their inferiority.

Black tactics for dealing with their position of inferiority always varied and led to disagreement. In the late nineteenth and early twentieth centuries, some advocated concentration on economic improvement (accommodationism) while others established NAACP to fight segregation.

Black activism dramatically increased as the twentieth century wore on, fuelled by unions, black newspapers, the Harlem Renaissance, organizations and slowly increasing sympathy from the federal government. Two world wars in which the USA claimed to be fighting for democracy increased black consciousness, and President Truman (1945–53) put civil rights on the national agenda with his call for legislation to end inequality. Truman began the process whereby minorities would gain equal employment rights. The increasingly liberal Supreme Court responded to NAACP suits with important rulings that culminated in *Brown* (1954). *Brown* undermined all justification for segregation and the 'separate but equal' doctrine espoused by the Supreme Court in 1896, but the court had no powers of enforcement and the desegregation of schools was a slow process, fiercely resisted by many whites. The murder of Emmett Till and the arrest of Rosa Parks demonstrated continuing Southern black vulnerability. However, Parks' arrest triggered the first great demonstration of mass activism, the Montgomery bus boycott, which brought Martin Luther King Jr to national attention and resulted in the desegregation of Montgomery's buses. Although not particularly sympathetic to African Americans, President Eisenhower felt he had to send in troops to protect the nine children who tried to enter Central High School in Little Rock, Arkansas, and to introduce civil rights bills that became feeble but precedent-setting acts in 1957 and 1960.

The Montgomery bus boycott was followed by a series of black campaigns that eventually resulted in the 1964 Civil Rights Act, which ended *de jure* segregation, and the 1965 Voting Rights Act, which gave African Americans political influence. These campaigns included the 1960 sit-ins, which led to the birth of SNCC, and CORE's 1961 Freedom Rides, which led to the desegregation of interstate transport. In 1963, SCLC's Birmingham campaign and the March on Washington played an important part in the eventual passage of the 1964 act and SCLC's Selma campaign was vital in the passage of the 1965 act. The campaigns were not always immediately successful, as with the Albany movement (1961–2), and were often plagued by unpunished violence, as with SNCC's grassroots work in Mississippi. Nevertheless, persistent black activism brought about the demise of Jim Crow. Perhaps equally important was President Johnson's determination to create a more equal society.

✅ Examination advice

How to answer 'to what extent' questions

The command term <u>to what extent</u> is a popular one in IB exams. You are asked to evaluate one argument or idea over another. Stronger essays will also address more than one interpretation. This is often a good question in which to discuss how different historians have viewed the issue.

Example

<u>To what extent</u> were civil rights movements divided in the 1960s?

1 Beyond stating the degree to which you agree with the premise, you must focus on the words <u>civil rights movements</u> and <u>divided</u> in the question. Remember, you will need to make a judgement about the degree to which the movements were divided.

2 First take at least five minutes to write a short outline. In order to gauge the degree of division, you should point out the goals of each group, their plans for actions, and how and when the groups co-operated with one another. In some instances, the movements appealed to different sectors and regional areas in the USA. An example of an outline is given below.

> * *NAACP: [As elsewhere, you do not need to write out the complete spelling of such an organization beyond the first mention of the group.]*
> *Goals/Actions: tried to obtain racial equality through use of the courts. After* **Brown v. Board of Education** *decision (1954), NAACP found it difficult to operate in the South. One of the oldest civil rights movements. Some animosity between leader Roy Wilkins and Martin Luther King Jr. Wilkins did participate in 1963 March on Washington.*
> * *CORE:*
> *Goals/Actions: organized sit-ins to combat* **de facto** *segregation in Chicago. Tried direct non-violent actions in the beginning but failed to mobilize many and failed to garner publicity. Organized successful Freedom Rides (1963). SNCC helped out when many CORE members were imprisoned. CORE insisted on being seen as the prime mover behind the success of Freedom Rides in ending segregation in interstate transport.*
> * *SCLC:*
> *Goals/Actions: stressed mass actions over litigation. Based mostly in southern states, where the aim was to end* **de jure** *segregation and gain equality.*

1963 March on Washington showed co-operation between SCLC and
NAACP. Selma to Montgomery March was evidence of SCLC and
SNCC co-operation. Martin Luther King, Jr leader.

- *SNCC:*
Goals/Actions: More locally based than national. Worked to
empower ordinary African Americans. 1961 Albany Movement
showed discord among SNCC, SCLC, and NAACP. Strong local action
in Mississippi (1960 Freedom Summer). More militant. Younger
members than other groups.

3 In the introduction, be sure to mention the main civil rights movements
   such as the Congress of Racial Equality (CORE), National Association for
   the Advancement of Colored Peoples (NAACP), Southern Christian
   Leadership Conference (SCLC) and the Student Nonviolent Coordinating
   Committee (SNCC). Briefly mention instances of division and unity. An
   example of a good introductory paragraph for this question is given below.

In the 1960s, several civil rights groups were active in trying to
secure equal rights for African Americans, particularly those living
in the Southern states. These groups included the Congress of Racial
Equality (CORE), National Association for the Advancement of
Colored Peoples (NAACP), Southern Christian Leadership Conference
(SCLC) and the Student Nonviolent Coordinating Committee (SNCC).
Because of differences in strategies, goals, leadership, and geographic
focus it was very difficult for the groups to work together effectively
in all situations. This was clearly demonstrated when the Albany
Movement failed in 1961. Nonetheless, there were instances when two
or more of the movements did co-ordinate efforts and did achieve
success such as during the March on Washington in 1963.

4 In the body of the essay, you need to discuss each of the points you raised
   in the introduction. Devote at least a paragraph to each one. It would be a
   good idea to order these in terms of which ones you think are most
   important. Be sure to make the connection between the points you raise
   and the major thrust of your argument. An example of how one of the
   points could be addressed is given below.

The Albany Movement in 1961 was an effort to force authorities in Albany, Georgia to desegregate public facilities. The SNCC took the lead and led sit-ins at the local bus terminal. In ensuing demonstrations hundreds of activists were arrested. SNCC had hoped to promote local action but the arrival of Dr King and others from the SCLC meant that attention was drawn away from the SNCC. King led a march and then signed an agreement with white city officials. After King departed, the officials reneged on the agreement. Continued infighting among several of the civil rights groups led to a series of smaller and smaller demonstrations and left a disheartened and divided movement in Albany.

5 In the conclusion offer final remarks on the extent to which the civil rights groups were not unified. Avoid adding any new information or themes in your concluding thoughts. An example of a good concluding paragraph is given below.

*In conclusion, it is clear that the civil rights movements in the 1960s were sometimes in opposition to one another. Some leaders felt that the best tactic was to attack segregation through the courts while others wished to force white intransigence and violence into the open. This lack of unity meant that some marches and demonstrations failed to achieve their goals. At the same time, there were instances when groups did come together to great effect. While divisions sometimes slowed the process of desegregation, the tide had clearly turned in the USA and the sum total of actions in Washington and throughout the South meant that the days of **de jure** racial separation were numbered.*

6 Now try writing a complete answer to the question following the advice above.

Examination practice

Below are three exam-style questions for you to practise on this topic.

1 Assess the impact of non-violent resistance to the success of the Civil
Rights Movement.
(For guidance on how to answer 'assess' questions, see pages 121–2.)

2 Evaluate the success of the NAACP at the Supreme Court.
(For guidance on how to answer 'evaluate' questions, see pages 171–3.)

3 Analyse the reasons for the rise of the Civil Rights Movement.
(For guidance on how to answer 'analyse' questions, see pages 51–2.)

CHAPTER 3

Martin, Malcolm and Black Power

This chapter focuses on the problems of the ghettos and the attempts made to deal with them by Martin Luther King Jr's Southern Christian Leadership Conference and the other civil rights organizations, and by the Black Power movement. The chapter compares and evaluates the achievements of King, Malcolm X and the Black Power movement. You need to consider the following questions throughout this chapter:

✪ What were King's contributions to the success of the Civil Rights Movement?

✪ Who or what played the most important role in the Civil Rights Movement?

✪ How and why were the Nation of Islam and Malcolm X important?

✪ Why and with what results did Black Power emerge?

✪ How new and successful was the Black Power movement?

① The role of Martin Luther King Jr in the Civil Rights Movement

▶ **Key question:** *What were King's contributions to the success of the Civil Rights Movement?*

Although the great Civil Rights Movement of 1955–65 helped to change the South, it did nothing for the problems of the Northern, Midwestern and Western ghettos. As King would see in Los Angeles in 1965 and Chicago in 1966, ghetto life was soul destroying. Housing was poor, amenities were few. Those born in the ghetto found it hard to break out of the cycle of poverty. Only 32 per cent of ghetto pupils finished high school, compared to 56 per cent of white children. Ghetto schools did not provide a solid educational foundation for good jobs. In addition, automation decreased the number of factory jobs for unskilled workers in the 1950s and 1960s, which led to a disproportionate amount of black unemployment. In the early 1960s, African Americans constituted just over 10 per cent of the US population but 46 per cent of the unemployed. Some ghettos, including Chicago's, had 50–70 per cent black youth unemployment.

Going West: Watts 1965

In August 1965, the nation's attention focused on the ghettos when riots erupted in Los Angeles' Watts ghetto. Black mobs set fire to several blocks of stores. Local churchmen asked King for help.

Despite previous unsuccessful attempts to calm black rioters in New York, where some residents of Harlem called him an Uncle Tom and the mayor had proved unhelpful, King felt it was his duty to go to Watts. The scenes of devastation shocked him. He told the press this had been 'a class revolt of underprivileged against privileged … the main issue is economic'. Previously King had thought of 'freedom' in terms of ending segregation and exercising the vote. Now King began to define 'freedom' in terms of economic equality rather than political equality. He was turning to **socialism**, calling for 'a better distribution of the wealth' of the USA.

> **What was the significance of the Watts riots?**

 **KEY TERM**

Socialism Political philosophy that society should be as equitable as possible in terms of economic and social standing.

SOURCE A

Bayard Rustin, King's ex-Communist friend, recalled the impact of the Watts riots on King in 1965. Quoted in *Bearing the Cross* by David Garrow, published by William Morrow, New York, USA, 1999, page 439.

[King was] absolutely undone, and he looked at me and said, 'You know, Bayard, I worked to get these people the right to eat hamburgers, and now I've got to do something … to help them get the money to buy it' … I think it was the first time he really understood.

> To what extent would you trust Rustin's assessment in Source A of the impact of the Watts riots on King?

SOURCE B

Two Watts residents speaking after the riots. 1. Quoted in *Martin and Malcolm and America* by James Cone, published by Orbis Books, New York, USA, 1991 page 222. 2. Quoted in *The Modern Presidency and Civil Rights* by Garth Pauley, published by Texas A&M University Press, College Station, Texas, USA, 2001, page 194.

1. *King, and all his talk about non-violence, did not mean much. Watts had respect for King, but the talk about non-violence made us laugh. Watts wasn't suffering from segregation, or the lack of civil rights. You didn't have two drinking fountains …*

2. *[When Johnson signed the civil rights bill in 1964] nobody even thought about it in Watts … It had nothing to do with us.*

> Read Source B. Using your own knowledge, explain why Watts residents would have laughed about non-violence and been unimpressed by the Civil Rights Act.

Going North: Chicago 1966

After Southern blacks had sought and gained primarily political and social rights, King turned North, where the problem was more economic. The struggle in the South had not helped black Northerners as he had hoped and he wanted do something to stop the increasing tendency towards violence and radicalism amongst some black groups. He sought a Northern

> **What was the significance of SCLC's Chicago campaign?**

ghetto on which the Southern Christian Leadership Conference (SCLC) (see pages 72–3) could concentrate and chose Chicago because:

- Chicago was the USA's second largest city, with three million people, 700,000 of whom were black. Concentrated in the South Side and West Side ghettos, black Chicagoans suffered severe employment, housing and education problems. Chicago's black schools were so overcrowded that students attended in half-day shifts. SCLC said, 'if Northern problems can be solved there, they can be solved anywhere'.
- Other great Northern cities were effectively shut off to King. He was told to keep out of New York City by Harlem congressman Adam Clayton Powell and out of Philadelphia by the local NAACP leader. Although Chicago activists warned SCLC not to just 'come in and take over', they did so relatively amicably.
- Chicago had a tradition of sporadic protest. Inspired by the Southern sit-ins, CORE (see pages 56 and 74) was revitalized in 1960. In 1961, there were 'wade-ins' in protest against the customary segregation of South Side beach. In October 1963, over half of Chicago's half a million black students boycotted their inferior segregated schools for a day in protest, although no improvement had resulted.
- Chicago's influential religious community supported the Civil Rights Movement.
- Chicago's Mayor Daley relied heavily on black voters and was not racist. He had total political domination. If he could be won over, things could get done. Chicago could become an inspirational symbol.

However, throughout the winter of 1965–6, King and his lieutenant, Andrew Young, were unsure of what to do in Chicago. Young talked vaguely of mobilizing Chicago blacks, and 'pulling things together'. In late spring 1966, SCLC finally focused on discrimination in housing sales, which stopped blacks moving out of the ghettos' slums.

King and life in Chicago

SCLC rented a West Side ghetto flat for King's use during the campaign. When the landlord found out who his new tenant was, an army of repairmen moved in to make it habitable. Chicagoans joked that the easiest way for King to improve ghetto housing would be for him to move from building to building. King led reporters around rat-infested, unheated ghetto dwellings. King and his aides dramatically seized a Chicago slum building and, dressed in work clothes, began repairing it. King told the press that SCLC had collected the tenants' rents to finance this. When he said that moral questions were more important than legal ones in this case, the press greatly criticized his justification of illegality.

The campaign was not going well. Local Chicago activists and SCLC members failed to get on and the lack of a clearly defined issue did not help. The July 1966 Chicago rally turnout was 30,000, disappointingly below the anticipated 100,000. The subsequent meeting between King and Daley was unproductive. King said Daley did too little, Daley said he did his best.

King's family neared disintegration as they sampled Chicago ghetto life. There were neither pools nor parks in which his children could escape the suffocating heat of their small, airless flat. The surrounding streets were too crowded and dangerous to play in. King's children screamed and fought each other, as never before. With the temperature near 100°F (38°C), the police shut off the water spouting from a fire hydrant that black youths had been using to cool themselves. After some youths were arrested, angry blacks ran through the streets. King persuaded the police to release the youngsters and encouraged ministers to join him in walking the ghetto streets to try to calm people. Black crowds derided and walked away from him, but he persuaded Mayor Daley to make fire hydrants and pools available.

De facto segregation in housing

Chicago whites feared black neighbours would hit property values, increase crime and threaten cultural homogeneity, so when 500 black marchers defiantly and provocatively entered a white Chicago neighbourhood to publicize the fact that they could not as yet reside there, they were greeted with rocks, bottles, and cries of 'apes', 'cannibals', 'savages' and 'the only way to stop [them] is to exterminate them'. Several such incidents occurred. The police, shocked by cries of 'nigger lovers' from fellow whites, did little to protect marchers. There was considerable violence. When a rock hit King, it made the national press and the marches became more peaceful. On one occasion, 800 policemen protected 700 marchers.

The riots caused $2 million worth of damage. Many influential whites blamed King and invited him to leave. King blamed Daley. 'A non-violent movement cannot maintain its following unless it brings about change', he said, warning that discriminatory house-selling practices would lead to 'Negro cities ringed with white suburbs', which was dangerous: hatred and fear developed when people were thus separated. The *Chicago Tribune* denounced King as a 'paid professional agitator' and asked how he could justify demonstrations that turned violent. He said demonstrations might stop greater violence and that the problem was not the marches but the conditions that caused people to march. He pointed out that:

We don't have much money … [or] education, and we don't have political power. We have only our bodies and you are asking us to give up the one thing that we have when you say, 'Don't march' … We're trying to keep the issue so alive that it will be acted on. Our marching feet have brought us a long way, and if we hadn't marched I don't think we'd be here today. [Quoted in Confronting the Color Line *by Alan Anderson and George Pickering, University of Georgia Press, 2007, page 253.]*

Assessment of SCLC in Chicago

King departed Chicago in autumn 1966, leaving dynamic young Jesse Jackson in charge of 'Operation Breadbasket', which successfully used economic boycotts to help increase black employment. Because of the threat of black marches into racist white areas, Daley agreed to promote integrated housing in Chicago, but the agreement was a mere 'paper victory' (*Chicago Daily News*) and most African Americans remained stranded in the ghetto. Although SCLC obtained a $4 million federal grant to improve Chicago housing and left behind a significant legacy of community action, the local black community felt SCLC had 'sold out' and lapsed into apathy. An SCLC staffer in Chicago said the voter registration drive there was 'a nightmare', 'largely because of division in the Negro leadership' and partly because black Chicagoans were uninterested: 'I have never seen such hopelessness … A lot of people won't even talk to us.'

Many became disillusioned and turned to **Black Power**. Chicago's race relations had always been poor. King could be considered to have worsened the situation. Black hopes were raised then dashed, and there was a white backlash. Whites increasingly thought of black people as troublemakers on welfare.

Reasons for failure in Chicago

The *New Republic* said, 'so far, King has been pretty much of a failure at organizing' and one of King's closest admirers described the Chicago venture as a 'fiasco' and 'disaster'. It failed because:

- SCLC had been inadequately briefed and ill-prepared – they even lacked warm clothing for the Chicago winter.
- The Meredith March (see page 96) distracted SCLC in mid-1966.
- SCLC could not effect a social and economic revolution in Chicago within months. Ella Baker (see page 73) always said SCLC's failure to develop grassroots participation often led to disaster. She felt King went into Chicago hoping to effect a miraculous transformation without educating and organizing the local population for a long-term haul after he and the media had gone, although King was in fact realistic (see Source C).
- In contrast to Montgomery and Selma (see pages 62–6 and 82–3), Chicago's near million black population was too large to mobilize.
- NAACP was unhelpful, as were some of the local black churches, radical Black Muslims (see pages 102–4), and black conservatives, who loathed SCLC's attempt to recruit and convert violent young gang members. African American Congressman William Dawson, who had represented Chicago since the Second World War, disliked mass action, which he thought caused trouble. Most slum land was owned by blacks, who resented King's criticism of slum landlords.
- SCLC never called in outside help in Chicago, as it had in Selma.
- Mayor Daley outwitted the SCLC. His police protected the marchers. He stopped the marches by threatening fines (which the SCLC could not afford) rather than filling the jails.
- The federal government did not help the Chicago Freedom Movement, because Mayor Daley was a political ally of President Johnson. Johnson was alienated by King's criticism of the **Vietnam War** (see box on page 95).

🔑 KEY TERM

Black Power
A controversial term, with different meanings, such as black pride, black economic self-sufficiency, black violence, black separatism, black nationalism, black political power, black working-class revolution, black domination.

Vietnam War War between non-Communist South Vietnam (supported by the USA) and Communist North Vietnam and its allies in the South (1954–75).

Martin Luther King and the Vietnam War

African Americans resented the disproportionate number of black casualties in the Vietnam War and felt kinship with the poor, non-white Vietnamese. When King saw a picture of Vietnamese children with burn wounds from US napalm bombs in January 1967 he became publicly critical. He said that President Johnson's **Great Society** poverty programme had raised hopes for the inhabitants of the inner-city ghettos, but now the funds were being diverted to the war. In a 1967 speech, he said young black males, 'crippled by our society', were being sent to:

… guarantee liberties in Southeast Asia which they had not found in Southwest Georgia and East Harlem … We have been repeatedly faced with the cruel irony of watching Negro and white boys on TV screens as they kill and die together for a nation that has been unable to seat them together in the same schools. I could never again raise my voice against the violence of the oppressed in the ghettos without having first spoken clearly to the greatest purveyor of violence in the world today – my own government.

King's anti-Vietnam War stance was disliked by 48 per cent of African Americans, because it alienated President Johnson. 'I know it can hurt SCLC, but I feel better', said King. 'I was politically unwise, but morally wise.' Sixty per cent of African Americans believed his opposition hurt the Civil Rights Movement.

 **KEY TERM**

Great Society President Johnson in 1965 declared a 'war on poverty' and called for a revolutionary programme of social welfare legislation that involved unprecedented federal expenditure on education, medical care for the elderly, and an expanded Social Security Program.

- The anti-Vietnam War movement was taking funds and energies from the Civil Rights Movement.
- National press coverage of King's Chicago Freedom Movement was limited. Black marchers attempting to register to vote in Selma gained national sympathy, black marchers going into white neighbourhoods did not. When CORE defied King and led a march into the working-class white suburb of Cicero, marchers clashed violently with hecklers. Whites were tired of black protests that led to violence, tired of black ghetto riots (see pages 108–9) and resistant to radical change that affected their property rights.

SOURCE C

Martin Luther King Jr speaking in 1968 on the difference between his campaign in the South and in the North, quoted in *Twentieth Century Shapes of Baptist Social Ethics* by Larry McSwain and William Lloyd Allen, published by Mercer University Press, Georgia, USA, 2008, page 195.

It's much easier to integrate lunch counters than it is to eradicate slums. It's much easier to guarantee the right to vote than it is to guarantee an annual minimum income and create jobs.

Using Source C and your own knowledge, explain why it could be argued that it was 'easier' for King to achieve successes in the South than in the North.

What was the
significance of the
Meredith March?

 **KEY TERM**

Howard Prestigious African
American university in
Washington, DC.

The Meredith March 1966

Famous as the University of Mississippi's first black student (1962), James Meredith began a 220-mile (350-km) walk from Memphis to Mississippi's capital Jackson, to encourage black people to vote. When he was shot on the second day and temporarily immobilized, black organizations declared that they would continue his walk. King and 20 others set off and there were 400 marchers by the third day, including the new SNCC leader, Stokely Carmichael. Born in the West Indies, brought up in Harlem and educated at **Howard**, Carmichael was a founder member of SNCC. Charismatic, handsome and a good organizer, he was involved in SNCC's voter registration campaigns in Mississippi (see page 80).

Divisions on the Meredith March

Black divisions damaged the march. NAACP wanted it to focus national attention on a new civil rights bill and withdrew when Carmichael criticized the bill. King welcomed white participants, SNCC rejected them. SNCC and CORE had become increasingly militant following the lack of federal protection for their voter registration projects in the 'Mississippi Freedom Summer' of 1964 (see page 80). As white bystanders waved Confederate flags, shouted obscenities and threw things at the marchers, SNCC people sang:

Jingle bells, shotgun shells, Freedom all the way
Oh what fun it is to blast, A [white] trooper man away.

Carmichael was arrested and on release urged burning 'every courthouse in Mississippi' and demanded 'black power' (see page 94). Crowds took up the chant of 'black power', while King and SCLC tried to encourage chants of 'freedom now'. King feared the words 'black power' would alienate white sympathizers and encourage a white backlash. Although he had reluctantly agreed to the black paramilitary group Deacons for Defense providing security, King was tired of violence and urged blacks to avoid violent retaliation against tear gas. As in Selma (see pages 82–3), Johnson refused King's pleas to send in federal troops.

Meanwhile, Meredith felt excluded and began a march of his own. Some SCLC leaders joined him to disguise the split. The 15,000 main marchers ended at Jackson with rival chants of 'black power' and 'freedom now'.

Results and significance of the march

King despaired: 'I don't know what I'm going to do. The government has got to give me some victories if I'm going to keep people non-violent.' He felt he could no longer co-operate with SNCC, and told the press, 'Because Stokely Carmichael chose the march as an arena for a debate over black power, we did not get to emphasize the evils of Mississippi and the need for the 1966 Civil Rights Act.' He admitted that blacks were 'very, very close' to a public split. NAACP no longer wanted to co-operate with SCLC or SNCC. Now it seemed that leadership might pass into the hands of extremists such as Carmichael who rejected non-violence.

Where Do We Go From Here?

← **Was King 'Martin Loser King' after 1967?**

After the Chicago debacle, King was depressed, unsure what to do next and marginalized by black extremists such as Carmichael, who called for black and white separation and said blacks should use 'any means necessary' to obtain their rights. Black extremists, the white backlash and the distraction of white liberals by the Vietnam War resulted in the collapse of the civil rights coalition that had achieved so much.

Affirmative action

In his book *Where Do We Go From Here?* (1967), King highlighted the problem: giving blacks the vote had not cost money, but improving the ghettos would be expensive. No one wanted higher taxation. King urged demonstrations to seek **affirmative action**, on the grounds that 'a society that has done something against the Negro for hundreds of years must now do something special for him, in order to equip him to compete on a just and equal basis'. King also urged blacks to broaden their movement and bring Hispanics, Native Americans and poor whites into the war on poverty.

> **KEY TERM**
>
> **Affirmative action** Positive discrimination to help those who have had a disadvantageous start in life.

The Poor People's Campaign

King planned to bring all the poor together to camp out in Washington, DC in a Poor People's Campaign. His final strategy (to represent a wider constituency) and his final tactics (yet another protest) were, in the climate of the time, unwise and unrealistic. 'It just isn't working. People aren't responding', he admitted. Even friends and colleagues opposed the idea. Even sympathizers expected it to fail, end in violence and generate an even greater white backlash. Adam Clayton Powell christened him 'Martin Loser King'.

Memphis

In March 1968, King was asked to visit Memphis, Tennessee, to support black sanitation workers faced with discrimination from the city authorities. King joined a protest march. When a radical black power minority got violent and broke shop windows, King was exhausted, confused, frightened and in despair:

Maybe we just have to admit that the day of violence is here, and maybe we have to just give up and let violence take its course. The nation won't listen to our voice. Maybe it will heed the voice of violence.

Within hours, he was dead.

Assassination aftermath

King's assassination triggered ghetto riots across the USA. Civil rights leaders called for calm, although Stokely Carmichael (see page 96) sought a more emphatic response. There were mixed feelings in white USA: some grief, some guilt, some joy. President Johnson declared a day of national mourning and Congress was inspired to pass the Fair Housing Act, which tried but failed to end discrimination in the sale of housing. In death, King became a somewhat sanitized hero, whose radicalism and faults (such as his womanizing) were swept under the carpet.

How important was King?

Martin Luther King Jr: conclusions

With his protests, inspiration and organization, King played a vital role in the demise of Jim Crow in the South. While he was just something of a figurehead for the Montgomery bus boycott, it gained him national prominence. Protesters recognized his value in terms of inspiration and publicity, as with the sit-ins and freedom rides (see page 73), and it is to King's credit that he was willing to be led as well as to be leader. While A. Philip Randolph masterminded the March on Washington (see page 78), King's unforgettable speech was its highlight. Although King's organizational skills often appeared limited, he successfully orchestrated Birmingham (see page 76), which along with the March on Washington, played a big part in encouraging the Kennedy administration to support what became the 1964 Civil Rights Act. King also masterminded Selma (see page 82), which was key in the passage of the Voting Rights Act. His manipulation of white violence and belief in the effectiveness of mass protest were essential in changing the focus of black activism from litigation. NAACP's litigation strategy had probably gone as far as it could go and it took mass action to make a reality of the anti-segregation principles enshrined in *Brown*.

King did not achieve the crucial legislation of 1964–5 all on his own. Black protesters, organizations such as NAACP, CORE and SNCC, Churches, local community organizations, and thousands of unsung field workers also played a vital part in producing the legislation by which Southern segregation had been shattered and a mass black electorate had gained a voice in the political process. The federal government, especially the Supreme Court, and President Lyndon Johnson, had played an important role, as had white extremists (President Kennedy joked that Bull Connor was a hero of the Civil Rights Movement).

King failed in Chicago, but the problems faced by the black population, particularly in the ghettos, were great and long-standing. After his death and after the rise of the Black Power movement, the federal government, continuing in the direction signposted by Presidents Kennedy and Johnson, supported affirmative action, and it could be argued that either King and the Civil Rights Movement, or the Black Power movement, or both, were crucial to the introduction of that policy.

King's radicalism

Contemporaries who accused King of deferring to white authority figures were usually young 'black power' militants who rejected non-violence (see page 110). He in turn criticized them, telling the *New York Times* 'black power' was dangerous, provocative and cost the Civil Rights Movement support. King knew violence stood little chance against the military strength of the US government. Moderate in comparison, even King aroused hatred and unrelenting opposition among many whites.

King was no Uncle Tom. He frequently criticized presidential policies. Some of his demonstrations were deliberately provocative. They invited white violence, making nonsense of his advocacy of non-violence. Within the Southern context, King was a political radical who sought the vote for the disenfranchised and a social radical who sought racial equality. The Northern ghettos confirmed his economic radicalism: 'something is wrong with the economic system of our nation … with capitalism'. King's tactics could be considered revolutionary, particularly with his Poor People's Campaign (see page 97), which he wanted to cause 'massive dislocation', so as to force Congress to act. By the winter of 1967–8 the Johnson administration considered King a revolutionary who advocated 'criminal [not civil] disobedience'. Like President Kennedy before him, Johnson was happy to have the Federal Bureau of Investigation (FBI) monitor King (they bugged his hotel rooms and informed his wife about his sexual liaisons). In 1995 King's family had a bitter argument with the federal National Park Service, which played down the radicalism of King's later career in information handed out at Atlanta's King National Historic site.

Successes
- Inspirational figure in Montgomery bus boycott
- Willing to be led, e.g. sit-ins, freedom rides
- March on Washington 1963 – inspirational speech
- Birmingham 1963 – helped get 1964 Civil Rights Act
- Selma 1965 – helped get 1965 Voting Rights Act
- Changed tactics from litigation to mass protest

Failures
- Considered an Uncle Tom
- Albany Movement 1961
- St Augustine 1964
- Chicago 1966
- Meredith March, 1966
- Poor People's Campaign

SUMMARY DIAGRAM

The role of Martin Luther King in the Civil Rights Movement

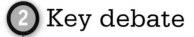

② Key debate

> ▸ **Key question:** *Who or what played the most important role in the Civil Rights Movement?*

A major debate on the Civil Rights Movement is over the relative importance of 'top-down' forces (leaders such as King, presidents, Supreme Court and Congress) compared to each other and to activists who operated at a grassroots level.

Did Martin make the movement?

The relative importance of King's contribution has always been controversial: Ella Baker insisted 'the movement made Martin rather than Martin making the movement' and historian Professor Clayborne Carson (1987) contended that:

If King had never lived, the black struggle would have followed a course of development similar to the one it did. The Montgomery bus boycott would have occurred, because King did not initiate it. Black students ... had sources of tactical and ideological inspiration besides King.

Journalist Fred Powledge (1991) covered the movement, and lamented:

In the minds of untold numbers of Americans, for example, the Rev Dr Martin Luther King Jr, was the Civil Rights Movement. Thought it up, led it, produced its victories, became its sole martyr. Schoolchildren – including Black schoolchildren – are taught this.

However, many historians agree that 'no person was more important' than King in the 'revolution in Southern race relations' brought about by the Civil Rights Movement (Professor Anthony Badger in a 1998 lecture).

How important were factors other than King?

In the debate as to whether local communities or national organizations played the more important part in the Civil Rights Movement, Steven Lawson (1998) contended that the fate of the Civil Rights Movement depended on the national organizations, especially NAACP and SCLC: 'They could do what Black residents of local communities could not do alone: turn the civil rights struggle into a national cause for concern and prod the federal government' into action against Jim Crow.

In the debate as to whether black activism or the federal government played the more important role, historian Mark Newman (2004) emphasized the need to look at factors external to the black community: for example, NAACP litigated increasingly successfully, but that owed much to Franklin Roosevelt's liberal appointments to the Supreme Court. Steven Lawson (1998) argued that 'the federal government played an indispensable role ...

Without their crucial support, the struggle against white supremacy in the South still would have taken place but would have lacked the power and authority to defeat [segregationist] state governments' (for example, the Montgomery bus boycott had to continue until NAACP obtained the Supreme Court ruling against segregated buses). Historian Mary Dudziak (2000) wrote of the 'Cold War imperative': in the struggle against Communism, the USA did not want to be seen to be racist and undemocratic, although other historians, such as James Patterson (1996) emphasize how Cold War pressure for conformity and opposition to left-wing ideas hindered black activists.

Historians such as Aldon Morris (1984) stressed black **agency**, especially the role of the black Churches, although historian Clayborne Carson (1981) pointed out that the Church was frequently conservative and often held back activists.

Perhaps Lawson (1998) summed it up best when he said, 'The federal government made racial reform possible, but Blacks in the South made it necessary.'

While the above debates have raged for many years, the last two decades have seen (usually female) historians place a new emphasis on the importance of black women activists, beginning with Vicki Crawford and others (1993).

Did the Civil Rights Movement in the South disintegrate after Selma?

Some historians claim that the Civil Rights Movement in the South disintegrated soon after Selma. Adam Fairclough held that view in 1987, but by 1995 his study of Louisiana, confirmed by Stephen Tuck's study of Georgia (2001), suggested that there was 'continuity of protest' at the local level, for example, in challenging electoral abuses. NAACP membership and activism grew again, and SCLC was very active in early 1970s' Georgia.

③ The Nation of Islam and Malcolm X

▶ *Key question: How and why were the Nation of Islam and Malcolm X important?*

The Black Power movement of the 1960s did not develop out of nothing. The black separatist tradition emerged in the nineteenth century, when some black people advocated 'back to Africa'. Marcus Garvey's separatist **black nationalist** movement flourished briefly in the 1910s and 1920s (see

> **KEY TERM**
>
> **Agency** In this context, where black actions were influential, as opposed to black history being determined by white actions.

> **T O K**
>
> Is history made by individuals or by historical forces? Come up with examples for both arguments. (Logic, Social Sciences, Reason.)

> **KEY TERM**
>
> **Black nationalist** Favouring a separate black nation either within the USA or in Africa.

page 55). When Garvey's UNIA went into decline, the nationalist and separatist banner was taken up by the Black Muslim movement or Nation of Islam.

What did the Nation of Islam achieve?

Elijah Muhammad and the Nation of Islam

The Nation of Islam (a name suggesting a nation within the US nation) was founded by Wallace Fard in Detroit in 1930. When Fard mysteriously disappeared in 1934, leadership of the new religious group passed to Elijah Poole, born in Georgia in 1897. Under his adopted name of Elijah Muhammad, Poole led the Black Muslims of the Nation of Islam (NOI) from 1934 to 1975.

NOI beliefs and growth

Although Elijah Muhammad said he was the prophet of Allah, the 'Messenger of Islam', his teachings frequently differed from those of orthodox Islam. He rejected ideas of spiritual life after death. He claimed that Allah originally created people black, and that other races were created by an evil scientist, Yakub, whose last evil creation was the white race. Whites would rule the world for several thousand years, but then Allah would return and end their supremacy. The NOI aimed to provide blacks with an alternative to the white man's Christian religion, to persuade members to live a religious life, to increase black self-esteem, to keep blacks and whites separate and to encourage blacks to improve their economic situation.

From the 1930s to the 1950s, the NOI set up temples in northern black ghettos such as Detroit, New York and Chicago. In the 1950s, the NOI's most brilliant preacher, Malcolm X, attracted the attention and devotion of frustrated ghetto-dwellers with his rejection of integration and his bitter attacks on white Americans. A television documentary called *The Hate that Hate Produced* (1959) brought the Nation of Islam national prominence and white hostility. Addressing 10,000 people in Washington, DC in 1959, Elijah Muhammad attacked the 'turn the other cheek' philosophy of Christianity as perpetuating enslavement. He advocated separatism and armed self-defence against white aggression.

NOI and Black Power

The NOI's relations with the black power movement were ambivalent. Both groups favoured separatism, cultural revival and self-help, but Elijah Muhammad's dismissive attitude towards non-Muslim African culture alienated some Black Power activists, especially when he said in 1972, 'I am already civilized and I am ready to civilize Africa'. Elijah Muhammad hated what he called 'jungle styles', such as Afro haircuts or colourful African-style garments. Nevertheless, most Black Power advocates revered Elijah Muhammad and the NOI as forerunners of the new black nationalism.

Achievements of the NOI

Negative

Some of the Nation's solutions to black problems (a return to Africa or a separate black state in the Deep South) were unrealistic and NOI teachings exacerbated divisions between blacks and whites and between blacks. While the NOI derided Martin Luther King Jr as an Uncle Tom, a 'fool' who humiliatingly begged for access to a white-dominated world and urged non-violence on his defenceless followers, King described the NOI as a 'hate group'.

Positive

Estimates of NOI membership vary but it was possibly as high as 100,000 in 1960, and perhaps a quarter of a million by 1969. The Nation of Islam newspaper *Muhammad Speaks*, with its comforting message of separatism in self-defence, had a weekly circulation of 600,000 by the mid-1970s. The NOI attracted and inspired ghetto-dwellers because of its self-confidence and emphasis on racial pride and economic self-help. Elijah Muhammad and his son Wallace created many businesses, such as restaurants, bakeries and grocery stores. These symbolized black success and gave rare employment opportunities in the ghettos. The NOI expected converts to live a religious life, emphasizing marital chastity and the rejection of alcohol, tobacco and flamboyant clothing.

When Elijah Muhammad died in 1975, his obituaries in the white press were surprisingly favourable. *Newsweek* described him as 'a kind of prophetic voice in the flowering of black identity and pride' while the *Washington Post* said he inculcated 'pride in thousands of black derelicts, bums, and drug addicts, turning outlaws into useful, productive men and women'.

> **NOI: a postscript**
> After Elijah Muhammad's death, the NOI split into Wallace Muhammad's group, which followed more orthodox Islamic teachings, and Louis Farrakhan's group, which retained Elijah Muhammad's teachings.

Malcolm X 1925–65

← **What did Malcolm X achieve?**

After a difficult youth (see page 106), Malcolm became a criminal and was sentenced to 10 years' imprisonment in 1946.

Malcolm and the NOI

In prison, Malcolm converted to the NOI, which taught him 'The white man is the devil' – 'a perfect echo' of his 'lifelong experience', he said. Released in 1952, he adopted the name Malcolm X (the X replaced the African name that had been taken from his slave ancestors). He quickly became a leading figure within the NOI, recruiting thousands of new members in Detroit, Boston,

Philadelphia and New York, where in 1954 he became Minister of Temple Number 7 in Harlem.

After *The Hate that Hate Produced* was televised in 1959 (see page 102), Malcolm attracted national and international attention, especially when he said blacks should defend themselves 'by any means necessary'. Always critical of Martin Luther King Jr's 'non-violence', he christened the 1963 March on Washington the 'Farce on Washington', scoffing at the dream of integration: 'Imagine, you have the chance to go to the toilets with white folks!' He mocked Christianity, a religion 'designed to fill [black] hearts with the desire to be white … A white Jesus. A white virgin. White angels. White everything. But a black Devil of course.'

Malcolm's split from the NOI

In late 1963, Malcolm was suspended by Elijah Muhammad for making unpopular remarks about the assassination of President Kennedy. In March 1964, he announced his split with the NOI, disappointed by Elijah Muhammad's expensive lifestyle, romantic affairs and refusal to allow him to join those risking their lives in Birmingham in 1963. 'We spout our militant revolutionary rhetoric', said Malcolm, but 'when our own brothers are … killed, we do nothing'.

On an April 1964 pilgrimage to Mecca, Malcolm X established good relations with non-US Muslims of all colours and rejected the racial theology (see page 102) of the NOI. Opinions vary as to whether Malcolm's development was genuine or whether his 'sudden realization' of the 'true' Islam was a ploy to re-create his public image. In the next month he established the Organization of Afro-American Unity (OAAU), which aimed to unite all people of African descent and to promote political, social and economic independence for blacks. Like King, Malcolm moved towards socialism, propelled by economic inequality in the USA.

In February 1965, Malcolm was assassinated by NOI gunmen. He was important as the harbinger of Black Power of the 1960s and as a role model, inspiration and icon for discontented ghetto blacks. He also played a big part in the alienation of white USA.

The aims, methods and achievements of Malcolm X

Malcolm X aimed to improve the lives of black Americans. His main methods were to advertise and encourage critical thinking on race problems, and, some would say, to encourage racial hatred and violence. Towards the end of his life, Malcolm claimed, 'I'm here to remind the white man of the alternative to Dr King.'

Achievements: negative

Malcolm X's achievements are controversial. Thurgood Marshall (see page 56) was particularly critical of the NOI ('run by a bunch of thugs') and of Malcolm ('what did he achieve?'). Black baseball player Jackie Robinson pointed out that while King and others put their lives on the line in places like Birmingham, Malcolm stayed in safer places such as Harlem. Many considered him to be irresponsible and negative. While he criticized civil rights activists such as King, he never established organizations as effective or long lasting as the NAACP or SCLC. His suggestions that blacks were frequently left with no alternative other than violence seemed negative, irresponsible and unhelpful. *Time* magazine described him as 'an unashamed demagogue whose gospel was hatred and who in life and in death was a disaster to the Civil Rights Movement'.

Achievements: positive

Malcolm rightly drew early attention to the dreadful conditions in the USA's ghettos, and he brought US blacks more closely in contact with oppressed black people throughout the world. He became an iconic role model for black youths, particularly through his exploration of his feelings of rejection and his search for his identity in his *The Autobiography of Malcolm X* (1965). 'Primarily', said historian Claude Andrew Clegg (1997), 'he made black nationalism in its various forms appealing to the angry generation of black youths who came of age just as American segregation and European colonial empires were collapsing'. Perhaps most important of all, Malcolm inspired the new generation of black leaders such as SNCC's Stokely Carmichael and CORE's Floyd McKissick and the Black Power movement in general. He was the first really prominent advocate of separatism and what subsequently became known as Black Power during the great civil rights era.

SOURCE D

An extract from the *Saturday Evening Post*, September 1964 on Malcolm X's autobiography. The *Saturday Evening Post* is a US magazine.

If Malcolm were not a Negro, his autobiography would be little more than a journal of abnormal psychology, the story of a burglar, dope pusher, addict and jailbird – with a family history of insanity – who acquires messianic delusions and sets forth to preach an upside-down religion of 'brotherly hatred'.

Is Source D favourable or unfavourable to Malcolm and African Americans?

Martin and Malcolm: similarities and differences

← **How and why were Martin Luther King Jr and Malcolm X different?**

Although generally considered very different, the two most famous African American activists of the civil rights era, Martin Luther King Jr and Malcolm X, had much in common.

Family backgrounds

In many ways, Martin Luther King Jr (1929–68) and Malcolm X (1925–65) could not have been more different. King was a Southerner, born in Atlanta, Georgia, while Malcolm Little was born in the Midwest, in Omaha, Nebraska. King was born into the slowly growing black middle class, to a stable family headed by 'Daddy King', who, as a Church minister, was shielded from the worst traumas of the Great Depression years. In contrast, Malcolm's widowed mother could not cope with the poverty of those years and was committed to an insane asylum when Malcolm was 14 years old.

Youth and education

While King was able to go to college, albeit segregated, in Atlanta, Malcolm left school full of resentment at a teacher who told him that his ambition to become a lawyer was an unrealistic one for a black student.

King's childhood and student days were not totally idyllic. If as a child he wanted to see a film in central Atlanta, he could not buy a soda or a hot dog at a store's lunch counter. If a white shop served him, they would hand him his ice cream through a side window and in paper cups so no white would have to use anything that he had used. He had to drink from the 'colored'

SOURCE E

? Giving consideration to the caption to this photograph, and using your own knowledge of the relationship between Martin Luther King Jr and Malcolm X, is this photograph important to the historian of African American history?

Martin Luther King Jr (left) and Malcolm X met only once and accidentally. The meeting took place in the US Congress in March 1964 and they posed for this photograph.

water fountain, and use the 'colored' toilet. He had to sit in the 'colored' section at the back of the balcony in the movie theatre. King said it made him 'determined to hate every white person'.

Having received a poor quality education in Atlanta's segregated schools, King experienced further racial prejudice when he went North to college. When he demanded service in a Philadelphia restaurant, his plate arrived filled with sand. A New Jersey restaurant owner drew a gun on King when he refused to leave. King had problems getting student accommodation in Boston in 1951. Rooms were 'for rent until they found out I was a Negro and suddenly they had just been rented'.

Without much education, Malcolm's teenage years were far less happy than King's. Malcolm moved to Boston's black ghetto in 1941, where he took jobs traditionally open to African Americans, shoeshine boy and railway waiter. While King graduated from an inferior Southern college but a good Northern university, Malcolm graduated from the school of drug dealing, pimping, burgling and jail.

Different philosophies

Naturally their backgrounds greatly affected their philosophies. 'Daddy King' supported the NAACP (see page 55) and he and Martin believed in the American dream and sought integration into it. In contrast, Malcolm's father had supported UNIA (see page 55), and according to Malcolm, 'What is looked upon as an American dream for white people has long been an American nightmare for black people.' Because of this, Malcolm sought **separatism**. While King's first preoccupation was the segregated South, Malcolm's was always the ghettos.

Similarities

Although very different in many ways, Malcolm and Martin had much in common. Both aimed to improve the black situation and had many followers. Both were Church ministers, King in the Christian Church, Malcolm in the NOI. Both had great oratorical gifts and belief in the power of organizations, preaching and print, but whereas Malcolm justified black violence in the form of self-defence, King preferred to contrast peaceful black protest with violent white responses. Both were involved with influential organizations. Both had philosophies that changed, developed and made them more similar in their last years, when King became increasingly socialist ('You show me a capitalist and I'll show you a bloodsucker', said Malcolm) and Malcolm became less antagonistic towards whites. Both were controversial. Both were assassinated.

Most people would probably agree that King achieved far more, although the 1965 Voting Rights Act (see page 83) proved to be his last great triumph. Neither King nor Malcolm could solve the terrible problems of the ghetto.

KEY TERM

Separatism Desire for African Americans to live separate but equal lives from whites, in all-black communities or even in a black state or Africa.

Paying attention to the provenance, does Source F give a fair assessment of Malcolm?

SOURCE F

An extract from Martin Luther King Jr's interview with Alex Haley in *Playboy* magazine, January 1965. King talks about Malcolm X.

Maybe he does have some of the answers. I don't know how he feels now, but I know that I have often wished that he would talk less of violence, because violence is not going to solve our problem. And in his litany of articulating the despair of the Negro without offering any positive, creative alternative, I fear that Malcolm has done himself and our people a great disservice. Fiery, demagogic oratory in the black ghettos, urging Negroes to arm themselves and to prepare to engage in violence, as he has done, can reap nothing but grief.

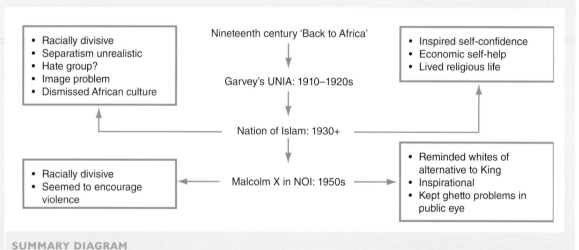

SUMMARY DIAGRAM

The Nation of Islam and Malcolm X

4 The rise of Black Power in the 1960s

▶ *Key question: Why and with what results did Black Power emerge?*

The origins of Black Power are controversial, but the influence of Malcolm X (see above), ghetto problems and the experiences of SNCC and CORE (many of whose members were Northerners) in Mississippi (see page 80) were all contributory factors.

Black Power and the ghettos

Why did Black Power appeal in the ghettos?

During the five so-called 'long hot summers' of 1964–8, US ghettos erupted. The first major race riot was in Watts (Los Angeles) in 1965. With 34 deaths, 1000 injuries, 3500 rioters and looters arrested, and over $40 million damage done to largely white-owned businesses, the Watts riots gained national attention. There were 238 other race riots in over 200 US cities from 1964 to 1968. Virtually every large US city outside the South had a race riot, for example, Newark, New Jersey (1967), and Detroit, Michigan (1967). Some had several, for example, Oakland, California (1965 and 1966), Cleveland, Ohio (1966 and 1968), and Chicago, Illinois (1966 and 1968). There was certainly a 'copycat' element: 16 cities experienced serious riots in 1964, 64 in 1968. From 1964 to 1972, ghetto riots led to over 250 deaths (the fatalities mostly resulted from the police shooting rioters), 10,000 serious injuries, 60,000 arrests and a great deal of damage to ghetto businesses.

Out of the many city, state and federal government investigations into the violence, the most famous was the National Advisory Commission on Civil Disorders (commonly known as the Kerner Commission) set up by President Johnson. Like the other reports, the Kerner Report, released in February 1968, emphasized the social and economic deprivation in the ghettos, which had poor schools and housing and high unemployment (see page 90). The reports also noted that the violence was frequently triggered by black reaction to what were perceived as oppressive police policies and indifferent white political machines.

Suggested solutions for the problems in the ghettos

Leaders of the black community used different tactics to improve ghetto life. NAACP worked for integrated education, hoping it would provide better quality education for blacks and enable them to escape from the ghettos (see pages 57 and 60). A. Philip Randolph encouraged unionization and pressure on the federal government as the way towards equal pay and employment opportunities (see page 56). Martin Luther King Jr drew attention to ghetto problems in the Chicago Freedom Movement (see page 91). Reports such as the Kerner Report recommended increased expenditure on the ghettos, but most whites were unwilling to finance improvements.

Why whites were unwilling to help

US Cold War anti-Communism ensured that sympathy for the poor was often equated with sympathy for Communist doctrines of economic equality. White American unwillingness to help was also motivated by self-interest. Black entry into a white neighbourhood would cause property prices to plummet and black schoolchildren from deprived backgrounds might damage the educational and employment prospects of white children. White voters did not want to pay extra taxes to end ghetto poverty, particularly after the Vietnam War led to tax rises. Neither the federal government nor state nor city authorities wanted to bear the expensive burden of improving the ghettos.

Federal government expenditure
Great Society, 1963–9: $15.5 billion
Vietnam War, 1965–73: $120 billion

While whites increasingly perceived blacks as seeking 'handouts', blacks increasingly perceived whites as uninterested and unsympathetic. Not surprisingly then, the Black Power movement emerged out of the impoverished ghettos, for which by the late 1960s a new generation of black radicals were demanding improvements.

Ghetto rejection of the civil rights organizations

The civil rights organizations tried to respond to ghetto frustration. King and SCLC went to Chicago in 1966 (see page 91) and initiated the Poor People's Campaign in 1967 (see page 97). From 1964, CORE established 'Freedom Houses' in the ghettos to provide information and advice on education, employment, health and housing. The National Urban League (NUL) launched a programme to develop economic self-help strategies in the ghettos in 1968 and received $28 million from the Nixon administration in 1971. However, none of this was enough. Many ghetto inhabitants felt that organizations such as NAACP and SCLC knew little about ghetto life and were not much help in improving matters. Many younger black activists rejected 'de great lawd' Martin Luther King Jr's emphasis on the South, the 'white man's' Christian religion, and non-violence, none of which seemed to be contributing to progress in the ghettos. However, they recognized that civil rights activism had led to improvements, and were inspired to be active themselves, looking to new leaders such as Malcolm X and Stokely Carmichael, whose condoning of violence seemed a more appropriate response to white oppression than King's 'love thine enemy'.

The radicalization of SNCC and CORE

The radicalization of SNCC and CORE and their alienation from the older organizations were demonstrated in the Meredith March in 1966 (see page 96).

SNCC

In 1966, impatient with the slow progress toward equality, and disillusioned by the lack of federal protection in the Mississippi Freedom Summer (see page 80) and by the refusal of the Democratic Party to seat the MFDP delegates at Atlantic City (see page 80), SNCC turned to a more militant leader. John Lewis (see below) was replaced by Stokely Carmichael and in 1966, SNCC voted to expel whites. In 1967, Carmichael was replaced by the even more militant Henry 'Rap' Brown ('violence is as American as cherry pie'), who advocated armed self-defence and urged a black audience in Cambridge, Maryland, to take over white-owned stores in the ghettos, using violence if necessary. There was a race riot in Cambridge soon afterwards. At a rally in Oakland, California, in February 1968, SNCC merged with the Black Panthers (see page 112), the most radical of all black organizations.

John Lewis 1940–

When studying in Nashville for the ministry, Alabama-born John Lewis participated in sit-ins in 1960. His parents were 'shocked and ashamed' when he was jailed: 'My mother made no distinction between being jailed for drunkenness and being jailed for demonstrating for civil rights.' It was years before she forgave him. In 1961, he participated in the Freedom Rides. He was elected chairman of SNCC in 1963. A staunch advocate of non-violence, he was the youngest speaker at the 1963 March on Washington, where other black leaders dissuaded him from criticizing the Civil Rights Bill ('What is in the bill that will protect the homeless and starving?'). He co-ordinated the Mississippi Freedom Summer in 1964 and led marches in Selma in 1965, where 'Sheriff Clark's temper played right into our hands.' The only former civil rights leader to be elected to the US Congress, he has represented Georgia's fifth Congressional district since 1988. When Barack Obama was elected president in 2008, Lewis said:

If someone had told me this would be happening now, I would have told them they were crazy, out of their mind, they did not know what they were talking about … I just wish the others were around to see this day … To the people who were beaten, put in jail, were asked questions they could never answer to register to vote, it's amazing.

He was on the stage during President Obama's inauguration in 2009, the only surviving speaker of the March on Washington. The president signed a photograph for Lewis with: 'Because of you, John. Barack Obama.'

CORE

When James Farmer resigned leadership of CORE in December 1965, the radical Floyd McKissick was elected in his place. In 1966, the annual CORE convention, endorsed 'black power', and declared non-violence inappropriate if black people needed to defend themselves. The 1967 convention excised the word 'multiracial' from CORE's constitution. By 1968, whites were excluded from CORE's membership.

Definitions of Black Power

What was Black Power?

The phrase 'black power' first came to prominence during the Meredith March (see pages 96–7), when SNCC chairman Stokely Carmichael cried 'black power' in Greenwood, Mississippi. It meant different things to different people.

For some black people, Black Power meant black supremacy. In 1968, Elijah Muhammad said, 'Black power means the black people will rule the white people on earth as the white people have ruled the black people for the past six thousand years.'

During 1968–9, black car workers at the Chrysler, Ford and General Motors plants in Detroit, Michigan, thought Black Power meant a black working-class revolution. They united in a Black Power union, the League of Revolutionary Workers, which had a core of 80 activists and contributed to the militancy of black car workers and to the employment of more black foremen, before it imploded in 1971.

The older generation of civil rights leaders were hostile. NAACP leader Roy Wilkins felt Black Power supporters were racist and no better than the Ku Klux Klan. Martin Luther King Jr said, 'When you put black and power together, it sounds like you are trying to say black domination'. He called Black Power 'a slogan without a program'. When people persisted in using the phrase, King tried to give it more positive connotations: 'The Negro is in dire need of a sense of dignity and a sense of pride, and I think black power is an attempt to develop pride. And there is no doubt about the need for power – he can't get into the mainstream of society without it … Black power means instilling within the Negro a sense of belonging and appreciation of heritage, a racial pride … We must never be ashamed of being black.' SNCC's Floyd McKissick also attempted a positive definition: 'Black Power is not hatred' and 'did not mean black supremacy, did not mean exclusion of whites from the Negro revolution, and did not mean advocacy of violence and riots', but 'political power, economic power, and a new self-image for Negroes'.

Republican Nathan Wright believed Black Power meant economic power. He proposed a Black Power capitalist movement. He organized conferences in Newark (1967) and Philadelphia (1968), and won the support of SCLC and NUL. In 1968, Republican presidential candidate Richard Nixon said Black Power meant, 'more black ownership, for from this can flow the rest – black pride, black jobs, black opportunity and yes, black power'.

Clearly Black Power was amorphous and ever changing. The *New York Times* probably got it right: 'Nobody knows what the phrase "black power" really means'. SNCC's Cleveland Sellers said, 'There was a deliberate attempt to make it [black power] ambiguous … [so that] it meant everything to everybody.' One of the few areas of unanimity was the emphasis on black pride and black culture. Blacks frequently adopted Afro hairstyles and African garb. Black college students successfully agitated for the introduction of black studies programmes.

What did the Black Panthers achieve?

→ ## The establishment, aims and achievements of the Black Panthers

In 1966, the Black Panther Party for Self-Defence was established in Oakland, California, by Huey Newton and Bobby Seale. Newton explained that he chose the Panther as a symbol because the panther 'never attacks. But if anyone attacks him or backs him into a corner the panther comes up to wipe the aggressor or that attacker out.'

SOURCE G

The iconic photograph of Huey Newton in 1967.

Looking at Huey Newton's pose in Source G, what point was he trying to make? **?**

The aims of the Black Panthers

Greatly influenced by Malcolm X and by Communist revolutionaries such as **Che Guevara** and **Mao Zedong**, Newton and Seale's Black Panthers aimed to become involved in the global non-white working-class struggle. From 1969 to 1970 they forged links with liberation movements in Africa, Asia and South America, and aligned themselves with other radical groups in the USA, especially the Mexican 'Brown Berets' and Puerto Rican and Chinese-American radicals. The Black Panthers adopted a predominantly black paramilitary uniform, with berets and leather jackets. Their manifesto was radical and nationalistic, with demands and aims very similar to those of Garvey and Elijah Muhammad, including:

🔑 KEY TERM

Che Guevara An Argentine Communist who promoted revolution in Latin America and Africa.

Mao Zedong Leader of Communist China 1949–75.

- payment of compensation for slavery to black Americans by the federal government
- freedom for incarcerated blacks, who should be jailed only if tried by a black jury
- exemption of blacks from military service
- a United Nations supervised referendum of black Americans 'for the purpose of determining the will of black people as to their national destiny'
- less police brutality
- improvements in ghetto living conditions.

The achievements of the Black Panthers

Newton's biographer Hugh Pearson (1995) claimed the Black Panthers were 'little more than a temporary media phenomenon'. They never boasted more than 5000 members. However, with their 30 chapters, mostly in ghettos in the West and North (including Oakland, New York, Boston and Chicago), they won a great deal of respect, especially for their emphasis on self-help. They set up ghetto clinics to advise on health, welfare and legal rights. In 1970, the Southern California chapter of the Free Breakfast programme served up over 1700 meals weekly to the ghetto poor.

Black Panthers aimed to expose police brutality and harassment. Citing the Second Amendment to the US Constitution (which said that citizens had the right to carry arms), armed Black Panthers followed police cars in the ghettos, in order to expose police brutality. This led to some violent shoot-outs. In May 1967, Black Panthers surrounded and entered the California State Capitol Building in Sacramento, accusing the legislature of considering repressive legislation. Some plotted to blow up major department stores in New York City, according to one FBI infiltrator.

Case study: Fred Hampton – successful or unsuccessful?

Opinions of the Black Panthers and their achievements vary, as demonstrated by reactions to Fred Hampton (1948–68). Born in a Chicago suburb, he was an NAACP activist who joined the Black Panthers and organized a multiracial alliance that included Hispanic groups such as the Brown Berets and the Students for a Democratic Society (see page 177). The FBI monitored him closely from 1967 and he was shot in 1968 during a 4.45a.m. police raid on his flat. NAACP leader Roy Wilkins declared the killing illegal. Hampton's family brought a case against the city, state and federal governments, and years later were awarded $1.85 million in damages. In 1991 and 2004, Chicago City Council approved the celebration of a 'Fred Hampton Day'. In 2006, Chicago police officers voiced objections to a proposal that a Chicago street be named after him. Hampton's life is celebrated in rap music and hip-hop. Many see him as a hero who among other things calmed Chicago's warring gangs. Some see him as a troublemaker.

The decline of Black Power

Black Power 'peaked' in 1970, but this was followed by a swift decline. Why?

← **Why did the Black Power movement end in the 1970s?**

Divisions, disorganization and definitions

The Black Power movement was always relatively ill-defined and consequently poorly organized. Supporters had differing ideas as to what they meant by and wanted with Black Power, so as the years passed, the divisions became pronounced and open. For example, from 1967, SNCC was increasingly divided between black separatists and social revolutionaries who favoured multiracial co-operation in the struggle against poverty and inequality. While black power was an attractive slogan to discontented blacks, the movement never really produced a persuasive and effective blueprint for change. The Black Panthers' talk of violence brought down the effective wrath of the federal government on their heads. Similarly, Black Panther talk of socialism was ill-suited to the USA with its capitalist culture. Talk of a separate black nation within the USA was equally unrealistic.

Sexism

Feminism became very popular in the late 1960s, and appealed to many black women. Male Black Power advocates were often sexist. When female supporters found their Black Power activities limited because of their gender, they frequently concentrated on feminism instead.

Financial problems

White liberals had financed the major civil rights organizations. When SNCC and CORE became more militant and expelled whites, their funding suffered. By 1970, SNCC was reduced to only three active chapters (New York City, Atlanta and Cincinnati) and no full-time employees. The New York City chapter could not even afford a telephone. In December 1973, SNCC ceased to exist.

The Nixon administration

The worst problem for the Black Power movement was probably the Nixon administration's sustained and effective pursuit of Black Power leaders. Many Black Panthers had prison records from their pre-Panther days. Eldridge Cleaver, ranked 'No. 3' in the Black Panther hierarchy, had been released from prison in 1966, having served a sentence as a serial rapist. He justified his crimes as a righteous rebellion against 'white man's law', in the form of 'defiling his women'. The Black Panthers routinely engaged in petty crime, sought confrontation with, and advocated the killing of, the police. Not surprisingly, they suffered from police attention, some would say persecution. They were targeted and destroyed by the police and FBI from 1967 to 1969. By 1970, most of the Black Panther leadership was killed, imprisoned or in enforced exile.

Even civil rights activists were targeted. In 1972, for example, the 'Wilmington Ten' (all civil rights activists) were arrested and charged with arson in North Carolina. The jury contained three known Ku Klux Klan members and the FBI bribed witnesses hostile to the 10, who were given extensive jail sentences. Their convictions were overturned in 1980 by a federal appeals court.

Was Black Power a failure?

Achievements of the Black Power movement

The achievements of the Black Power movement are as controversial as the movement itself.

Success?

The movement raised the morale of many black Americans. A 1970 poll revealed that 64 per cent of African Americans took pride in the Black Panthers. Perhaps the main legacy with regard to black pride was the establishment of courses on black history and culture in US educational institutions. Groups such as the Black Panthers gave useful practical help to ghetto dwellers and it could be said that Black Power activists, like civil rights activists, kept the ghetto problems on the political agenda. Ghetto riots were surely one manifestation of the Black Power movement. King asked a group of Watts residents, 'How can you say you won, when 34 Negroes are dead, your community is destroyed, and whites are using the riots as an excuse for inaction?' They replied, 'We won because we made them pay attention to us.'

Failure?

It could be argued that Black Power contributed to the demise of what had been an effective Civil Rights Movement. The older generation of civil rights leaders lost support and momentum and their replacements failed to match their achievements. Under the leadership of its founder, James Farmer, CORE had played a vital role in non-violent protests such as sit-ins and freedom rides, which contributed to desegregation in the South. After the radical Floyd McKissick replaced Farmer in 1965, CORE achieved little. SNCC followed a similar line of development. However, it could also be argued that the Civil Rights Movement would have lost momentum and effectiveness without the development and rivalry of Black Power, because the Northern ghetto problem proved insoluble.

Like the older generation of civil rights leaders, Black Power adherents failed to find an answer to the ghetto problem and ghetto rioters and armed Black Panthers helped to decrease the white sympathy that had been a key to progress for the non-violent civil rights activists.

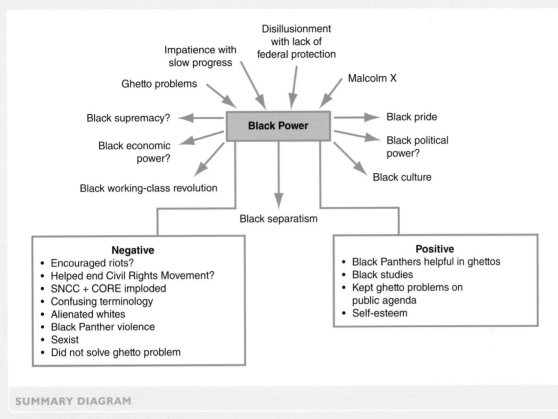

Impatience with
slow progress

Disillusionment
with lack of
federal protection

Ghetto problems

Malcolm X

Black supremacy? ← **Black Power** → Black pride

Black economic
power?

Black political
power?

Black working-class revolution

Black culture

Black separatism

Negative
- Encouraged riots?
- Helped end Civil Rights Movement?
- SNCC + CORE imploded
- Confusing terminology
- Alienated whites
- Black Panther violence
- Sexist
- Did not solve ghetto problem

Positive
- Black Panthers helpful in ghettos
- Black studies
- Kept ghetto problems on
  public agenda
- Self-esteem

SUMMARY DIAGRAM

The rise of Black Power in the 1960s

5 Key debate

> ▶ *Key question: How new and successful was the Black Power*
> *movement?*

From the start of their enslavement in the colonial USA, some black
Americans have sought self-determination and sovereignty. Historians John
Bracey, August Meier and Elliot Rudwick (1994) pointed out that nationalism
dominated the black community in several periods, one of which was the
mid-1960s to the early 1970s. However, this last separatist and nationalist
movement has not captured historians' interest and imagination in the

manner of the Civil Rights Movement. Historian Peniel Joseph (2001) tried to explain why scholars pay little attention to black power:

- American politics became increasingly conservative after the early 1970s.
- Scholars disliked the 'evil twin' that helped to wreck the Civil Rights Movement.
- There is little archive material.
- Mainstream scholars do not take the topic seriously.

UNIA: successful?

Historians' interpretations of the success or failure of Marcus Garvey and UNIA (see page 55) depend on how the historian views black nationalism. Liberal, **integrationist** black historian John Hope Franklin (1988) acknowledged UNIA's mass appeal, but nevertheless declared it an unrealistic movement, doomed to fail. However, historians such as Theodore Vincent (1972) stressed UNIA's influence on the Civil Rights Movement and Black Power.

Elijah Muhammad and Malcolm X: successful?

Biographies of controversial figures such as Elijah Muhammad and Malcolm X are frequently themselves controversial. In a balanced biography of Elijah Muhammad, Claude Andrew Clegg (1997) recognized his positive and negative achievements and characteristics. In sharp contrast, Bruce Perry's (1991) biography of Malcolm X, which attributed Malcolm's struggles to an unhappy home life and psychological damage, infuriated nationalist scholars who saw Malcolm as being within the long tradition of black nationalism in the USA. Historians' backgrounds similarly affect their interpretations of Malcolm's philosophical changes in his final year. The genuine nature and extent of his embrace of orthodox Islam are much debated.

In what many consider to be the definitive study of Malcolm X, Manning Marable (2011) considered Malcolm's conversion to orthodox Islam to be genuine. Marable regarded Malcolm's autobiography as skewed by his integrationist co-author, Alex Haley, who disliked and therefore censored Malcolm's radicalism. Marable contended that this censorship helps to explain why Malcolm's autobiography is so popular in schools and colleges. One thing scholars agree on is that Malcolm had a great and lasting impact.

Did the Black Power movement damage the Civil Rights Movement?

Many historians of the Black Power movement have been negative. For example, African American Clayborne Carson (1996) claimed that its militancy failed to produce greater power for black people and actually led to a decline in the ability of African Americans to affect the course of US politics. The Black Power movement promised more than the Civil Rights Movement but delivered less. Amid much negativity, most historians, such as William Van Deburg (1992), agreed that Black Power's greatest (some thought sole) contribution to the black community was intellectual and cultural, in university courses and in increased black self-esteem and identity. The inspirational impact of the movement on other groups, such as Native Americans, has long been recognized, as by Jeffrey Ogbar (2009). It even transcended national boundaries (see page 129).

A Civil Rights Movement followed by a Black Power movement?

Recent historians such as Peniel Joseph (2006, 2009) have advised care over the traditional chronological periodization of a civil rights era (1955–65) followed by a Black Power era (c.1966–72). Joseph (2006) emphasized a Black Power 'movement that parallels, and at times overlapped, the heroic civil rights era'. Several historians complain that this traditional view that the Civil Rights Movement was followed by a more assertive black movement led to a distorted view. According to the historian Sharon Harley (2009), the traditional but erroneous periodization meant historians ignored Gloria Richardson's leadership in Cambridge, Maryland, in the early 1960s, which emphasized self-defence. Timothy Tyson (2001) studied an even earlier advocate of self-defence in Robert Williams in Monroe, North Carolina, in the 1950s. Williams' uniquely militant NAACP chapter infuriated Roy Wilkins, although subsequently, as emphasized by historian Yohuru Williams (2009), Wilkins defended the Black Panthers, believing they were being destroyed by unconstitutional and illegal methods.

T O K What arguments can be made for the use of violence in the service of securing civil rights? (Ethics, Reason.)

SOURCE H

An extract from *Black Power's Powerful Legacy* by Peniel Joseph, 2006, quoted at www.penielejoseph.com/legacy.html

[The Black Power movement] transformed America's racial, social and political landscape … Ultimately, Black Power accelerated America's reckoning with its own uncomfortable, often ugly, racial past, and in the process spurred a debate over racial progress, citizenship, and democracy that would scandalize as much as it would change the nation.

With reference to Source H, do you suppose that a reader can sometimes guess the colour of a writer on movements such as Black Power? How much does our colour and philosophy affect what we write and believe about movements?

Chapter summary

Martin, Malcolm and Black Power

After Martin Luther King Jr's successful focus on segregation in the South, he turned to the problem of the Northern and Western ghettos. His Chicago campaign (1966) did little to alleviate the appalling situation in Chicago's ghetto areas. Knowing white voters did not want their economic well-being threatened by the taxation necessary to improve the ghettos or by African Americans moving into their neighbourhoods, Mayor Daley did little to help.

During the Meredith March (1966), African American divisions became public. Militants such as SNCC's Stokely Carmichael called for black power. King was depressed by black violence and the lack of enthusiasm for his Poor People's Campaign. He was assassinated in 1968.

The relative importance of King in the Civil Rights Movement successes has always been controversial. Other individuals, organizations and the federal government played an important part, but King was a uniquely inspirational leader who despite his weaknesses as an organizer orchestrated highly effective campaigns in Birmingham and Selma that contributed greatly the 1964 Civil Rights Act and the 1965 Voting Rights Act. His preference for the tactic of mass protests as opposed to litigation aroused considerable jealousy and unease in NAACP, and his moderation and religiosity irritated many believers in Black Power. Like the Black Power movement he had little success with the insoluble problems of the ghetto. Militants thought him an Uncle Tom, but like the founder of his religion, he was a revolutionary.

Black Power emerged out of a long tradition of black nationalism and separatism, demonstrated in Marcus Garvey's UNIA and the Nation of Islam (NOI). The most famous NOI minister was Malcolm X, whose bitter attacks on US whites gained him a great following among ghetto residents and hatred from whites. With its emphasis on black pride and economic self-sufficiency, the NOI inspired and aided many ghetto residents and contributed to the rise of Black Power, as did Malcolm.

Long critical of King's campaigns, Malcolm seemed to mellow after he left the NOI in the year before his assassination (1964). Although often accused of fomenting racial hatred and violence, he helped to keep ghetto conditions on the national agenda. He played an important part in making some African Americans more extreme, as did ghetto problems, the lack of federal protection for activists, and the slow pace of progress.

Martin Luther King Jr and Malcolm X had many differences. King was from a Southern, stable, strongly religious, middle-class family that supported NAACP. Malcolm came from an impoverished Midwestern family. His father joined UNIA. Both suffered from great discrimination, but while King graduated from good universities, Malcolm basically educated himself while in jail. Given their backgrounds, it is not surprising that King sought integration, while Malcolm sought separatism. While King advocated non-violent protest, Malcolm justified black violence, but they shared the same ultimate aim, to improve black lives. Some of their tactics were the same. Both preached, wrote, and joined and founded organizations.

Black Power was hard to define. It meant different things to different people – violent demonstrations, black pride, black economic self-sufficiency, black political power, black supremacy or black workers' rights. The most famous Black Power group was the separatist Black Panthers who worked to help the ghetto poor. One of their tactics was to expose police brutality towards African Americans, which, coupled with participation in crime, contributed greatly to the opposition of the white authorities to the group.

By 1970 the Black Power movement was in decline because of its vague aims, internal divisions, and the effective opposition of the Nixon administration. The movement had raised black morale and helped create a legacy of black studies in educational institutions. Some believe it caused irreparable damage to the Civil Rights Movement, others that the Civil Rights Movement had done all it could do when it brought about the end of Jim Crow. Further progress would have cost white USA too much. Recently, historians have reminded us that the Civil Rights Movement and the Black Power movement ran parallel.

✓ Examination advice

How to answer 'assess' questions

Questions that ask you to <u>assess</u> want you to make judgements that you can support with evidence, reasons and explanations. It is important for you to demonstrate why your own assessment is better than alternative ones.

Example

<u>Assess</u> the aims and success of the Black Panthers in the 1960s and early 1970s.

1 For this question, you need to consider what the Black Panthers hoped to achieve and how successful they were in reaching those goals. Be sure to focus on the Black Panthers specifically. Some students confuse Malcolm X and the Black Panthers. They are not the same. In order to tackle this question, think about what is being asked. There are essentially four points to consider:
   - Identify the goals and successes of the Black Panthers.
   - Only write in depth about the Black Panthers.
   - You might want to contrast the goals of the Panthers with other movements but this should not be your overriding concern.
   - Finally, discuss the aims and success of the Panthers in the specific time period stated. Your answer will not be helped by long references to what took place before and after the 1960s and early 1970s.

2 For questions that ask for both aims and successes, you might want to make a chart listing the two. Spend five minutes doing this before you begin to write your essay. Here is an example of what you might include:

Goals	Success
Become involved with worldwide struggle	Links made with other revolutionary groups in Africa, Asia, Latin America
Receive compensation for slavery	None
Freedom for jailed blacks	Did not happen
Exempt blacks from military service	Did not happen
Expose and decrease police brutality	Supporters say exposed the brutality but the authorities soon destroyed them
Improve ghetto living conditions	Medical, educational, legal, social centres set up
Provide means to defend black community	Panthers armed themselves
Replace old leadership	Young Panthers attracted urban supporters
UN referendum on self-determination	Did not happen

3 Your introduction should state your thesis which might be something like: 'The Black Panther Movement set itself ambitious goals most of which were not met.' An example of a good introductory paragraph for this question is given below.

Many young African Americans, particularly those living in the depressing ghettoes of major US cities, became impatient at the pace of change. They felt that the more established civil rights movements were out of touch with the realities faced by urban blacks. The Black Panther Party was established in 1966 and their ambitious programme included improving living conditions in ghettos, working with other revolutionary groups outside the USA, and defending the black community against perceived police brutality. Many of the goals of the movement were not met as the US government and police forces turned their power on the Black Panther Party and jailed and killed many of its members. However, the Panthers did create social, legal and health services in poor urban areas and were respected for these actions. Furthermore, the Panthers did raise awareness of the social and economic problems in ghettos even if remedies were not immediately forthcoming.

4 In the body of your essay, discuss one goal in each paragraph, assessing to what extent each was successful. One strategy would be to begin with the aims you think were the most important and end with those that were the least significant. It is also very important that you explain why or why not a specific goal was met. Remember that your essay will be judged on the quality and quantity of supporting evidence. Be sure to defend and explain your examples.

5 Now try writing a complete answer to the question following the advice above.

✒ Examination practice

Below are three exam-style questions for you to practise on this topic.

1 Compare and contrast Dr Martin Luther King Jr's and Malcolm X's strategies to create a more equal society.
(For guidance on how to answer 'compare and contrast' questions, see pages 235–8.)

2 Assess the importance of Dr Martin Luther King Jr's contributions to the Civil Rights Movement.

3 'The Civil Rights Movement ran out of steam by the early 1970s.' To what extent do you agree with this assessment?
(For guidance on how to answer 'To what extent' questions, see pages 86–9).

CHAPTER 4

Afro-Latin Americans

This chapter looks at the history of the descendants of African slaves brought to Latin America in the colonial period and the nineteenth century. It focuses on Brazil, where their descendants are most numerous. It looks at the origins of the new black movements after the 1960s, how they were influenced by movements elsewhere and the impact they had. This chapter compares and contrasts the Afro-Latin American and African American experiences. You need to consider the following questions throughout this chapter:

✪ What was the legacy of slavery?
✪ Why did the situation of Afro-Latin Americans improve in the early twentieth century?
✪ How successful was the late twentieth-century black Civil Rights Movement?
✪ Have Afro-Latin Americans attained equality through agency and racial democracy?

1 Afro-Latin Americans in the nineteenth century

▶ *Key question: What was the legacy of slavery?*

While 560,000 African slaves were imported into what became the USA, 5.7 million came to Latin America. As in the USA, slavery ended during the nineteenth century but the freed slaves and their descendants still suffered from racist laws and poverty.

Racism was justified by 'science', which claimed that the white race was superior. It was popularly believed that in order to become civilized and modernized, a country needed to be white, so some countries worked hard to 'whiten' their population by encouraging immigration from Europe. Through this 'whitening', the racial composition of Argentina, Brazil, Uruguay and Cuba was changed. Fictions furthered the process: in 1899, a Cuban patriotic commission exhumed the body of Afro-Cuban Antonio Maceo, hero of the Cuban war of independence against Spain. Scientists studied his skull and 'proved' that he was more white than black. In contrast to the 'whitened' nations, West Indian immigration 'blackened' countries such as Costa Rica, the Dominican Republic and Panama.

The Redemption of Ham, an 1895 painting by Modesto Brocos (1852–1936) in Brazil's Museu Nacional de Belas Artes.

? Study the three generations of a Brazilian family in *The Redemption of Cain* in Source A and think carefully about the title the artist used. Do you see any evidence of racism on the part of the artist?

2 Afro-Latin Americans in the twentieth century

▶ *Key question: Why did the situation of Afro-Latin Americans improve in the early twentieth century?*

🔑 **KEY TERM**

Afro-Latin Americans
Residents of Latin America with black ancestry, including those of mixed race.

As in the USA, the black population of Latin America suffered from, and sought an end to, racism and inequality during the twentieth century. As the century wore on, **Afro-Latin Americans** became more confident and empowered.

Afro-Latin Americans 1900–60s

Afro-Latin American progress and improvement in the first half of the twentieth century were due to sympathetic regimes, organizations such as labour unions, improved educational and job opportunities, and ideological and cultural developments.

Sympathetic regimes

In the 1930s and 1940s, a series of **populist regimes** gained power in countries such as Brazil, Cuba, Venezuela, Colombia and Costa Rica. The populist regimes promised racial equality and greater minority participation in national life. According to historian George Reid Andrews (2004), 'None of the populist regimes was able to fully realize these promises, but most carried through to at least some degree.'

Brazil and Costa Rica

After a military coup in 1930, the new Brazilian leader Getúlio Vargas (president 1930–7, dictator 1937–45 and elected president 1950–4) sought labour support. He did not mention Afro-Brazilians specifically, but cultivated his 'Father of the Poor' image and as most Afro-Brazilians were poor, they supported his Brazilian Labour Party (PTB). He employed many black civil servants at a time when employers openly excluded those not white.

Cuba and Venezuela

In a development not paralleled in the USA, some Afro-Latin Americans gained political power, as in Cuba and Venezuela. Under pressure from the Great Depression, the Machado dictatorship in Cuba was overthrown by the predominantly lower class Afro-Cuban Sergeants' Revolt. Their leader, Fulgencio Batista, dominated Cuban politics as elected president from 1940 to 1944, and dictator from 1952 to 1958. His two main sources of support were organized labour and the armed forces, both of which were predominantly Afro-Cuban. In contrast, Fidel Castro and the revolutionaries who overthrew Batista in 1959 were mostly middle-class whites. Nevertheless, Castro appealed to the poorer classes, and declared his commitment to racial equality. A US study of 1962 found Afro-Cuban workers more pro-Castro than white workers. Significantly, only 13 per cent of anti-Castro Cuban exiles in the 1960s were black or **mulatto**.

Afro-Venezuelans such as Rómulo Betancourt were prominent in the Acción Democrática (AD) Party, which combined with a group of junior officers to overthrow the military regime in 1945. Betancourt was president of the civilian–military junta from 1945 to 1948, during which period an unusual number of black and mulatto civil servants were appointed, prompting the next president, Rómulo Gallegos to comment, 'Now the blacks are ruling.' Betancourt was then elected president from 1959 to 1964.

Why did Afro-Latin Americans gain confidence in the early twentieth century?

KEY TERM

Populist regimes Governments that courted support from large groups such as labour unions and the poor.

Mulatto Of European–African descent.

Jorge Gaitán, a dark-skinned mulatto, whom Conservatives referred to as 'el negro Gaitán' (a racial epithet that he adopted with pride), was one of the most popular of Colombian politicians. Had Gaitán not been assassinated in 1948, he would probably have become Colombian president.

Labour unions and other organizations

As in the USA (see page 55), labour unions played an important part in Afro-Latin American empowerment. Populist politicians such as Vargas in Brazil, Batista in Cuba and Juan Perón in Argentina usually sought the support of the labour unions, in which black workers participated throughout Latin America. The unions adopted and promoted the idea of racial democracy (see page 127). There were also purely black organizations, such as the Brazilian Black Front (FNB), established in 1931, which organized large-scale protests against racial discrimination. However, unlike the NAACP (see page 55), the FNB never established itself as an effective political force because black ancestry was traditionally not something of which Brazilians were proud. Also, when Vargas ruled as a dictator after 1937 he banned all political parties and all discussions of race. He sought to portray Brazil as a white country in order to attract foreign investors.

Improved educational opportunities

During the twentieth century, the number of universities greatly increased. In 1950, only 51,000 out of 20 million Brazilian blacks and mulattos graduated from high school, and only 4000 from college. By 1999, out of a population of 70 million Afro-Brazilians, 3.3 million were high school graduates and 600,000 were college graduates. In 1950, only five black students had ever graduated from Uruguay's biggest university, but by 1966, two per cent of Afro-Uruguayans were college graduates. In socialist Cuba, racial disparities in education virtually disappeared. The number of Afro-Cubans with university degrees was in similar proportions to the number of white Cubans. By the 1970s, there were sufficient numbers of Costa Ricans of West Indian ancestry at the National University in San José to organize a national conference on the black situation. In the 1970s and 1980s, there was an influx of Afro-Venezuelans into the universities, and in 1993, the largest university, Universidad Central de Venezuela, was majority Afro-Venezuelan.

Improved employment opportunities

Once educated, Afro-Latin Americans became **white-collar workers** and populist leaders often gave them jobs. For example, Costa Rican José Figueres' Partido de Liberación Nacional (PLN) won electoral victories in 1952 and 1970 that owed much to voters of West Indian descent and employed many of them in the civil service. By 1987, 11.2 per cent of Afro-Brazilians were white-collar workers and constituted 23.5 per cent of the total white-collar labour force.

 **KEY TERM**

White-collar worker
Person who performs professional or office work rather than manual labour.

Ideological and cultural developments

The collapse of oligarchic governments during the Great Depression led to a rejection of 'whitening' and it became fashionable to embrace African and Indian culture as essential components of national heritage. The new ideology of 'racial democracy', closely associated with the rise of labour-based populism, claimed that Latin America was happily multiracial and multicultural. The ideology became popular, thanks in particular to the writings of white Brazilian Gilberto Freyre. Born in 1900, 12 years after the abolition of slavery in Brazil, Freyre spent much of his youth on sugar plantations owned by his mother's relations. In his 1933 book *Casa Grande e Senzala* (*The Big House and the Slave Quarters*) he argued that because of greater racial intermixing during the era of slavery, race relations were better in Brazil than in other slave-owning societies. He declared that from the time of slavery, a racial democracy was being constructed in Brazil. He created the idea (some say myth) that Brazil is one of the few truly mixed, non-racist nations. His ideas are widely taught in schools, including in the USA. He has been credited with having improved Brazilian race relations.

 **KEY TERM**

Miscegenation The mixing of races through marriage and interbreeding.

Merengue Music and dance created by Afro-Dominicans.

Carnaval Annual festival before the deprivations of Lent.

SOURCE B

An extract from the writings of Gilberto Freyre, quoted in *Black in Latin America* by African American historian Henry Louis Gates Jr, published by New York University Press, New York, USA, 2011, page 42.

*The truth is that in Brazil, contrary to what is to be observed in other American countries and in those parts of Africa that have been recently colonized by Europeans, the primitive culture – the Amerindian as well as the African – has not been isolated into hard, dry, indigestible lumps incapable of being assimilated by the European social system … Neither did the social relations between the two races, the conquering and the indigenous one, ever reach that point of sharp antipathy or hatred, the grating sound of which reaches our ears from all the countries that have been colonized by Anglo-Saxon Protestants. The friction here was smoothed by the lubricating oil of a deep-going **miscegenation**.*

Which part of this passage from Freyre in Source B do you suppose Gates said troubled him?

In some ways, it seemed believable that racial democracy had been achieved in the new mestizo-dominated societies in Mexico and Cuba and in majority mulatto Brazil, where what historians such as George Reid Andrews (2004) called 'brownness' was exalted and African-based cultural forms became fashionable. The Dominican Republic dictator Rafael Trujillo (1930–61) declared **merengue** the country's 'national music'. Countries such as Brazil and Cuba encouraged the previously restricted African elements of **Carnaval**. Even African-based religions became acceptable, especially when governments sought support from practitioners. For example, during the Second Republic (1946–64) and in the era of military rule (1965–85), Brazilian governments wooed leaders of religions such as Candomblé in order to gain the support of their 20 million followers.

Rafael Trujillo and whitening
Rafael Trujillo had black ancestry. His personal effects, which can be seen at the Santo Domingo National Museum of History and Geography, include white face powder.

Why and with what
results was there an
Afro-Latin American
Civil Rights
Movement after the
1960s?

→ New black movements after the 1960s

In much of Afro-Latin America there was a dramatic rise in racial
mobilization in the late twentieth century, a little later than in the USA.

A late 1980s' directory listed 343 Afro-Brazilian organizations, mostly in the
states of São Paulo, Rio de Janeiro, Minas Gerais and Bahia. Many were
cultural organizations such as samba schools that became politicized and
focused on civil rights. Because it had the largest black population and the
greatest tradition of black activism, Brazil had the most notable black
mobilization. Next came Colombia, where many organizations were
established in the 1970s, such as Cimarrón in Bogotá. While the mobilization
of the 1970s was primarily urban and focused on discrimination and
inequality, the mobilization of the 1980s included the rural black population.
Peasants and forest-dwellers were concerned about the fate of their
communal land, and their lobbying contributed to the relevant provisions in
the 1991 Colombian Constitution. Even countries with small black
populations, such as Costa Rica, Peru and Uruguay, saw an upsurge in black
activism in the 1970s and 1980s.

Owing to its close ties with the USA, Panama's black mobilization was
earlier. In the mid-1960s black activist Walter Smith created Movimiento
Afro-Panameño, which he based on the US Civil Rights Movement. His and
other organizations were supported and encouraged by President Omar
Torrijos, and Afro-Panamanians in turn supported him. These organizations
had run out of steam by 1980, but new ones emerged during General
Noriega's dictatorship in the 1980s. Their focus was cultural, but when
electoral democracy was restored in the 1990s, the focus was on racial
discrimination once more.

The new movements emerged because of the failure of governments to
deliver on promised equality, political conditions, foreign influence and
international events.

The failure to deliver equality

Governments had failed to deliver equality owing to a combination of
insufficient economic growth and racism. The Afro-Latin American middle
class had grown greatly since the Second World War thanks to the economic
development and socialist provision under populist governments, but
economic inequality and racism were not eradicated. During the 1940s and
1950s, there were many highly publicized incidents of racism. In 1950, a São
Paulo hotel refused to accommodate famous African American
choreographer Katherine Dunham, but gave a room to her white secretary.
Such incidents generated national discussions that led to anti-discrimination
legislation in Venezuela (1945), Brazil (1951), Panama (1956) and Costa Rica
(1960), but none of these laws was rigorously enforced.

In Brazil in 1987, black and brown poverty rates were twice those of whites, partly because half of Afro-Brazilian workers were employed in agriculture and service industries where no great education was needed and where employers retained great control over their workers. Many Afro-Brazilians lived in *favelas*. During Brazil's 1988–90 '**war on children**', 82 per cent of the 4600 murdered street children were Afro-Brazilian. The murders were often perpetrated by public and private security forces, usually commissioned by shopkeepers whose businesses suffered from the attention and presence of the impoverished children.

Educated Afro-Latin American workers faced barriers. In 1974, Afro-Costa Rican civil servant Garnet Britton said, 'There are now quite a few of us black professionals who by virtue of our ability and hard work are beginning to compete for the best jobs, and we are beginning to feel the opposition.' Mobilization was an inevitable response to this failure to deliver equality.

Political conditions

In Brazil, increasing opposition to the military dictatorship and the gradual return of civilian rule in the late 1970s and early 1980s created openings for opponents, including black civil rights activists. A similar situation occurred in Uruguay, when the military dictatorship ended in 1985. In Panama, Omar Torrijos took power in 1969. He sought support from West Indian Panamanians and in return supported black organizations. In Colombia, the peace talks with the many guerrilla groups in the 1980s and the new constitution in 1991, which recognized Colombia as a multi-ethnic society, gave Afro-Colombians opportunities to participate in national discussions.

Foreign influence

The Civil Rights Movement in the USA had a great influence on Afro-Latin Americans throughout the twentieth century, especially among English-speaking Costa Ricans and Afro-Panamanians who had studied or worked in the USA in the 1960s and 1970s or heard about Martin Luther King Jr and Malcolm X from African American soldiers in Panama. In 1967, Stokely Carmichael visited Cuba and told *Time* magazine, 'Castro is the greatest black man I know.' However, Castro found Carmichael and the Black Panther Eldridge Cleaver, who visited in 1968, 'difficult and argumentative', according to the historian Richard Gott (2004). US Communist Angela Davis's 1972 visit was far more successful (see Source C, page 130). Along with the US Civil Rights Movement, black liberation struggles in Portuguese Africa in the 1970s and in South Africa in the 1990s were an inspiration to Afro-Latin Americans.

KEY TERM

Favelas Shantytowns in Brazil.

War on children Brazilian street children were seen as a threat to the property and life of the more prosperous classes, who employed security forces to be rid of them, sometimes resulting in murder.

SOURCE C

West Indian-born Carlos Moore's description of the impact of Angela Davis's visit to Cuba in 1968, quoted in *Cuba: A New History* by Richard Gott, published by Yale University Press, New Haven, Connecticut, USA, 2004, page 230.

Starved as they had been for over a decade for positive symbols of self-identity, black Cubans had reacted to Angela Davis's beautiful, un-straightened 'Afro' hair. Here was someone everyone could identify with, without fearing being tagged as 'counter-revolutionary', or as a 'black racist'. Angela Davis was a Communist, heroine, a 'runaway' Negress, approved of by Cuba. She wore a lovely, 'loud'-colored, tight-fitting dress, and did not straighten her hair. She was black. She was defiant. She was revolutionary. She was beautiful, in a sense that Afro-Cubans understood in their secret code of blackness.

Jesse Jackson vs Vicente Fox

Memín Pinguín is a comic book character who first appeared in Mexico in the 1940s. In 2005, the Mexican government issued five commemorative stamps with his image. African American activist Jesse Jackson flew to Mexico to urge President Fox to recall the stamps and apologize for their content and issue. Fox said that Mexicans loved Memín Pinguín, never apologized, and that Jackson was viewing Mexican culture through US eyes and lacked understanding. In 2011, African American scholar Henry Louis Gates Jr interviewed West Indian-born Glyn Jemmott, who worked among Afro-Mexicans, who said that Mexicans recognize that one should not judge a character created in the 1940s by contemporary standards.

SOURCE D

The Memín Pinguín stamps.

International events

Afro-Latin American activists gained inspiration from transnational meetings, beginning with Colombia in 1977, then Panama (1980), Brazil (1982 and 1995), Ecuador (1984) and Uruguay (1994). These meetings focused on inequality and how to combat it. Participants gained awareness on the availability of grants and loans from US and European foundations and the Inter-American Development Bank. Influenced by liberation theology (see page 13) and anxious to maintain the loyalty of black and mulatto members, the Catholic Church created *Pastorales Negroes* (black missions) that worked closely with local black organizations. They offered organizational experience and promoted self-belief. As in the USA, the Church, whether Christian or African-based, played a big role in black empowerment.

The United Nations

Afro-Latin American activists were also inspired by the United Nations (UN). The 1996 report by the UN Commission on Human Rights on racial discrimination and inequality in Brazil helped persuade President Fernando Henrique Cardoso to include proposals for affirmative action in his national human rights programme. Similar UN findings in Uruguay in 1999 led the José Battle administration to publicly acknowledge discrimination and to propose affirmative action. The 2001 UN Conference against Racism in South Africa energized Afro-Latin American organizations, and put pressure on national governments, prompting the establishment of the Brazilian National Council to Combat Discrimination (2010) and affirmative action programmes in several Brazilian government departments. The 2001 conference also encouraged Panama to pass anti-discrimination legislation in 2005.

Numbers of Afro-Latin Americans

← **Why is it difficult to find accurate statistics on Afro-Latin Americans?**

Obtaining exact statistics on the numbers of Afro-Latin Americans can prove difficult. For example, an apparent fall in the Afro-Brazilian population in the 2000 census could have been due to the 'Don't Let Your Color Pass as White' campaign for the previous census by black activists, who tried to persuade Afro-Brazilians to report themselves as brown (racially mixed 'browns' outnumber black people throughout Latin America) or black for the census. There was no such campaign in 2000. With the exception of Brazil (where 70 per cent of Afro-Latin Americans live), Cuba and Puerto Rico, other Latin American countries with large black/mulatto populations, such as Colombia, the Dominican Republic and Venezuela, ignore race as a category in censuses. Furthermore, many Afro-Latin Americans are reluctant to admit black ancestry, as noted by the historian George Reid Andrews (see Source E).

SOURCE E

An extract from *Afro-Latin America: 1800–2000* by George Reid Andrews, published by Oxford University Press, New York, USA, 2004, page 55.

As the citizens of present-day Afro-Latin America struggle to escape the economic heritage of poverty and dependency left by plantation agriculture, they do so under the shadow of the social heritage of racial and class inequality left by slavery. This requires them to define their relationship to 'blackness', the most visible and obvious indicator of low social status.

According to Source E, why are many Afro-Latin Americans reluctant to admit black ancestry? Could the content of Source E be said to describe the situation in the USA?

Afro-Latin American populations in 2000.

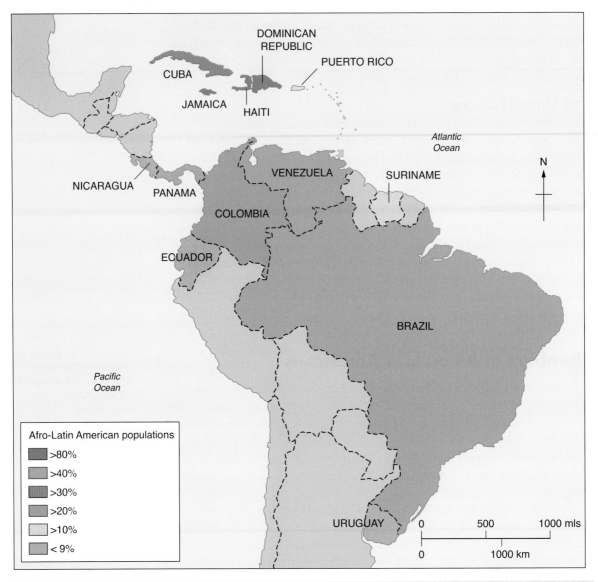

Afro-Latin American populations

- >80%
- >40%
- >30%
- >20%
- >10%
- < 9%

Look at Source F. Rank the Latin American nations according to the highest percentage of Afro-Latin Americans in their population.

By 2000, there were around 110 million Afro-Latin Americans. They constituted roughly 22 per cent of the Latin American population, nearly one half of the national population in Brazil, and a significant proportion in other countries (see Source F, page 132). There are Afro-Latin Americans in every Latin American country.

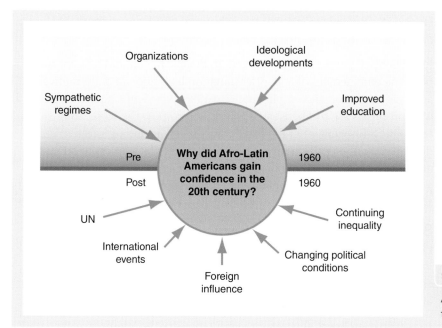

SUMMARY DIAGRAM

Afro-Latin Americans in the twentieth century

③ The impact of the Afro-Latin American Civil Rights Movement

▶ **Key question:** *How successful was the late twentieth-century black Civil Rights Movement?*

The racial democracy writers of the 1930s and 1940s were confident that there was no racism in Latin America, and many people believed their claims. However, Afro-Latin Americans knew better and wanted Latin American racism acknowledged. In a development similar to, but later than that in the USA, Brazil, Colombia, Costa Rica and Panama were forced to recognize racism by late twentieth-century black activism. Such countries then tried to improve the situation.

Brazil and the recognition of racism

During the 1988 commemorations of the centennial of the abolition of slavery in Brazil, the government, press and Catholic Church acknowledged racial inequality with unprecedented honesty and called for reform. As a result, greatly strengthened anti-discrimination legislation was incorporated into the Brazilian constitution and into local laws in states such as Rio de Janeiro. A new national agency, the Palmares Foundation, was established to direct federal funds towards the black population.

In 1995, black organizations marched on Brasilía to demand help for the poor, the enforcement of anti-discrimination legislation and affirmative action in education and employment. In 1996, President Cardoso responded with proposals for 'compensatory policies to promote the social and economic advancement of the black community', including 'positive discrimination' and 'affirmative action' to increase black access to education and employment. Although his proposals were ignored by Congress, government agencies, universities and private firms practised affirmative action by 2001.

Brazilian success against racism

Historian George Reid Andrews (2004) considered Brazil 'the most impressive case of attempted redress of racial grievances', with Colombia a close second. In contrast, countries such as Venezuela, Ecuador and Peru lacked similar laws and programmes.

However, even Brazil illustrated the limitations of the attempt to combat racism. The anti-discrimination law of 1988 resulted in a great many court cases, but virtually no convictions prior to 1995. The budgets and staff for the Palmares Foundation and other agencies were inadequate. The black Civil Rights Movement had reignited and revolutionized the debate about racial equality yet for the most part failed to achieve it, although there were encouraging signs.

Afro-Brazilian politicians

Afro-Brazilians became more politically prominent. In 1990, three out of the 27 elected state governors were black. In 1994 there were two black women senators. In the city of Salvador, 80 per cent black and mulatto and the 'capital' of Afro-Brazil, only around 10 per cent of city councillors were black in the 1970s and 1980s but by 1992 the proportion had reached nearly 50 per cent. In 1987, there were only five Afro-Brazilian legislators. By 1999, three per cent of Brazilian legislators were black or mulatto, although that was still a testament to inequality in a country roughly half Afro-Brazilian. These statistics were far less encouraging than those in the USA, the difference being that Brazilians were usually reluctant to admit the connection between racism and the fact that the poorest people were those with the darkest skin.

> **Afro-Latin American politicians in the Dominican Republic and Venezuela**
>
> Afro-Latin American politicians also attained prominence in other countries. In the Dominican Republic, José Francisco Peña Gómez was a serious contender for the presidency in 1994. In Venezuela in the early 1990s, one black candidate defeated another to be mayor of Caracas, and in 1994 'el negro Claudio' Fermín was the country's first black presidential candidate. **Pardo** Hugo Chávez became president in 1998, although he suffered barely veiled racist attacks from the opposition.

🔑 KEY TERM

Pardo Mixed-race.

Comparing Brazil and the USA

A major difference between Afro-Brazilians and African Americans was that Afro-Brazilians were in the majority. Historian Teresa Meade (2010) noted two further differences. First, race was less of a political issue in Brazil (see Source G). Second, Brazil does not have the same history of violence against blacks in order to maintain white supremacy. Historian Lisa Brock commented that being black in Brazil was being on the bottom looking up, whereas being black in the USA was being on the outside looking in. That Afro-Brazilian sense or conviction of integration perhaps explains the differences noted by Meade. The greatest similarities were the legacies of poverty and racism left by enslavement, and the fact that the twentieth-century struggle for improvement had some but not total success, especially in economic terms.

SOURCE G

An extract from *A Brief History of Brazil* by Teresa Meade, published by Checkmark Books, New York, USA, 2010, pages 140–1.

Brazil has never had a Civil Rights Movement comparable to the one in the United States that challenged discriminatory laws. Brazil also differs in that many schoolchildren in North America learn about black leaders such as Martin Luther King Jr., Malcolm X, or Rosa Parks along with their study of recent history. In Brazil, children learn of great artists and writers, such as Machado de Assis, who happens to be a mulatto, but whose race generally passes unmentioned.

Using your own knowledge, can you explain the differences noted in Source G? **?**

Continuing inequality

The black Civil Rights Movement failed because the movement could not mobilize the whole Afro-Latin American population and because of racism.

← **Why did the black Civil Rights Movement fail?**

The failure to mobilize all Afro-Latin Americans

Divisions of gender, colour and class damaged black mobilization:

- Women felt that issues such as women's health and the problems of single mothers were never seriously considered and many created separate organizations, such as Criola in Brazil.
- Most Afro-Latin Americans considered themselves brown rather than black.
- Some Afro-Latin Americans did not want to admit that they were black and victimized. Some felt that the Civil Rights Movement itself was racist in its emphasis on blackness.
- Most of the activists were middle class, who felt prejudice more keenly than those at the bottom of society who simply thought about food and survival.
- The poorest Afro-Latin Americans generally thought that the best prospect of aid came not from the protest organizations but from local élites, political parties, the Church and labour unions. They feared that activism could actually alienate such groups, which had been helpful in the past.
- Some felt that the growth of an Afro-Latin American middle class suggested that individual effort paid off.

Persistent racism

Afro-Latin Americans remained poor and still suffered racial and class inequality.

Brazil

Late twentieth-century Afro-Brazilian workers were disproportionately at the lowest wage and skill levels, with disproportionately low rates of promotion and high rates of firing and disciplining. On paper, workers in the rubber and cement industry were equally educated, but white salaries were 50 per cent higher than black salaries. Despite the anti-discrimination legislation of 1953, discrimination persisted in the Brazilian workforce and increased during the 1970s and 1980s. Middle-class Afro-Brazilians were frequently confined to jobs in the state sector. Governments failed to root out discrimination in the private sector (see Source H). Even in 2002, Brazilian newspapers carried job advertisements for private companies that sought 'good appearance'. This was coded language that meant Afro-Brazilians should not apply (whiter skin was considered more attractive). In 2003, the Brazilian Congress responded to the Brazilian Black Movement's pressure and discussed a law to reserve 20 per cent of university and civil service places for Afro-Brazilians, a discussion that demonstrated the inequality prevalent in those sectors.

Cuba

Socialist Cuba demonstrated how racism was deeply rooted. In the first 30 years of the Castro regime (1959–89), apparently successful efforts were made to eliminate racial inequalities. However, when Soviet aid ended in the 1990s, the Cuban economy struggled. Castro allowed the liberalization of state control. That led to increased competition for employment, and to a resurgence of racism. Afro-Cubans were not properly represented in the professions and politics. In a situation similar to that in the USA, Afro-Cuban youths made up more than one half of the *jóvenes desvinculados*, or alienated youths, who rejected work or study. Castro himself acknowledged that racism had not been eradicated, and in 2011, Professor Esteban Morales told a *USA Today* reporter that Cuba still struggled with racism, for which he blamed individual Cubans rather than the government.

A similar resurgence of racism occurred in the 1990s in Brazil, Colombia, Uruguay and Costa Rica, where middle- and upper-class racist skinhead groups attacked Afro-Latin Americans. Neoliberalism (see page 21) assisted the restoration of democracy but also increased competitiveness and racism.

Comparisons with the USA suggest that the legacy of slavery and racism is, sadly, impossible to overcome, even when those of African descent are in the majority, as in Brazil.

SOURCE H

An extract from *Afro-Latin America: 1800–2000* by George Reid Andrews, published by Oxford University Press, New York, USA, 2004, page 181.

This theme emerges repeatedly in interviews with educated Afro-Latin Americans: either how they nearly gave up in the face of the obstacles that faced them, or in fact did so. An Afro-Brazilian journalist recalls how 'my brothers and sisters, tired and resigned to the situation, never understood why I worked in the mornings at the market and then went to study'. 'Study for what? It won't get you anywhere', they said. An Afro-Uruguayan woman interviewed in the mid-1950s recalls how 'I developed an inferiority complex among my colleagues at work. They knew that I was studying and they would say: "That negra actually thinks she's going to amount to something".' Another Afro-Uruguayan informant recalls a friend whose classmates constantly discouraged her from continuing in school: "'Look, it doesn't make sense for you to go on. If you graduate, you'll only have problems. How are you going to pursue a profession, being black?" So often did they say this to her that ultimately she became discouraged and abandoned her studies.'

What can you infer about opportunities for Afro-Latin Americans from the interviewees quoted in Source H?

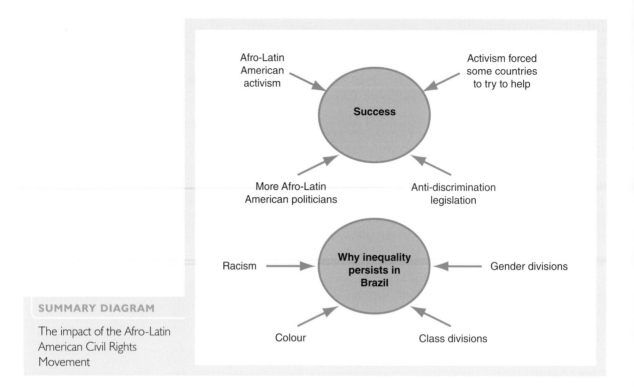

④ Key debate

> ▶ **Key question:** *Have Afro-Latin Americans attained equality through agency and racial democracy?*

Have Afro-Latin Americans been masters of their own fate?

In the 1960s and 1970s, historians such as Leslie Rout (1976) tended to stress the social, economic and political constraints on black action, but from the late twentieth century, there was a greater focus on slave and free black 'agency', as in Henry Louis Gates Jr (2011). Among slaves, agency was demonstrated by the slaves who fled, rebelled, stole, assaulted, negotiated with their masters for better conditions, worked slowly, appealed to the courts, and used African cultural practices. However, their efforts were frequently futile.

Racial democracy: a myth?

The first significant statement of racial democracy thought was Mexico's José Vasconcelos' *The Cosmic Race* (1925). Even more famous was the Brazilian Gilberto Freyre's *Masters and Slaves* (1933). Similar works were produced by the Cuban Fernando Ortiz (1940) and the Venezuelan Carlos Sisto (1935). These believers in racial democracy rejected whitening, and claimed that they lived in happily multiracial and multicultural societies. They argued this state of affairs had its roots in the more benevolent nature of Latin American slavery compared to that of the USA. They claimed that there had been a great 'levelling' during wars for independence, when blacks and whites fought together to help bring down the colonial order.

Afro-Brazilian intellectual and politician Abdias do Nascimento (1977) wrote that the idea of racial democracy was a myth. He said that because of that myth, Brazil never had a Civil Rights Movement that could fight against *de jure* segregation (as in the USA), because Brazilian racism was informal. African American historian Henry Louis Gates Jr (2011) interviewed Afro-Brazilians such as Abdias do Nascimento (he said that racial democracy was 'a joke' that Brazil 'likes to spread around the world') and rapper MV Bill, who also described racial democracy as 'a myth' and pointed Gates to the slums and prisons, populated mostly by impoverished Afro-Brazilians. Gates' own observations confirmed their view. Mexican anthropologist Sagrario Cruz-Carretero (2011) used the words 'pigmentocracy' and 'negrometer' to sum up the way skin colour locates people in society throughout the Americas.

By the late twentieth century, it remained clear that Brazilian racism had not been eradicated as noted by historians such as George Reid Andrews (2004), Boris Fausto (2006) and Teresa Meade (2010).

> **T O K**
>
> What would the characteristics of a 'racial democracy' be? Are there examples of racial democracy in the real world? Why might this be a difficult ideal to attain? (Perception, Language, Reason, Social Sciences.)

Chapter summary

Afro-Latin Americans

Ten times as many slaves were imported into South America as into North America. Each Latin American country has Afro-Latin Americans, who constitute over 20 per cent of the Latin American population. They are a numerical majority in Brazil.

In the early twentieth century, the descendants of slaves suffered from poverty and the humiliation of 'whitening' population movements, but they gained confidence during the first half of the twentieth century. Populist politicians sought the support of labour unions, which contained Afro-Latin American members. Some Afro-Latin Americans gained political power, for example, Fulgencio Batista in Cuba. The expansion of universal education benefited Afro-Latin Americans,

and better education led to better jobs. Afro-Latin American culture became fashionable in the first half of the twentieth century, as did the belief (some say the myth) that Latin America was a racial democracy. However, Afro-Latin Americans invariably remained among the poorest members of society, which, coupled with the influence of the US Civil Rights Movement, transnational conferences and the UN, contributed to the development of an Afro-Latin American Civil Rights Movement after the 1960s.

The situation of Afro-Latin Americans improved greatly during the twentieth century but they remained socially and economically inferior. This was partly due to frequent unwillingness to admit to 'blackness', which was different from the contemporary US experience. It was also due to the difficulties associated with the legacy of slavery and racism, which was similar to the US experience, and to class and gender divisions and a preoccupation with basic survival.

✅ Examination advice

How to answer 'Why' questions

Questions that ask <u>why</u> are prompting you to consider a variety of explanations. Each of these will need to be explained fully. It is also possible to disagree with the basic premise of the question. If you choose this path, you must be prepared to offer substantial counter-arguments.

Example

<u>Why</u> were there social and economic improvements in the lives of Afro-Latin Americans in *one* country of the region in the second half of the twentieth century?

1 To answer this question successfully, you should first explain what social and economic improvements were made for Afro-Latin Americans after 1945. For each be sure to explain the reasons for the specific improvement. Some reasons might be because the government in question hoped to appeal to the poorer (and darker) sectors in society, outside influences such as the seeming success of civil rights movements in the USA, and the growth of labour unions and other mass organizations. Because the question does not identify which country you will use, it is up to you to choose the one for which you think you have the most supporting evidence. Brazil might be a good choice.

2 Before writing the answer you should write out an outline – allow around five minutes to do this. For this question, you could include supporting evidence such as:

- Sympathetic and populist regimes such as that of Getúlio Vargas.
- Growth of cultural associations.
- As a reaction to continued poverty and racism, especially in the private sector.
- Afro-Brazilians made up more than half the population.
- Influence of 1960s' civil rights movements in the USA.
- Transnational meetings with those of African descent from other Latin American countries.
- Exposure of myth of Brazil as a racial democracy in the 1970s.
- After centenary of abolition of slavery (1988), growing focus on slow pace of change.
- UN reports such as the 1996 one on racial discrimination and racial inequality in Brazil led to affirmative action.

3   In your introduction, you should cite the major social and economic advances made after 1950 and then mention the reasons why there had been changes.
4   In the body of your essay, write at least one paragraph on each of the major themes you raised in your introduction. A good example is given below.

In 1995, Afro-Brazilians marched on Brasília, the nation's capital, to push for assistance in combating poverty and discrimination. The progressive president, Fernando Henrique Cardoso, responded by proposing affirmative action measures to turn back the centuries of lack of access to education and employment faced by blacks in Brazil. The Congress did not endorse these proposals but publicizing the conditions did translate into some positive changes. Universities and government institutions began to set aside spaces for aspiring Afro-Brazilians, ignoring the traditional colour barrier.

5   Now try writing a complete answer to the question following the advice above.

 # Examination practice

Below are two exam-style questions for you to practise on this topic.

1   To what extent is the idea of 'racial democracy' in Latin America a myth? (For guidance on how to answer 'to what extent' questions, see pages 86–7.)

2   Compare and contrast how two countries in the region addressed racial inequality. (For guidance on how to answer 'compare and contrast' questions, see pages 235–8.)

CHAPTER 5

Role of governments in Civil Rights Movements in the Americas

This chapter uses two case studies to illustrate the role of government in the acquisition of civil rights by non-white populations. In the USA, the federal system played an important role in dictating the pace, which was fastest when all branches of the federal government were in agreement. In Bolivia, oppressed people were in the majority but that did not guarantee their civil rights. As in the USA, oppressed people pressured the government, and once enfranchised, their majority status resulted in more sympathetic governments. You need to consider the following questions throughout this chapter:

⊗ What role has the US government played in relation to the civil rights of non-white minorities?

⊗ What role has the Bolivian government played in relation to the civil rights of the indigenous majority?

⊗ Were Latin American constitutional guarantees of indigenous rights due to activism?

During the twentieth century, the civil rights situation throughout the Americas usually improved. The role of governments in that process of change varied. Some national governments were simply repressive, as in Guatemala in the 1970s and 1980s (see pages 21–5). Others were unhelpful for reasons of national unity, as with the Sandinistas in Nicaragua in the 1980s (see page 18) and the Trudeau government in Canada in the 1960s and 1970s (see pages 41–3). Sometimes regional governments were resistant to the national government's policies on minorities, as in Canada (see page 46). Some governments responded positively to activism, as in Bolivia in 1952 (see below), while others did not, as in Mexico (see page 21). All governments had the capacity to help or hinder Civil Rights Movements, but there were other factors that played a role in change, particularly activism. The USA shows how government at all levels, whether federal, state or municipal, played a crucial role in helping and hindering civil rights for minorities, while Bolivia shows how a majority can struggle to obtain civil rights.

① The US government and civil rights

▶ **Key question:** *What role has the US government played in relation to the civil rights of non-white minorities?*

In order to avoid colonial-style tyranny, the **Founding Fathers** ensured that their new government would be characterized by a system of checks and balances among the three branches of the federal government (the executive, legislature and judiciary; see page 34) and between federal and state governments. This governmental system dramatically affected the pace of change.

KEY TERM

Founding Fathers The men who drew up the US Constitution in 1787.

Government and change in nineteenth-century USA

Most members of minority groups lacked basic civil rights for much of the nineteenth century (see pages 27 and 54). Until the Civil War (1861–5), slavery was supported primarily by Southern state governments, with the acquiescence of the federal government. When national unity was at risk, the federal government ended slavery, more as a by-product of war than as inherently desirable. When Northerners grew tired of the South and its race problem, white-dominated Southern state governments reintroduced race control, in the form of Jim Crow. The Supreme Court's 'separate but equal' ruling in *Plessy v. Ferguson* (1896) showed that state governments and the federal government were in agreement.

◀ To what extent did the US government respect the civil rights of minorities before 1900?

During the nineteenth century, government was the motor behind the changing situation of African Americans who, in the face of racism and the lack of educational and economic opportunities, were rarely masters of their own fate. The government was similarly behind the changing situation of Native Americans, who were a problem to be removed through battle and segregation on reservations. Their civil rights were not on the US government agenda.

Government and change in the USA 1900–61

NAACP and the Supreme Court and Congress

In the first half of the twentieth century, the NAACP worked through the law courts (see pages 55–6 and 59) to erode Jim Crow and 'separate but equal'. The great problem with Supreme Court rulings was that the court lacked enforcement powers: although it might declare an action unconstitutional, it would depend on Congress, the president or state governments to make a reality of the decision. In the first half of the twentieth century, Congress was disinclined to protect black civil rights. Southern Democrats dominated

◀ To what extent and why did minorities gain greater equality 1900–61?

Senate committees and helped to ensure the defeat of anti-lynching and anti-poll tax bills during the presidency of Franklin Roosevelt.

President Franklin Roosevelt 1933–45

Franklin Roosevelt was the most sympathetic president US minorities had yet seen, but even he was reluctant to make any effort to help obtain civil rights for them. His New Deal (see page 55) helped many impoverished African Americans, without being specifically designed for them. Under pressure from black labour leader A. Philip Randolph, who threatened to bring wartime Washington to a standstill, Roosevelt refused to desegregate the armed forces but established FEPC to promote equality of employment in defence industries (see page 56). Change was clearly in the air. Roosevelt had several black advisers, the so-called Black Cabinet. However, it took Roosevelt's successor to put the White House squarely behind full citizenship for African Americans.

Like African Americans, Hispanics suffered segregation in the South. Future President Lyndon Johnson told how in the 1920s he taught Mexican Americans 'mired in the slums', 'lashed by prejudice' and 'buried half alive in illiteracy', in a segregated school in 'one of the crummiest little towns in Texas'. The Roosevelt administration was unhelpful to Hispanic Americans, but improved conditions on Native American reservations were far less controversial, and the administration began the restoration of tribal self-government and of respect for Native American culture (see pages 27–8).

The Truman years 1945–53

As president, Truman brought the position of African Americans into the national debate when he asked Congress to implement his civil rights commission's recommendations (1947) (see page 58). He used his executive powers to obtain greater equality in employment (see page 58).

Why Truman put civil rights on the agenda

Truman was a decent human being, aware of the need to live up to the US claim to be the beacon of freedom in the Cold War, and motivated partly by political considerations. Northern Democrats wanted the black vote and urged him on. Truman's adviser Clark Clifford told him that many politicians believed 'the Northern Negro vote today holds the balance of power in presidential elections' because the black population 'vote in a bloc' and was geographically concentrated in 'pivotal, large and closely contested electoral states such as New York, Illinois, Pennsylvania, Ohio and Michigan.'

Truman carried an unprecedented two-thirds of the black vote in the 1948 presidential election, which played a big part in his victories in electorally vital states such as California and Illinois. However, Truman's civil rights stance cost him many Southern Democrat votes when the **Dixiecrats** left the Democratic party in 1948 and fielded their own presidential candidate, Strom Thurmond, who thought it un-American 'to force us to admit the

 KEY TERM

Dixiecrat Breakaway Southern Democrat party founded in 1948.

144

Negro into our homes, our eating places, our swimming pools and our theaters' and never publicly acknowledged his mixed-race daughter.

There is much debate (see pages 100–1) as to whether the president and the Supreme Court would have done anything without pressure from black organizations. Basically, there was mutual interdependence. It was NAACP litigation that obtained Supreme Court rulings that eroded the justification for Jim Crow, but the organization needed sympathetic justices, who in turn could only respond to litigation.

What progress was made in the Truman years?

Progress was made on civil rights in the Truman years, although more in the realm of principle than in practice. In 1947, Truman established a civil rights committee that issued a report called 'To Secure These Rights'. The report called for an end to segregation and pointed out the hypocrisy of a nation that viewed itself as a beacon of liberty. This and Supreme Court rulings against segregated transport and education in 1950 (see page 59) meant that two branches of the federal government had come out strongly against the constitutionality of segregation. However, Supreme Court decisions lacked powers of enforcement and the success of Truman's efforts varied:

- some came to nothing, as when Congress, dominated by Republicans and Southern Democrats, rejected the proposed legislation in 'To Secure These Rights' and hampered a fairer distribution of federal funds to black schools
- some were minimally effective, as with CGCC (see page 58), which could only recommend rather than enforce
- some took time to come to fruition, as with the desegregation of the army, which was only sped up under the pressure of the **Korean War** (1950–3).

Jim Crow still reigned supreme in the South, suggesting that for the moment the forces ranged against change remained in the ascendant. This was because white Southern politicians sought to maintain white supremacy in the South and because public opinion slowed down progress on civil rights. Things could not and would not be changed overnight. Polls in 1949–50 showed that while many voters favoured abolition of the poll tax, only 33 per cent favoured the fair employment bill. Southern state governments remained determinedly white and segregationist.

In the Truman years, the federal government was clearly the key to progress, with the executive and judicial branches pressured by NAACP and pushing for change, and the third branch (and Southern state governments) successfully resisting it.

The Eisenhower years 1953–61

The importance of a presidential lead in civil rights issues was demonstrated under Eisenhower who, in sharp contrast to Truman, usually resisted change. Despite calling for an end to racial discrimination in his first State of the Union address (February 1953), he disapproved of *Brown* and was only

> **KEY TERM**
>
> **Korean War** The USA, South Korea and the United Nations fought against Communist North Korea and China in 1950–3.

forced into upholding the ruling by white mob action in Little Rock in 1957 (see pages 68–71). In 1954, he said, 'It is all very well to talk about school integration, but you may also be talking about social disintegration. We cannot demand perfection in these moral questions. All we can do is keep working towards a goal.'

Eisenhower refused to condemn either white Southern politicians (all but three of whom signed the pro-segregation Southern Manifesto), or the murder of Emmett Till (see page 61), or the University of Alabama's defiance of a federal court order that said it should admit its first African American student, Autherine Lucy. Eisenhower said, 'if we attempt merely by passing a lot of laws to force someone to like someone else, we are just going to get into trouble'.

In comparison to the Truman years, change during the Eisenhower years was more clearly prompted by black activism (see pages 59–66). The Montgomery bus boycott and the NAACP obtained the 1956 Supreme Court ruling (*Browder v. Gayle*) that segregation on buses was unconstitutional. The activism did not always achieve immediate success. The actions of the brave young 'Little Rock nine' demonstrated how Supreme Court rulings such as *Brown* met tremendous grassroots resistance in practice (see pages 68–9).

The contrasting fate of Native Americans in the Eisenhower years, when Congress 'terminated' some reservations and increased state government jurisdiction over others (see pages 28–9), suggest that it was black activism that finally caused the Eisenhower administration to draw up civil rights legislation in 1956. Although Eisenhower's bills were greatly diluted (see pages 71–2) they were significant in that a reluctant Congress was finally forced to acknowledge that there were dreadful problems in the South.

Was President Kennedy more pro-civil rights than President Johnson?

Presidents Kennedy 1961–3 and Johnson 1963–9

President Kennedy

Kennedy's presidency was notable for a dramatic rise in black activism and the introduction of an important civil rights bill that was securely stuck in Congress at the president's death. This raises the question of the relationship between the activism and the introduction of the bill.

The most famous examples of black activism during the Kennedy presidency were:

- the Freedom Rides (see page 74)
- SNCC's voter registration campaign in Mississippi (see page 80)
- James Meredith's successful but violently resisted attempt to be the University of Mississippi's first black student (1962)
- Birmingham (see page 76)
- the March on Washington (see page 78).

In response to much of this activism, groups of Southern whites demonstrated a widely publicized disregard for law and order that prompted federal intervention. Attorney General Robert Kennedy reacted after the Freedom Riders were dragged off buses and beaten up, as in Anniston, Alabama. When the administration had Meredith escorted into university by 500 marshals, and a third were injured by a racist mob, the president sent in the National Guard and the army.

The Kennedy administration's responses were often unenthusiastic. Robert Kennedy condemned white attacks on would-be black voters during SNCC's campaign in Mississippi, but subsequently defended federal government inactivity, when he said the federal government could not interfere with local law enforcement unless there was a total breakdown of law and order. The president said SNCC 'sons of bitches' were unnecessarily provocative: 'SNCC has got an investment in violence'. Similarly, for much of the summer of 1963 the administration opposed the proposed March on Washington. Some historians claim Kennedy aides were ready to 'pull the plug' on the public address system if anyone criticized the administration's tardiness in introducing the civil rights bill.

Why was President Kennedy unhelpful?

Kennedy was slow to help African Americans because of congressional and white opposition.

Congress

In his presidential election campaign Kennedy had promised that discrimination in housing could be ended at a 'stroke of the presidential pen', but once elected he did nothing. Disappointed African Americans inundated the White House with pens in order to jog his memory, but Kennedy thought that Congress would reject other more important legislation if he were to push the issue. Also, with the congressional elections of 1962 looming, Northern Democratic congressmen did not want their white voters upset by the thought of living next door to black people. After those elections, Kennedy issued a half-hearted executive order that applied only to future federal housing facilities. It was always difficult for Kennedy to obtain congressional co-operation: the 1962 administration literacy bill (enabling African Americans with a sixth-grade education to vote) failed due to Southern opposition.

White opinion

The political dangers of presidential activism on civil rights were demonstrated by polls in September 1963: 89 per cent of African Americans approved of Kennedy's presidency, but 70 per cent of Southern whites and 50 per cent of all Americans felt he was moving too fast on integration. Kennedy's approval rating in the South dropped from 60 per cent in March 1963 to 44 per cent in September 1963 because of his support for the civil rights bill.

Kennedy's presidency demonstrated that while the Supreme Court could rule repeatedly on the demise of Jim Crow, white resistance, Southern state governments and Congress kept segregation alive. Arguably, black persistence was killing it slowly. Kennedy admitted that segregationist behaviour in Birmingham in 1963, which disturbed many white moderates, was crucial in his support for the bill, which was struggling in Congress at his death.

President Johnson

The Johnson presidency was a great turning point in African American history. First, the 1964 Civil Rights Act and the 1965 Voting Rights Act finally ended *de jure* segregation and ensured that African Americans could vote in the South. Second, the Northern ghetto riots reminded Americans that there were other problems, such as *de facto* segregation, poverty and unemployment. Johnson's legislative reforms of 1964–5 (see pages 83–4) were a remarkable achievement that illustrated what could be done when a congressional majority finally agreed with the president and the Supreme Court that the black situation in the South was unacceptable (Southern Democrats voted against the bill).

Using Sources A–C and your own knowledge, account for Johnson's different tone and content in each.

SOURCE A

Extracts from Robert Parker's recollections of working for Lyndon Johnson as a part-time servant at private dinner parties in Washington in the 1940s, quoted in *Lone Star Rising: Lyndon Johnson and his Times*, Volume I by Robert Dallek, published by Oxford University Press, New York, USA, 1991, page 276.

[It was a] painful experience. [I feared] the pain and humiliation he could inflict at a moment's notice … In front of his guests Johnson would often 'nigger' at me. He especially liked to put on a show for [Mississippi] Senator Bilbo, who used to lecture: 'the only way to treat a nigger is to kick him' … I used to dread being around Johnson when Bilbo was present, because I knew it meant that Johnson would play racist. That was the LBJ I hated. Privately, he was a different man as long as I didn't do anything to make him angry. He'd call me 'boy' almost affectionately. Sometimes I felt that he was treating me almost as an equal … Although I never heard him speak publicly about black men without saying 'nigger', I never heard him say 'nigger woman'. In fact, he always used to call his black cook, Zephyr Wright, a college graduate who couldn't find any other work, 'Miss Wright' or 'sweetheart.'

SOURCE B

An extract from President Johnson's 1964 words to Walker Stone, prominent conservative editor of the Scripps Howard newspapers, quoted in whitehousetapes.net/clips/1964_0106_stone/trans2.swf

I'm gonna try to teach these nigras that don't know anything how to work for themselves instead of just breedin'; I'm gonna try to teach these Mexicans who can't talk English to learn it so they can work for themselves … and get off of our taxpayers' back.

SOURCE C

An extract from President Johnson's speech to Congress to encourage them to pass the 1965 voting rights bill, quoted in uspolitics.about.com/od/speeches/a/lbj_1965_15_mar.htm

Rarely are we met with a challenge … to the values and the purposes and the meaning of our beloved Nation. The issue of equal rights for American Negroes is such an issue … The command of the Constitution is plain … It is wrong – deadly wrong – to deny any of your fellow Americans the right to vote in this country … A century has passed, more than a hundred years, since the Negro was freed. And he is not fully free tonight … A century has passed, more than a hundred years, since equality was promised. And yet the Negro is not equal … The real hero of this struggle is the American Negro. His actions and protests, his courage to risk safety and even to risk his life, have awakened the conscience of this Nation … He has called upon us to make good the promise of America. And who among us can say that we would have made the same progress were it not for his persistent bravery, and his faith in American democracy?

Quoting phrases from Source C, suggest to whom you think it would appeal. **?**

Why Johnson could not do more for African Americans

Johnson had done more for African Americans than any other president, but after 1965, Congress, local officials, black violence and the cost of the Vietnam War made further progress difficult.

Congress and white opinion

In 1966, Congress rejected an administration civil rights bill, one aim of which was to prohibit housing discrimination. Polls showed 70 per cent of white voters opposed large numbers of blacks living in their neighbourhood, especially after the Watts riots and Stokely Carmichael's call for 'black power' (see page 96). Johnson's proposed bill resulted in some of the worst hate mail of his presidency. When housing discrimination was finally prohibited in the 1968 Fair Housing Act, passed by Congress in the aftermath of Martin Luther King Jr's assassination, the law proved difficult to enforce owing to white resistance. Johnson found it hard to sustain national and congressional support for his war on poverty. He was angry with congressmen who jokingly called his rat extermination bill a 'civil rats bill' and suggested he send in a federal cat army. Johnson pointed out that slum children suffered terribly from rat bites.

Local officials

Johnson had to rely on local and state authorities, officials and employees to carry out his programmes. They were sometimes reluctant to co-operate, as in Chicago. The 1964 Civil Rights Act said federal funding should not be given to *de jure* and *de facto* segregated schools, but Mayor Daley was a valuable political ally, so he got his funds and kept his segregated schools. This pattern was repeated in other Northern cities.

Ghetto riots, Black Power and the white backlash

The ghetto riots of 1964–8 (see pages 108–9) caused a white backlash. As television showed black youths shouting 'burn, burn, burn', whites feared that black militants were driving the USA into a race war. Throughout California, gun sales to suburban whites soared. Tired of being blamed for the black predicament, whites were turning against blacks and against Johnson's reform programme. A 1965 poll showed 88 per cent of whites advocated black self-improvement, more education and harder work, rather than government help. A 1966 poll showed 90 per cent opposed new civil rights legislation. In a 1967 poll, 52 per cent said Johnson was going 'too fast' on integration, and only 10 per cent said 'not fast enough'.

The Vietnam War and rising taxes

The expense and distraction of the Vietnam War contributed to Johnson's inability to do more in his War on Poverty (see page 95). In 1965, the federal government deficit was $1.6 billion; by 1968 it was $25.3 billion. Tax rises were mostly due to the war, but white taxpayers put a great deal of blame on federal expenditure on the poor, which had increased by nearly 50 per cent. In 1967, the Democratic governor of Missouri told Johnson that 'public disenchantment with the civil rights programs' was a major reason why he and the Democrats were so unpopular. White Americans were tired of paying out for Johnson's War on Poverty. The programmes were expensive and it appeared that political radicals were hijacking them.

Attempting the impossible

Johnson recognized that he could not work miracles. In June 1966, he told a task force set up to report on black problems that 'The dilemma that you deal with is too deeply rooted in pride and prejudice, too profound and too complex, and too critical to our future for any one man or any one administration to ever resolve.'

He knew there was a limit to the amount of legislation that any administration could pass, particularly if most of the population were beginning to resist it. 'It's a little like whiskey', said Johnson. 'It is good. But if you drink too much it comes up on you.' 'We have come too far too fast during your administration', a leading Democrat told him.

Johnson: conclusions

The Johnson presidency seemed to prove yet again that the federal government was the crucial factor in generating change, but that while it could be prodded by black activism of the Civil Rights Movement style, Black Power was probably counter-productive. Johnson's presidency also suggested that the cost of change had to be taken into account. Northerners were happy enough to see the end of Jim Crow in the South – giving African Americans the vote and letting them sit alongside Southern whites in a restaurant or on a bus cost nothing. However, allowing them to move in next door or financing ghetto improvement were different matters. Even an exceptionally helpful president such as Johnson found that impossible. Nevertheless, Johnson had one final success in his promotion of civil rights when he put affirmative action firmly on the national political agenda.

In a commencement address to Howard University students in 1965, Johnson said that positive discrimination (also known as affirmative action) was needed to help the black population:

You do not take a person who, for years, has been hobbled by chains and liberate him, bring him up to the starting line of race and then say, 'you are free to compete with all the others', and still justly believe that you have been completely fair. Thus it is not enough just to open the gates of opportunity. All our citizens must have the ability to walk through those gates. This is the next and the more profound stage of the battle for civil rights.

Affirmative action

← ....
| **Did the federal**
| **government remain**
| **the key to progress**
| **for minorities?**
....

During the 1970s, two branches of the federal government were particularly crucial in the promotion of affirmative action. The Supreme Court ruled in favour of affirmative action in, for example, *Griggs v. Duke Power Company* (1971). President Richard Nixon (1969–74) embraced affirmative action and his 1972 Equal Employment Opportunity Act gave the Equal Employment Opportunities Commission set up by Kennedy greater powers of enforcement. Despite opposition from Congress and the labour unions, Nixon helped to ensure that over 250,000 companies with federal contracts employed a fair proportion of minority workers. Nixon's support for affirmative action encouraged universities to give priority to minority applicants.

Bakke and the white backlash

Marine veteran Alan Bakke challenged the University of California at Davis for rejecting his application to medical school, while minority candidates with lower scores gained places. The California Supreme Court ruled in his favour, but the US Supreme Court (*Bakke v. Regents of the University of California*, 1978) upheld the university's affirmative action.

Bakke's challenge to affirmative action was indicative of the white conservative reaction that had set in against affirmative action by the late 1970s. Many voters were opposed to the policy, as was the administration of Republican President Ronald Reagan (1981–9). In 1983, Reagan's Secretary of the Interior, James G. Watt, had to resign because of comments about affirmative action (see Source D, page 152).

Secretary of the Interior James G. Watt's description of the commission with which he dealt in 1983, quoted in www.nytimes.com/1983/09/23/watt-asks-that-reagan-forgive-offensive-remark-about-panel.html

We have every kind of mix we can have. I have a black, a woman, two Jews and a cripple. And we have talent.

> What can you infer about affirmative action in the Reagan years from Source D?

African Americans considered Reagan to be totally unsympathetic to their civil rights. Reagan appointed 368 federal judges, out of whom only seven were African American, 15 Hispanic and two Asian American. Reagan had one black cabinet member but failed to recognize him at a meeting six months after he appointed him.

The conservative Supreme Court

In 1991, President George H.W. Bush (1989–93) appointed African American Clarence Thomas to the Supreme Court as a replacement for Thurgood Marshall (see page 56). Although Thomas had benefited greatly from affirmative action, through which he had gained a place at Yale Law School, he made it quite clear that he rejected affirmative action as a means to attain racial equality.

> What point is Source E trying to make about the impact of affirmative action on universities?

SOURCE E

A cartoon published in a US newspaper in 1997.

GOSH, IT WORKS! SINCE WE ENDED AFFIRMATIVE ACTION HERE ON CAMPUS, I NEVER NOTICE ANYONE'S SKIN COLOR ANYMORE!

A Supreme Court dominated by liberal justices had been vital in rulings helpful to minorities, but in the late 1970s the court became more conservative and less sympathetic. Aware of the court's increasing conservatism, President Bill Clinton (1993–2001) voiced qualified support for affirmative action ('Mend it don't end it'). During his presidency, affirmative action remained the norm in major companies and universities. For example, 12 per cent of college students were African American, which reflected their percentage of the overall US population. However, in the early twenty-first century, the court expressed doubt as to whether affirmative action should be continued.

Ethnic minorities and white liberals believe affirmative action has not yet erased inequality. In the early twenty-first century, African American and Native American poverty and unemployment rates remained twice as high as those of whites. As always, the key to change is the federal government.

	President	Congress	Supreme Court	State/local government
Pre-Civil War	✗	✗	✗	✗
Civil War and Reconstruction	✓	✓	–	–
Jim Crow	✗	✗	✗	✗
1933–45	–	✗	✓	✗
Truman years	✓	✗	✓	✗
Eisenhower years	✗	✗	✓	✗
Kennedy years	–	✗	✓	✗
Johnson years	✓	–	✓	–
Nixon years	–	–	✓	–
Reagan/Bush years	✗	–	✗	–
Clinton years	✓	–	✗	–
Early 21st century	✗	✗	✗	✗

SUMMARY DIAGRAM

The US government and civil rights

2 The Bolivian government and civil rights

▶ **Key question:** *What role has the Bolivian government played in relation to the civil rights of the indigenous majority?*

KEY TERM

Cholos Bolivian mestizos or indigenous Bolivians who are city dwellers or more prosperous farmers, speaking both Spanish and an indigenous language.

Chaco War War between Bolivia and Paraguay 1932–5.

Bolivia remains what historian Herbert Klein (2003) described as 'the most Indian of the American republics', where Spanish speakers are a minority and indigenous languages dominate (see the map on page 155). This makes it a particularly interesting case study. The two largest indigenous groups are the Aymara, who constitute between 20 and 25 per cent of the population, and are concentrated in the Province of La Paz, and the Quechua, who constitute between 35 and 40 per cent, and are mostly found in Cochabamba and Sucre. **Cholos** now constitute between 30 and 40 per cent of Bolivia's population, and their numbers are growing as Bolivia develops slowly into a mestizo nation. 'Whites' number between five and 15 per cent: many look like their indigenous ancestors but are counted as white because they are upper-class, Spanish-speaking, westernized and eat non-indigenous food.

To what extent did Bolivian governments respect minority rights before 1945?

→ The indigenous population before 1945

With rebellions unparalleled in the colonial Americas, the indigenous population of what became Bolivia did not passively accept the Spanish conquest. In 1780, over 100,000 rebelled in vain for the restoration of the Inca monarchy and of indigenous rights and powers.

The new republic

Life did not improve for the indigenous population under the newly independent republic. The dominant white élite manoeuvred to deny non-whites any power. In order to enforce mid-nineteenth-century legislation that deprived the indigenous population of communal lands, the army killed thousands. The indigenous tribes' resentment was demonstrated in their 1899 revolt against heavy taxation, forced labour and land loss, when they massacred, ritually sacrificed and ate some government soldiers. The government response was brutal. The civil rights of the indigenous population were simply not on the political agenda.

The early twentieth century

While late nineteenth- and early twentieth-century governments incorporated the middle class and urban workers into political society, the indigenous population remained resentful, impoverished and exploited. In 1921 and 1927 there were violent indigenous uprisings in the Andean highlands. Tens of thousands of highland conscripts died in the **Chaco War** (1932–5), when the fighting was left to the indigenous populations. The government was as careless with their education as with their lives, but,

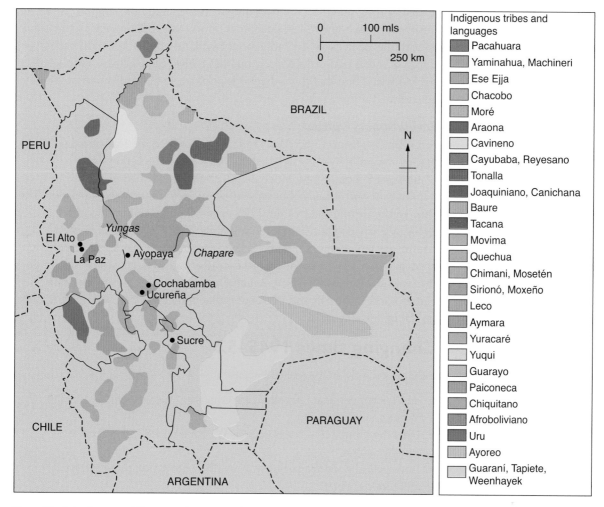

Map of Bolivia showing different indigenous tribes and languages and places of particular significance in the struggle for civil rights

because there was no public education available prior to the 1930s, indigenous culture survived in the countryside. There were also promising signs of change.

Warisata and indigemismo

Teachers trained at the teacher training school established at Warisata in 1928 encouraged the indigenous population of the highlands to organize to fight for land reform and their rights. The school was a centre of *indigenismo* (see page 11).

The military reformist governments of 1936–9

In 1937, Colonel Germán Busch's reformist military government called a constitutional convention. Some of the more radical delegates proposed laws to protect indigenous communities and their communal lands, and to abolish forced labour on the **haciendas**. They gained little support. However, the convention approved an education reform law that provided many rural educational centres for the indigenous highland population and Busch's Office of Indigenous Education promoted *indigenista* teachers, although some advised him that the indigenous population needed land more than education.

Revolutionary parties

After the disastrous Chaco War (1932–5) discredited the traditional political parties, several new ones were established. Víctor Paz Estenssoro's Nationalist Revolutionary Movement (MNR), established in 1941, was nationalistic and socialist, but initially silent on the indigenous question. The Party of the Revolutionary Left (PIR), established by Communists in the 1940s, was divided between internationalist, pro-Soviet members and nationalist pro-indigent members. The Revolutionary Workers' Party (POR), established in 1934, was the first to use what would be a popular slogan in the National Revolution of 1952, 'Land to the Indian, mines to the state'. Parties such as the PIR and POR put indigenous problems and rights firmly on the political agenda.

> **Why and with what results did indigenous civil rights become an issue 1945–52?**

Changing times 1945–52

Indigenous activism increased because:

- Busch's educational reforms made education more widely available to the indigenous population.
- Teachers trained at schools such as Warisata raised indigenous consciousness.
- New radical political parties such as PIR were sympathetic to the indigenous tribes.
- Indigenous peasants began to organize themselves, as in the successful peasant co-operative movement in Cochabamba.
- In 1943, Quechua-speaking Major Gualberto Villarroel led a group of reformist military officers in a coup. In collaboration with the MNR, his government assembled over 100 indigenous leaders in Bolivia's first National Indigenous Congress (1945), which discussed land reform and indigenous servitude and greatly increased indigenous consciousness.

The first National Indigenous Congress 1945

The government's attitude towards the 1945 National Indigenous Congress was ambivalent. Bolivian anthropologist Jorge Dandler (1987) showed that the government justified its call for the 1945 National Indigenous Congress as a way to channel agitation over indigenous rights, removed indigenous leaders such as Antonio Alvarez Mamani with claims that they were not truly indigenous, and replaced them with a government-appointed non-indigenous chairman of the Congress.

Nevertheless, the summoning of an indigenous conference was 'a provocative, indeed revolutionary, political move', according to historian Waltraud Morales (2010). Its very existence represented a questioning of the old order. President Villarroel's sympathetic speech to Congress promised better educational facilities, the abolition of the hated labour service obligations, and better housing, clothing, food and healthcare. The Congress demonstrated a rare indigenous unity when the participants demanded the end of discriminatory laws, the end of compulsory labour service, and indigenous access to segregated public places. MNR activist Hernán Siles Zuazo told the delegates that the land problem was Bolivia's greatest challenge and that a major MNR platform was that 'the land should belong to those who work it'. He recognized that land redistribution would take many years to achieve but, 'I believe that this Congress is the first step.' Probably the greatest achievement of the Congress was the sense of unity that it engendered among the many different indigenous groups. In the face of attempted sabotage by the great landowners, indigenous communities throughout Bolivia had organized mass meetings and regional congresses in order to prepare for the National Congress.

President Villarroel's reforming decrees constituted 'a truly revolutionary act', according to historian Herbert Klein, 2003, but were never put into force. After the Congress raised indigenous consciousness, large-scale indigenous marches occurred in the centre of cities such as La Paz. This mobilization terrified conservatives, particularly great landowners, who feared the abolition of forced labour obligations. Villarroel was overthrown in 1946 and the army reintroduced forced indigenous labour. Raised indigenous expectations then contributed to the great uprising of Ayopaya (1947), in which several thousand people attacked haciendas until the armed forces crushed them. Nevertheless, despite widespread persecution between 1946 and 1952, the long-term foundations for indigenous self-help were being laid.

The National Revolution 1952

> ← What were the causes and results of the National Revolution of 1952?

Historically, most agricultural land in Bolivia belonged to a few great landowners. During the eighteenth and nineteenth centuries, independent indigenous communities struggled to keep communal lands and by 1950, six per cent of landowners owned 92 per cent of cultivable land.

Between 1946 and 1951, the conservative, repressive oligarchy reversed the major reforms that the military socialists and the MNR had introduced, used military repression against its opponents and fraudulently deprived the MNR of a presidential election victory in 1951. With politics particularly fractious, the economy hit by the collapse of tin prices, and many politicized by Bolivia's defeat in the Chaco War and the National Indigenous Congress, the MNR, supported by the workers and middle class, led a successful National Revolution in 1952. Victor Paz Estenssoro became Bolivia's first revolutionary president.

Results and significance of the National Revolution

The new government introduced political, social and economic reforms that greatly decreased the exploitation of the indigenous population, who were finally given political power and land. The MNR had long called for universal suffrage, nationalization of the mines and, most radical of all, land reform.

Universal suffrage

Before 1950 the indigenous majority had not been allowed to vote. A new electoral law abolished literacy tests and discriminatory property restrictions and raised the electorate from 200,000 to 1,000,000. Most new voters were illiterate indigenous peasants, miners and factory workers.

Peasant initiative and land reform

Despite open rebellion and litigation, the peasants had not made a reality of the reforms their hero President Villarroel had decreed in 1945. The great landowners had ignored the laws and repressed the peasantry, punishing those who had attended the National Indigenous Congress by doubling their workload or by firing them. In spring 1952, an independent and spontaneous indigenous land reform movement broke out near Cochabamba, where peasants began to seize land. Rural unions in Cochabamba had been organized by returning indigenous war veterans after the Chaco War in 1936. These peasant unions were concentrated in the town of Ucureña, which became exceptionally militant and well organized, thanks to the Party of the Revolutionary Left (PIR), which dominated the unions. The unionized peasants of Ucureña, led by José Rojas, joined the MNR but sought more radical agrarian reform in return.

Although always ambivalent about agrarian reform and uneasy about growing indigenous autonomy, the MNR had to speed up and radicalize its land reform policy when peasant land seizures spread. Contemporaries concluded that if the peasants had not taken the initiative through land seizures, the Agrarian Reform Law of 1953 might not have been signed.

The Agrarian Reform Law 1953

The Agrarian Reform Law legalized the peasant land seizures. The law confiscated and redistributed the largest estates, and abolished compulsory labour and the unpaid transport of hacienda produce to urban markets by the peasants' animals. It restored the communal lands seized in the previous century, redistributing 24 million acres to 237,000 people by 1955, and 29 million to 289,000 others by 1970.

The agricultural reform had its disadvantages. Only larger estates were redistributed, and they were divided into small inefficient holdings where, without capital input, productivity declined. The transfer of titles got bogged down in the bureaucracy. However, the positives outweighed the negatives. After 1952, the indigenous peoples were voters and property owners.

Educational reform

The 1953 educational reform decree re-established the right to universal education, and the government pledged to extend this to the indigenous population, whom the landowners had previously prevented from accessing education.

The Ministry of Peasant Affairs and MNR peasant unions

The MNR created the Ministry of Peasant Affairs, which sent out organizing teams to rural areas, and created and financed the first national rural union, the Bolivian National Confederation (*Confederación Nacional de Trabajadores Campesinos de Bolivia* or CNTCB). Within months of the revolution there were over 1000 peasant unions with 20,000 members in the Department of Cochabamba alone. By 1961 there were 7500 peasant unions in Bolivia, all affiliated to the MNR.

The indigenous groups were traditionally suspicious of political parties, but after the land reform they became passive, content with their lands. The MNR worked through the unions to keep their loyalty. The party also made symbolic gestures, as when it abolished the word 'Indian' from official language because of its colonial connotations.

By the time the national government collapsed in 1964, the indigenous population's situation had greatly improved. The government had played a big part in this, but so had activists, and it seems likely that the government would not have been as helpful without prompting from the underprivileged.

Military governments 1964–82

By 1964, the National Revolution and the MNR were on the verge of disintegration. An excessively broad coalition of conflicting interest groups, MNR's local leaders had become increasingly corrupt. From 1964 to 1982 Bolivia was dominated by counter-revolutionary military governments.

Under the MNR government, the Bolivian army had been made to aid national development. Its tasks had included the incorporation of the indigenous population into national life, and educated individuals were encouraged to join the army. So, the military governments between 1964 and 1982 were sometimes sympathetic to the 'original peoples'.

← **How and why did military governments help the indigenous population?**

General René Barrientos Ortuño

In 1964, a military junta headed by General René Barrientos Ortuño (1919–69) came to power. Barrientos, a Quechua-speaker nicknamed the 'peasant president', promised to aid the peasants. His helicopter took him to many remote villages where he won over the local leaders. In 1966 he signed the Military–Peasant Pact and redistributed land to the peasants, who in turn pledged to defend the military against leftists. Satisfied by agrarian reform and land titles, the peasants had become conservative and malleable.

Maximum leader
Recognition of one leader as superior to all other tribal leaders.

Katarismo Bolivian movement to re-create Aymara ethnic solidarity.

Central Obrero Boliviano (COB) National labour union set up in the early days of the revolutionary MNR government to represent the general voice of Bolivian workers.

Barrientos continued the policy of co-opting, controlling and mobilizing the peasants, and introduced the policy of personal ties with the caciques, who recognized him as sole '**maximum leader**' of the peasantry. Peasant loyalty to the regime, based on the fear that they might lose their land rights, was such that in 1967 the Guaraní tribe betrayed the sympathetic Argentine Communist revolutionary Che Guevara to the authorities.

Hugo Banzer Suárez

In 1971, Hugo Banzer Suárez became president and then dictator. On the one hand, his government (1971–8) repressed the indigenous population, killing over 100 peasants in the Massacre of Tolata after 100 peasant syndicates blocked Cochabamba's main road in protest against food prices in 1974. This was the first major clash between the peasantry and the military since 1952. On the other hand, Banzer worked to renew the Military–Peasant Pact. He removed independent minded leaders of the peasant syndicates and replaced them with pro-government caciques, but redistributed over 15 million hectares (37 million acres) of land to peasant families.

Significantly then, even military dictators had to take the interests of the majority indigenous population into account. Their sheer numbers played an important role in the maintenance of some rights. Inevitably, some were members of the army, which helped to ensure that the military had some sympathy for the indigenous population.

The *kataristas* and the CSUTCB

Founded in the early 1970s by students of Aymara descent in La Paz and by young Aymara peasants in the highlands, the **karismo** movement worked for Aymara ethnic solidarity. In 1973 several groups affiliated to the *katarismo* movement met in La Paz and published the Tiwanaku Manifesto in which the indigenous population described themselves as 'foreigners in their own fatherland'. The manifesto rejected the integrationist politics of the government as denying the ethnic integrity of two-thirds of Bolivia's population. *Kataristas* published a biography of Tupac Katari, who had rebelled against the Spanish colonial government in 1781. They used leaflets and radio programmes to create and confirm his iconic status. An organization for peasant women was named after his wife, Bartolina Sísa. It organized congresses and mobilized women to demand better working conditions, unionization, and better treatment for indigenous women by politicians and male family members.

Although the *katarista* movement was intensely divided over ideology and poorly organized, by the late 1970s it had taken over most of the official government peasant unions and organized the Confederation of Peasants Unions of Bolivia (*Confederacíon Sindical Unica de Trabajadores Campesinos de Bolivia* or CSUTCB). By 1981, the *kataristas* controlled the Aymara peasant unions and gained representation on the national labour union, the Bolivian Labour Central (**Central Obrero Boliviano, COB**). In 1981, the indigenous

Tupac Katari Revolutionary Movement (MRTKL) leader, Genaro Flores, became the first indigenous peasant leader of the COB.

The return of civilian government

After 1982, Bolivia returned to democracy but was plagued by successive economic crises that led many unemployed miners and peasants into coca cultivation and some into the drug trade.

← How sympathetic was the civilian élite to indigenous rights?

Coca and cocaine

Particularly easy to grow, cultivate and sell, coca has great religious and medicinal significance for the Aymara and Quechua. Miners traditionally chewed the leaves between shifts in order to calm their stomachs and ease their pain. It was found that when they stopped chewing them, the loss of the vitamins contained in the leaf caused their teeth to fall out. Extensively processed coca leaves become cocaine, so from 1961 the United Nations (UN) called for the outlawing of coca tea and traditional coca leaf chewing, which infuriated the Bolivian population.

From 1964 onwards, with the connivance of the military regime, drug cartels paid poor indigenous peasants to grow coca. When the international cocaine trade became exceptionally lucrative in the early 1980s, the production of coca leaves tripled, but Paz Estenssoro's coalition (1985–9) criminalized coca leaf cultivation and, assisted by US military advisers and 150 special US troops, used military force against growers. The cocaine problem and policies of the USA helped to politicize the indigenous population of Bolivia. In the 1980s and 1990s, indigenous peasant associations opposed the government's coca eradication programme and use of military force against growers. Peasant tactics included strategic roadblocks, hunger strikes, mass rallies with 'chew-ins' of coca leaves, marches and occupations, which combined to force the government to compromise. Federations of coca-leaf growers insisted that national sovereignty and Andean culture were at issue in the struggle against the government's eradication and criminalization policies.

From 1988 Evo Morales headed the biggest coca growers' federation. The Peasant Coca Growers Union became very influential in the CSUTCB, which dominated the COB. The peasant and labour movements were very close to the leftist parties, and gained representation in the National Congress in 1989. Morales became leader of the Movement toward Socialism (MAS). In 2002 the Chamber of Deputies expelled him because his repeated attacks on the government's anti-drug policy were deemed seriously unethical. His expulsion triggered widespread peasant protests and anti-US feeling. The US ambassador's public criticism of Morales in 2002 probably helped him to gain more votes in the presidential election. The coca-leaf war greatly affected the political mobilization and empowerment of the indigenous peasantry, the largest group of voters in Bolivia.

A multi-ethnic and pluricultural society

In the 1989 elections it became clear that indigenous rights groups were becoming increasingly popular. When the government of Gonzalo Sánchez de Lozada of the MNR came to power in 1993, it allied with several other parties, including the indigenous Tupac Katari Party (see page 160). Well aware of the electoral importance of indigenous groups, Sánchez de Lozada chose as his vice president the Aymara leader of Tupac Katari, Víctor Hugo Cárdenas, whose wife wore indigenous dress for political and social events.

Sánchez de Lozada introduced several laws that affected the indigenous population. In the Constitutional Amendments Law of 1994, Bolivia was defined as a multi-ethnic and pluricultural society, and an independent human rights ombudsman was set up to monitor abuses. Sánchez de Lozada also introduced bilingual and multicultural educational reforms, along with several new agencies to monitor ethnic and gender issues. His 1994 Law of Popular Participation devolved power to the localities, and established over 300 municipalities, among which were indigenous villages that now had their traditional governing units recognized by the government. According to historian Waltraud Morales (2010), this 'transformed the political landscape' in that 85 per cent of municipalities had rural and often indigenous majorities and now received significant federal funding (critics claimed that these local governing bodies did not do well, thanks to insufficient funding, inertia, mismanagement and corruption). Along with the recognition of traditional local laws, the new constitution guaranteed traditional land rights. However, the majority indigenous population still felt politically alienated.

Indigenous political alienation

In the 1997 election, only one of the presidential candidates of the main parties had an indigenous background. Three of the vice presidential candidates represented the indigenous groups, but overall the indigenous populations considered themselves poorly represented in the presidential race. Their sense of alienation from the political process increased with President Banzer's 'zero coca' policy, which led to violent clashes that pitted the military against the coca growers and the powerful Cochabamba-Chapare unions, and with the Water Wars.

Water Wars 1999–2002

Over 40 per cent of Bolivians lacked proper sanitation, and 15–30 per cent did not have access to drinkable water. The primarily mestizo and indigenous population of Cochabamba viewed access to water as a basic human right, which led to the Cochabamba Water Wars. When the water utility was privatized and put in the hands of a large multinational corporation, 30,000 people took to the streets in 2001 to protest and brought the centre of the city of Cochabamba to a standstill for five days. President Banzer (1997–2001) sent in troops, which aroused international condemnation of human rights violations. The poverty-stricken population was right to be fearful as the price of the privatized water rocketed. The next president, Jorge Quiroga Ramírez (2001–2), was forced to suspend both the water privatization contract and the 'zero coca' policy.

The Water Wars demonstrated that being the numerical majority in a democracy did not necessarily give the indigenous population what they wanted, but that sheer weight of numbers deployed in popular protest and supported by the international community could improve a situation.

Evo Morales

In what historian Waltraud Morales (2010) called a 'historic and revolutionary' election in December 2005, socialist Evo Morales, charismatic spokesman of Bolivia's majority indigenous population and other traditionally marginalized groups, became Bolivia's first indigenous president.

> ← **What is the significance of Bolivia's first indigenous president?**

The 'indigenous populist' Morales first gained fame in the 1990s as the spokesperson of the peasant-based coca growers' association. He stood for the presidency in 2002. Opponents described him as a **Marxist** and a drug trafficker, but he was only narrowly defeated. Morales' MAS party and the other pro-coca party, Felipe Quispe Huanca's Pachakuti Indigenous Movement, led the opposition to the MNR-dominated government.

> **KEY TERM**
>
> **Marxist** Someone who believes in Marx and Engels' political, economic and social principles.

Reasons for Morales' electoral victory in 2005

Morales was victorious in the 2005 presidential election because of the constitutional reforms of 1994–5, the continued alienation of the indigenous population, more water wars, and his personal charisma and policies.

The reforms of 1994–5
The constitutional reforms of 1994–5 devolved power to new governmental units that empowered the indigenous population by giving them greater experience, responsibility and political awareness. This contributed to renewed militancy and grassroots activism that proved important when the population felt alienated.

The alienation of the indigenous population
In spite of the radical reconstruction of 1952, economic and political power had gradually become dominated by a 'new oligarchy' that dominated politics after the restoration of democracy. Their neoliberal (see page 21) economic policies increased the poverty of the mestizo and indigenous populations: their privatization of major state-owned enterprises in the 1990s led to large-scale unemployment and displacement, especially in the highlands. Despite the redistribution of land after the National Revolution, ownership had become more narrowly distributed again, as impoverished *campesinos* left the countryside and migrated to the cities, where they suffered unemployment, overcrowding, exploitation and poverty.

Economic and political discontent led to renewed militancy and grassroots activism: hundreds of autonomous organizations and movements at all levels of society were determined to make Bolivia more inclusive and more democratic. Furthermore, all Bolivian political parties had to respond to indigenous peasants who still constituted the majority of the population and electorate. Despite their poverty and a high proportion of illiteracy, they could produce a high voter turnout when mobilized. The peasant unions played an important part in that mobilization, which benefited Morales.

Evo Morales: leadership and policies

Morales was an inspirational opposition leader and his promised policies (see Source F) were popular. He called for:

- the nationalization of Bolivia's oil and gas reserves
- an assembly to rewrite the constitution and give more rights and power to the 'original peoples'
- a national referendum on regional autonomy
- land redistribution.

He won the votes of the indigenous population, trade union activists, women's organizations and student groups.

According to Source F, what problems faced Bolivia in 2005 and what were the solutions?

SOURCE F

Extracts from interviews with Evo Morales, 2005 and 2007. Quoted in 1. www.inthesetimes.com/article/2438/ and 2. news.bbc.co.uk/1/hi/world/americas/7035944.stm

1. *The majority of people in this country – people from more than 30 indigenous groups – did not participate in the foundation of Bolivia in 1825. We have to refound Bolivia in order to end the colonial state, to live united in diversity, to put all our resources under state control, and to make people participate and give them the right to make decisions … Our Constitution says that Bolivia is a multi-ethnic democratic country, but that is only in theory. If we can win we have to change the country, not only in theory but in reality …*

2. *We believe in a democratic revolution, an indigenous revolution, to claim back our land and all of our natural resources …*

Water and gas wars

Large-scale protests over the privatization of water (2004–5) and natural gas (2003, 2005) severely damaged three presidencies. In 2004–5, the indigenous city of El Alto (near La Paz) initiated the second great Water War. The feisty Aymara population brought the city to a standstill in protest against connection rates of $400, at a time when many families earned less than that in the year. The El Alto Water War was led by the Aymara President of the Federation of Neighbourhood Councils of El Alto, Abel Mamani. In 2006, the transnational water company ended its operations in La Paz. Internationally there was great sympathy for people demonstrating for water rights in the face of police using tear gas and guns. Similarly, a gas dispute in May 2005 brought La Paz to a standstill, as 80,000 protesters fought against the police. Most of the 80,000 were Aymara, encouraged by Morales and Quispe. This prompted the government to call the December 2005 election.

The significance of Morales' election

Historian Waltraud Morales (2010), believing 'endemic racism' was Bolivia's 'largely unacknowledged' but 'oldest social and cultural problem', considered Evo Morales' victory in 2005 exceptionally significant because it promised, 'for the first time in decades … a real voice to the country's humble and largely indigenous citizens, many underserved by state and society and living in impoverished rural and urban communities. It represented the triumphant culmination of the more than 500 year struggle against white European aggression and domination'. His victory was greeted with joy among the majority indigenous population. At last one of their own had gained the presidency and it raised their hopes for greater social and economic equality and respect for their identity and culture. Morales' election signalled a peaceful democratic transition of power from the non-indigenous ruling élites to the Andean indigenous majority.

In the 2001 census, 62 per cent of Bolivians described themselves as indigenous. Before the National Revolution of 1952 they suffered social exclusion and were considered totally inferior. Although the reforms of the National Revolution improved their situation, racism and discrimination continued, even after the 1994 claims of a multi-ethnic and pluricultural society.

The election of Morales, with his embrace of indigenous identity, made being 'Indian' a source of pride. As the nation's first democratically elected indigenous president, most Bolivians and foreigners described him as the first 'Indian' president, although some queried the 'Indian' tag because while he spoke Aymara as a child, he was not fluent in the language and had adopted Cholo culture. Aymara leaders Felipe Quispe Huanca of the Pachakuti Indigenous Movement and former Vice President Victor Hugo Cárdenas criticized him as insufficiently 'Indian', although white opponents called him 'that Indian'.

Morales' unofficial indigenous inauguration in January 2006 was a spectacular Andean ceremony at the top of the Kalasaya temple with a crowd of tens of thousands of mostly indigenous supporters. Morales wore a wreath of coca leaves, dressed in the style of pre-conquest Andean priests and nobles, and thanked the Andean Mother Earth deity. He held a staff with a condor head, which symbolizes indigenous rule. Even at his official inauguration in La Paz the next day, he wore a handwoven Andean jacket.

Problems in early twenty-first century Bolivia

With a unique 85 per cent turnout, Morales won 54 per cent of the popular vote, the first time any Bolivian president was elected by an outright majority. These statistics gave him a powerful mandate, but he still faced a great deal of opposition.

SOURCE G

Bolivian President Evo Morales (left) on a state visit, meeting South African President Thabo Mbeki (right) on 11 January 2006.

Racism

Morales' election did not solve Bolivian racial problems. According to historian Teresa Meade (2010), the attempt of the prosperous whites and mestizos of the eastern provinces of Bolivia to separate from the Bolivia of Morales 'has everything to do with racial prejudice'.

Economic and social inequality

In the UN Human Development Index (HDI), which is based on life expectancy, adult literacy and living standards, only Haiti and Guatemala ranked lower than Bolivia in Latin America. The extent of economic inequality within Bolivia was the greatest in Latin America, and the seventh highest in the world. Morales inherited an economic and political system dominated by an élite group of wealthy 'whites' unwilling to see wealth and power redistributed and anxious to maintain traditional social inequality.

The 2006 Constituent Assembly was dominated by Morales' supporters. It contained a record number of indigenous delegates and in 2007 passed a new constitution (see Source H) that:

- was among the world's first to enshrine the principles of the UN Declaration on the Rights of Indigenous Peoples
- reiterated that Bolivia was a plurinational state
- increased indigenous rights in relation to land and cultivation
- gave the indigenous population more seats in the legislature
- gave a judicial system based on customary law equal status to the established legal system
- established self-governing homelands for 36 indigenous nations
- introduced affirmative action in order to provide more jobs for the indigenous population.

Although the constitution was approved by 61 per cent of voters in 2009, others bitterly opposed it. The decentralization reforms of 1994–5 that had helped to mobilize indigenous political power had strengthened municipal and local government. In the more prosperous areas of Bolivia, especially the Media Luna (Half Moon), this new governmental structure encouraged opposition to reform and threats of secession.

SOURCE H

Extracts from the *Constitution of the Plurinational State of Bolivia … 2009*, translated by Luis Francisco Valle at www.bolivianconstitution.com

Article 1: Bolivia is constituted in a Social, unitary State of Plurinational Communitarian Law, free, independent, sovereign, democratic, intercultural, decentralised and with autonomies. Bolivia is founded in plurality and in political, economic, legal, cultural and linguistic pluralism, with the integrating process of the country.

Article 2: Given the pre-colonial existence of the indigenous originary [sic] farmer nations and people and their ancestral domain over their territories, their free determination is guaranteed within the framework of the unity of the State, which consists in their right to autonomy, to self-government, to their culture, to the recognition of their institutions and to the consolidation of their territorial entities, in accordance to this Constitution and to the law.

Article 3: The Bolivian nation is formed by the totality of the Bolivian males and females, the indigenous originary farmer nations and people, and the intercultural and Afro-Bolivian communities which all together make up the Bolivian people …

Article 5. I. The official languages of the State are the Spanish language and all of the languages of the indigenous originary farmer nations and people, that include the languages aymara, araona, naure [there follows a list totalling 36 indigenous languages].

What can you infer from the extracts from the Bolivian constitution in Source H about civil rights issues in pre-2009 Bolivia? Suggest reasons why some Bolivians would criticize these articles.

Coca

A final domestic problem facing twenty-first century Bolivia was summed up by Evo Morales: 'Let me chew my coca leaves' (see Source I). The eradication policies of Bolivian governments between 1988 and 2005 led to the impoverishment and incarceration of many coca growers who were not involved in the drug trade (few peasants did the actual processing of the coca leaves into cocaine). International opposition to coca growing was great.

How far would you agree that Source I gives a good justification for the cultivation of coca in Bolivia?

SOURCE I

Extracts from Bolivian President Evo Morales' interviews about coca cultivation. Quoted in 1. *A Brief History of Bolivia* by Waltraud Morales, published by Facts on File, New York, USA, 2010, pages 260–1 and 2. Profile: Evo Morales, BBC News Online, 14 December 2008.

1. *No to zero coca leaf, yes to zero cocaine … coca is not cocaine [but a] healthful Andean tradition … [Coca is] an important symbol in the history and identity of the indigenous cultures of the Andes …*

2. *I am not a drug trafficker. I am a coca grower. I cultivate the coca leaf, which is a natural product. I do not refine [it into] cocaine, and neither cocaine or drugs have ever been part of the Andean culture.*

	'Whites'	Indigenous population
Colonial period	Conquerors	Conquered; rebellions failed
New Republics	Dominant politically and economically	Heavily taxed, forced labour, land loss, rebellions failed
Early 20th century	Still dominant	*Indigenismo*, rise of more sympathetic parties
First National Indigenous Congress	Government more sympathetic, élite angry	Greater consciousness, confidence, education, organization
1946–51 Repression	Conservative oligarchy	Marking time
1952 National Revolution	MNR government grants vote, land reform	Great organizational experience. Life improved. Land restored (some)
1964–82 Military governments	Military sympathetic	Military–peasant pact. More organizations
Democracy	Governments struggled with economy. Devolved power to localities	Great poverty ⟶ coca growing. 'Indian' rights parties increasingly popular. Still felt alienated. Water wars
Evo Morales	Old white élite resistant, threatened secession	'One of their own' as president

SUMMARY DIAGRAM

The Bolivian government and civil rights

Similar	USA	Bolivia
	Fought against colonial powers but oppressed non-whites	
	More respectful of indigenous culture from 1930s	
	Delayed non-white voting as long as possible	
	Greater civil rights consciousness after Second World War	
	Unions important in forcing government to change	
	Wars eventually improved non-white lives	
	Often repressed non-white militancy	
	Constitution talks of equality	
	Government vital in civil rights	
	Even government cannot obliterate centuries of racism/deprivation	
	Non-whites remain among the poorest	
	Elected non-white president after 2000; conservative racist opposition	

Different	USA	Bolivia
	Long very wealthy	Long very poor
	Federal government system long significant	Federal government system only recently significant
	Non-whites in minority	Non-whites in majority
	Non-whites did not form own political party	Non-whites developed own political party
	Obama does not emphasize race	Morales emphasizes race

Diagrammatic comparison of civil rights in the USA and Bolivia

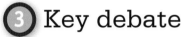

Key debate

▶ *Key question: Were Latin American constitutional guarantees of indigenous rights due to activism?*

Focusing on the constitutional reforms of the late twentieth century that recognized the plurinational and pluricultural nature of many Latin American states, historian Donna Lee Van Cott (2000) argued that 'in no case in Latin America was the demand for special rights and recognition the most important reason for the decision to reform the political constitution.'

In contrast, Jaime Arocha (1998) argued that the rights given to the indigenous and black population of Colombia in 1991 were a concession that their activism forced out of a reluctant and indifferent Constituent Assembly.

Peter Wade (2008) played down black agency and said rights for black groups in Colombia and Nicaragua 'in a sense rode on the coattails of rights for indigenous groups', but concluded that ethnic mobilization was 'clearly important', if not the 'most important' factor in the wave of constitutional reform that recognized indigenous and Afro-Latin American rights. He found it hard to believe that the writers of the new constitutions would have included such rights without non-white activism, but he also emphasized that the governments were very much motivated by other factors such as the international climate and the desire to co-opt and control ethnic movements.

When governments
'do the right thing,'
does it matter what
their motives are?
(Ethics, Reason)

T O K

With regard to indigenous participation in government, C.R. Hale (2004) gave a cautionary reminder: 'it would be a mistake to equate the increasing indigenous presence in the corridors of power with indigenous empowerment' in 'the era of the "*indio permitido*" or "permissible Indian", who can go so far but no further.'

Overall, in Latin America as in the USA, it would seem that indigenous and black agency forced governments that otherwise would have done little or nothing, to guarantee the civil rights of those groups. After all, it is a rare élite that voluntarily gives away power.

Chapter summary

Role of governments in Civil Rights Movements in the Americas

Civil rights became more respected in the twentieth-century Americas. The USA illustrates a federal system of government's crucial role over minority civil rights. Bolivia shows a majority can struggle to gain equality even when enfranchised.

The nineteenth-century US federal government initially accepted slavery in the Southern states, then forced greater racial equality upon the South, then allowed the reassertion of white supremacy. In the early twentieth century, African Americans made some progress towards equality thanks to NAACP litigation and to sympathetic presidents, especially Truman (1945–53). Segregation nevertheless continued, thanks to white political domination in the South and Southern Democrats' importance in the US Senate. Even when the Supreme Court ruled segregation unconstitutional in *Brown* (1954), Southern white resistance forced a reluctant President Eisenhower (1953–61) to intervene in Little Rock. Eisenhower and Kennedy (1961–3) responded to African American activism with Civil Rights Acts (1957, 1960) and a civil rights bill that finally became an act (1963) under the sympathetic Johnson (1963–9). Black activism also encouraged the 1965 Voting Rights Act.

After 1965, Johnson was unable to help African Americans, because of opposition from Congress, local officials and the white population who, faced with black violence and the expensive Vietnam War, did not want to pay to improve black ghettos. Johnson urged affirmative action, which was introduced under President Nixon (1969–74). However, from the late 1970s a conservative white backlash gathered momentum. In 2000, black poverty and unemployment rates remained twice as high as those of whites.

Unlike the black population of the USA, Bolivia's indigenous people were in the majority. Their lands, rights and culture were despised in colonial times and under the new republic in the nineteenth and early twentieth centuries.

Indigenous rights became an issue in the 1930s. The combination of new political parties sympathetic to the impoverished indigenous population, the first National Indigenous Congress (1945) and the greater availability of education helped to mobilize the indigenous population, whose organizations mushroomed.

During Bolivia's National Revolution (1952), indigenous peasants seized land. The seizures were recognized by the reformist government. Bolivian military governments (1964–82) were often sympathetic to the indigenous population, whose sheer weight of numbers ensured that even dictators felt it unwise to ignore them.

Exasperated by threats to their water and their cultivation of coca, the indigenous population were crucial in the election of Aymara Evo Morales to the presidency in 2005. Significantly, the wealthy white minority of the lowland regions threatened secession.

✅ Examination advice

How to answer 'evaluate' questions

For questions that contain the command term <u>evaluate</u>, you are asked to make judgements. You should judge the available evidence and identify and discuss the most convincing elements of the argument, in addition to explaining the limitations of other elements.

Example

<u>Evaluate</u> the role the US government played in relation to the civil rights of African Americans from 1945 to 1965.

1 For this question you should aim to make judgements about the role different US governments or presidencies played in relation to the civil rights of African Americans. It is unlikely that the roles would have been the same with each president so part of your task is to discuss what each president did for civil rights. Explain why he pushed for certain actions or why he remained inactive. Because the question provides a specific timeline, be sure to cover the presidencies of Truman, Eisenhower, Kennedy and Johnson. Do not spend valuable time on discussing earlier or later presidents. Stronger answers will include evidence of the historical context of presidential actions. In other words, what Lyndon Johnson did in 1964 and 1965 was different from what Harry Truman was able to accomplish in 1945; this was partly due to the actions of the civil rights movement and the receptiveness of the US public to change, as well as how willing Congress was to overturn decades of *de jure* segregation.
2 Before writing the answer you should produce an outline – allow around five minutes to do this. You might want to organize your thoughts by dividing up each presidential term. You could include evidence such as:

President Truman (1945–53):
* *Truman needed the northern black vote.*
* *He created a committee to investigate civil rights in the USA. The report, 'To Secure These Rights', was an indictment of race relations.*
* *He banned segregation in the armed forces by executive decree in 1948. It would take two years to be enacted.*
* *NAACP kept up pressure with court cases.*
* *Overall, a helpful and crucial role, although limited by the obstructive role of Congress. Local government role still vital.*

President Eisenhower (1953–61)
* *Called for an end to segregation in his first State of the Union address (1953).*

▶

- Often forced to act because of outside forces such as mob action in Arkansas in 1957 and black activism.
- Did not like Supreme Court decisions such as **Brown v. Board of Education.**
- Congress forced to acknowledge that there were serious racial problems in the South.
- 1956 civil rights legislation was weak, tepid.
- Overall, a helpful role was somewhat forced on him.

President Kennedy (1961–3)

- During his presidency there was a huge rise in black activism. (Freedom Rides, Mississippi voter registration drives, Birmingham, March on Washington.)
- Southern white actions in which law and order was disregarded forced Kennedy to act.
- Generally, Kennedy was slow to act.
- Kennedy concerned about 1962 Congressional elections – he did not want to endanger Democratic chances in elections.
- His 1962 literacy bill which would have allowed African Americans with a sixth-grade education to be able to vote was not passed.
- 1963 Civil Rights bill did not go nearly far enough for Civil Rights leaders.
- Overall, a reactive role – needed black prompting.

President Johnson (1963–9)

- 1964 Civil Rights Act.
- 1965 Voting Rights Act.
- Congress finally acted with the Executive (president) and Judicial (courts) branches of government to enact meaningful change.
- Inability to stop US cities from burning. Problems in ghettoes continued.
- Unparalleled role in the presidential promotion of racial segregation in the South. Limited role in the Northern ghettos.

3 In your introduction, you will need to state your thesis. This might be: 'the various US governments from 1945 to 1965 could not avoid the growing problems associated with racial discrimination. However, the degree to which each tried to bring equal rights to African American citizens varied greatly'. When you write your introduction, do not waste time by restating the question. Just be sure to number your answer correctly.

An example of a good introductory paragraph for this question is given below.

Great changes in the political, economic and social status of African Americans took place between 1945 and 1965. Presidents Truman, Eisenhower, Kennedy and Johnson could not avoid the growing problems associated with racial discrimination. However, the degree to which each tried to bring equal rights to African American citizens varied greatly. Presidents Truman and Johnson seemed to act out of conviction while Eisenhower and Kennedy seemed to be pushed to action because of violent white backlashes threatening law and order. Other key factors in the governments' actions included the quickening pace of civil rights actions, whether or not Congress was willing to stand for change or the status quo and what political price a president was willing to pay in order to do what he thought was right.

4 In the body of your essay, devote at least one paragraph to each of the topics you raised in your introduction. This is your opportunity to support your thesis with appropriate evidence. Be sure to explicitly state how your supporting evidence ties into the question asked. If there is any counter-evidence, explain how and why it is of less importance than what you have chosen to focus on.

5 A well-constructed essay will end with a conclusion. Here you will tie together your essay by stating your conclusions. These concluding statements should support your thesis. Remember, do not bring any new ideas up here.

6 Now try writing a complete answer to the question following the advice above.

🖊 Examination practice

Below are two exam-style questions for you to practise on this topic.

1 Assess the role of the Bolivian government in guaranteeing equal civil rights for its citizens.
(For guidance on how to answer 'assess' questions, see pages 121–2.)

2 Why was President Johnson's civil rights programme derailed by the end of his term in office?
(For guidance on how to answer 'why' questions, see pages 140–1.)

CHAPTER 6

Youth culture and protests of the 1960s and 1970s

This chapter looks at the protests and the counterculture of disaffected youth in the Americas in the 1960s and 1970s. Focusing on case studies of the USA, Canada and Mexico, it explains student motives and grievances, describes student actions and government reactions, and evaluates their impact. You need to consider the following questions throughout this chapter:

✪ Why, in what ways and with what results did the young in the USA rebel?

✪ How 'new', effective and widespread was 1960s' US student radicalism?

✪ Why, to what extent and with what results did Canadian students adopt the counterculture?

✪ Why, to what extent and with what results did Latin American youth rebel?

① Youth culture and protests in the USA

▶ **Key question:** *Why, in what ways and with what results did the young in the USA rebel?*

> **Why and how did students protest 1961–9?**

→ ## Student protests 1961–9

In the 1960s, demographic change, an inspirational president, the Civil Rights Movement, conservative university authorities and the Vietnam War caused much student protest.

Demographic change
By the 1960s, the student population had rocketed. In 1960, 22 per cent of young people were students, by 1975 it was 35 per cent. With mutual inspiration and safety in numbers, and without jobs to lose or families to support, they thought they should and could protest without risk.

President Kennedy 1961–3
In his inaugural address in 1961, President Kennedy said, 'Ask not what your country can do for you; ask what you can do for your country.' When he suggested 'peace and war', 'ignorance and prejudice' and 'poverty and

surplus' as issues that people could take up, many students followed where he led. Anything seemed possible in this optimistic and affluent society, with its charismatic and idealistic young president.

The Civil Rights Movement

The African American struggle (see Chapter 2) inspired awareness of rights and activism. The first mass student demonstrations resulted from student participation in the Civil Rights Movement: in May 1960, thousands of students demonstrated against **HUAC** hearings in San Francisco (HUAC had targeted San Francisco because of local sympathy for the Civil Rights Movement).

College authorities and practices

Student radicalism erupted in the University of California at Berkeley. In 1964, the university authorities tried to restrict the distribution of political literature on campus. Thousands of students occupied the administration building until the police ejected them and made 800 arrests. The leader of Berkeley's Free Speech Movement (FSM), Mario Savio, compared the university to a machine and urged students to put 'bodies against the gears, against the wheels and machinery, and make it stop until we are free'. FSM's slogan was 'You can't trust anyone over 30'. The students gained considerable support from the Berkeley faculty and the university gave in on free speech, but the students remained restless. In 1965 there was another flareup when a student was arrested for displaying the word 'f**k'.

The Berkeley protests triggered nationwide student protests. Students had no formal voice in university governments and complained that the universities were impersonal, bureaucratic, and tried to regulate student behaviour (the age of majority was still 21 so universities served *in loco parentis*). Students who opposed the Vietnam War disliked universities doing research for government defence agencies.

Columbia University protests

Spring 1968 saw a great number of campus protests, beginning at Columbia University, New York, which received federal funding for work that assisted the government in Vietnam. One student wrote to Columbia's president that 'society is sick and you and your capitalism are the sickness'. The protests were triggered when the university, which had already encroached on African American and Hispanic homes, tried to build a new gym adjacent to Harlem, with a separate backdoor entrance for Harlem residents. Student protest focused on racism and the Vietnam War. A small group occupied college buildings, ransacked the president's office, and held three officials hostage for 24 hours. The university called in hundreds of New York City police with clubs who hit innocent spectators as well as the student occupiers. Most Columbia students went on a protest strike. The university shut down for that term, but abandoned the gym and many defence contracts. Hundreds of similar occupations across the USA followed.

> **⚷ KEY TERM**
>
> **HUAC** House Un-American Activities Committee, which pursued Communists in the 1940s and 1950s and others considered to threaten internal security in the 1960s and 1970s.

Pentagon Home of US Department of Defense.

Draft Conscription; compulsory call-up to the nation's armed forces.

ROTC College-based programme to train officers for armed forces (Reserve Officer Training Corps).

Counterculture Alternative lifestyle to that of the dominant culture.

Beat Generation Post-Second World War writers who rejected materialism and experimented sexually and with drugs.

Hippies Young people (often students) in the 1960s who rejected the beliefs and fashions of the older generation, and favoured free love and drugs.

The Vietnam War

Idealistic students were often pacifist. Established in 1959, the Student Peace Union had 3000 members by 1962. The escalating Vietnam War, which gave the students a single cause on which to fix their dissatisfaction with their parents' generation and with the ruling élite, mobilized thousands more. In 1964, 1000 students from Yale University staged a protest march in New York City. During 1965, many universities held a 'teach-in', with anti-war lectures and debates: 20,000 participated in Berkeley. The protests frequently led to disorder, as in 1965 when 8000 marchers (many from Berkeley) clashed with the Oakland police and vandalized cars and buildings.

In 1967, the New Left (see page 177) organized the National Mobilization Committee to End the War (the Mobe), which organized a high-profile demonstration in Washington as part of the Stop the Draft Week. Their favourite slogan was 'Hell no, we won't go'. Over 100,000 attended the march, and prominent political and social radical Abbie Hoffman led a crowd that tried to levitate the **Pentagon**. **Draft** cards were publicly burned throughout the country. Several thousand Berkeley radicals tried to close down the Oakland draft headquarters. The police attacked them with clubs. The demonstrators retaliated with cans, bottles and smoke bombs. They put thousands of ball-bearings on the street to stop police on horseback. The demonstrators brought the streets around the draft headquarters to a standstill, escaped from 2000 police officers, then vandalized cars, parking meters, news stands and trees. Many were high on drugs. By 1968, many protests were violent. **ROTC** offices and other campus buildings were burned or bombed across the USA.

The counterculture

Some students demonstrated contempt for contemporary USA in public protests while others adopted an alternative lifestyle (the **counterculture**) to that of the dominant culture. The roots of the counterculture lay in the 1950s' **Beat Generation**, with its spontaneity, drugs, free love and general defiance of authority and convention. Rejecting US society's emphasis on individualism, competitiveness and materialism, some students in the 1960s favoured communal living, harmony and the uniform of faded blue jeans. They listened to music that reaffirmed their beliefs, singing *We Shall Overcome* with Joan Baez, *All You Need is Love* with the Beatles, and anti-war songs. While their parents drank alcohol, which was socially acceptable, the students smoked cannabis, which was not. The more extreme exponents of the counterculture, '**hippies**', graduated from cannabis to stronger drugs such as LSD (lysergic acid diethylamide).

Hippies

In the mid-1960s, a group of alienated young people moved into the Haight-Ashbury area of San Francisco, where they wore 'alternative' clothes (British 'mod' fashions, granny gowns, Indian kaftans), attended '**happenings**',

smoked and sold cannabis, adopted new names (Blue Flash, Coyote, Apache) and grew their hair. In spring 1967, they announced a 'Summer of Love'. Around 75,000 hippies visited Haight-Ashbury, which became a centre of a bohemian lifestyle and was re-christened 'Hashbury' because of the popularity of **hash**. In autumn 1967, *Time* magazine reported that 'hippie enclaves' had blossomed in every major US city. New York's East Village had poetry readings, experimental theatre and underground publications such as *F**k You: A Magazine of the Arts. Time* estimated that there might be 300,000 hippies.

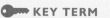

KEY TERM

Hash A resin prepared from cannabis.

Sex and drugs

In 1967, Republican politician Ronald Reagan told reporters that student protesters' activities 'can be summed up in three words: Sex, Drugs and Treason'. The common contemporary consensus was that hippies enjoyed premarital and extramarital sex more often and more openly than previous generations. Greater female sexual freedom was facilitated by the new oral contraceptive, 'the pill'.

A favourite hippie drug was cannabis, which induced relaxation and happiness. LSD was a synthetic drug that produced colourful hallucinations and inspired much psychedelic art and some rock music. Many musicians preferred heroin, which was far more addictive and physically damaging. Some liked to combine several addictive substances, such as alcohol, cocaine and barbiturates. Harvard University professor Dr Timothy Leary discovered hallucinogenic mushrooms on a visit to Mexico. His *Psychedelic Review* openly advocated the use of drugs – Leary advised students, 'Turn on, tune in drop out.' Harvard fired him.

> **Hairy problems**
> Following a drugs raid on a party in Norman, Oklahoma, two of those arrested and charged were put in a mental hospital for observation because of their long hair.

SDS and the New Left

Inspired by 1930s' working-class radicals, the Beat Generation and student participation in the Civil Rights Movement, Tom Hayden and other University of Michigan students established the Students for a Democratic Society (SDS) in 1960. In 1962, representatives of SDS, SNCC (see page 73), CORE (see page 56) and the Student Peace Union (see page 176) met at Port Huron, Michigan. Their Port Huron Statement (see Source A, page 178) called on college students to change the political and social system, and to liberate the poor, the non-whites and all enslaved by conformity. SDS emphasized the potential of the individual, currently stifled by the impersonal nature of the big universities, bureaucracy and the centralization

How significant was the New Left?

of all power. They called for 'participatory democracy' and looked forward to the emergence of a '**New Left** ... consisting of younger people' to awaken Americans from 'national apathy'.

SOURCE A

An extract from the Port Huron Statement, written by student activists (especially Tom Hayden), adopted at the SDS annual convention in 1962, quoted at www.h-net.org/~hst306/documents/huron.html.

We are people of this generation, bred in at least modest comfort, housed now in universities, looking uncomfortably to the world we inherit ... We began to see complicated and disturbing paradoxes in our surrounding America. The declaration 'all men are created equal ...' rang hollow before the facts of Negro life in the South and the big cities of the North. The proclaimed peaceful intentions of the United States contradicted its economic and military investments in this Cold War status quo ... While two-thirds of mankind suffers undernourishment, our own upper classes revel amidst superfluous abundance.

SDS became increasingly politically active, attacking racism, the military–industrial complex, and in particular, the Vietnam War. SDS's 1965 anti-war demonstration in Washington, DC drew national attention.

The New Left and other movements

The counterculture and the New Left often overlapped but were not synonymous. The counterculture distracted possible New Left recruits and alienated potential sympathizers such as US labour, who might otherwise have supported the New Left's anti-capitalism.

Other organizations affiliated to the New Left included the **Yippies** (see below) and SNCC. However, the alliance with African Americans was uneasy, as demonstrated by divisions amongst the 2000 delegates at the National Conference for the New Politics (1967) in Chicago, who tried unsuccessfully to create a unifying political party. Indeed, by 1968 the New Left was increasingly divided. Different groups seemed to be trying to outdo each other in a radicalism that only served to antagonize most Americans.

→ The Democratic National Convention in Chicago, August 1968

In 1968, the Mobe (see page 176) and Abbie Hoffman's (Youth International Party (Yippies), desirous to show contempt for the US political process, called on young people to come to Chicago to disrupt the Democratic National Convention. They spread rumours that they were going to put LSD in the city's water supply.

Around 30,000 members of the New Left arrived in Chicago. Mayor Daley mobilized around 12,000 police and banned marches. The Yippies produced a candidate for president, 'Pigasus', a squealing, rotund young pig. Some threw bags of urine at the police, who removed their badges and nameplates and

---

? According to Source A, why were the student activists of SDS dissatisfied with their own country?

KEY TERM

New Left Term used by SDS to differentiate themselves from the Communist Old Left of the 1930s.

Yippies Radical student group that wanted to pit the politics of freedom and disorder against the machine-dominated politics of the Democratic Party at Chicago in 1968.

What was the significance of the Chicago riots?

---

retaliated with clubs and gas. One congressman accused radicals of wanting 'pot instead of patriotism' and 'riots instead of reason'.

SOURCE B

A sign welcoming delegates to the 1968 Democratic National Convention with a group of police officers in the foreground.

What can you infer about US politics and society in 1968 from Source B?

SOURCE C

A British journalist writing about the Chicago riots, quoted in *The Unfinished Journey: America Since World War II* by William Chafe, published by Oxford University Press, New York, USA, 2003, page 363.

The kids screamed and were beaten to the ground by cops who had completely lost their cool ... They were rapped in the genitals by cops swinging billies [clubs].

What would you want to know about the journalist before you trusted the contention in Source C that the police had 'completely lost their cool'?

The results of the student actions in Chicago

Events in Chicago confirmed, and sometimes perhaps caused, many voters' support for the presidential candidate for law and order in 1968, the

Republican Richard Nixon. Many Americans were tired of students, protests and violence. Polls recorded 56 per cent approval of police actions against the protesters. 'We just seem to be headed towards a collapse of everything', said one small-town Californian newspaper.

Historian William Chafe (2010) described Nixon's victory in 1968 as a 'watershed'. Traditional US values had been reasserted. The left had become increasingly extreme, and reaction had set in on the right, although this did not mean the end of student unrest.

How much student unrest was there in the Nixon years and how did he deal with it?

Student unrest in the Nixon years 1969–74

Student protests continued under Nixon. Sometimes, the older generation joined in, as in the 1969 **Moratorium**, the USA's greatest ever anti-war protest. Tens of thousands marched on the White House and in every major city. The deputy attorney general believed students constituted the most important group of protesters ('We just can't wait to beat up those … kids'). **Middle America** was hostile: a 1969 poll showed that 84 per cent believed student protesters, along with black militants, were treated 'too leniently'.

Some students did more than march:

- Out of 2179 bombings or attempted bombings from 1969 to 1970, 56 per cent involved students.
- Radical students blew up buildings at the University of Colorado because scholarship funds for black students were frozen.
- Anti-capitalist students in San Diego, California, set fire to banks.
- Ohio State students demanded the admission of more black students and the abolition of ROTC. In a six-hour battle with the police, seven students were shot, 13 injured and 600 arrested, after which Ohio's governor called in the National Guard.
- A pro-Black Panthers demonstration set Yale Law School library books on fire.

Kent State

When Nixon invaded Cambodia in search of Communist sanctuaries in spring 1970, anti-war protests erupted again in over 80 per cent of US universities. Police and National Guardsmen frequently clashed with students, most famously at Kent State, Ohio, where students had rioted in the central business district and firebombed the ROTC building. When Kent State students held a peaceful protest rally, the National Guard shot four dead and wounded 11. Two of the girls had simply being walking to their classes.

Days later, two more students were killed and 12 wounded at Jackson State, Mississippi, when police opened fire on the women's dormitory. Some Americans felt the government was deliberately murdering dissenters, but

---

KEY TERM

Moratorium In this context, suspension of normal activities to facilitate nationwide anti-Vietnam War protests in 1969.

Middle America A term invented by the media to describe ordinary, patriotic, middle-income US citizens.

Middle America agreed with Nixon, who criticized 'these bums … blowing up the campuses'. Over half of Americans blamed the students for what had happened at Kent State.

Stopping the demonstrators

Anti-war demonstrators were convinced that Nixon was another Hitler who planned to send troops into the campuses. He did not. Instead, he halted federal scholarships and loans for convicted student criminals or those who had 'seriously' violated campus regulations, adjusted the draft (August 1972) so that students aged over 20 were no longer threatened, secretly monitored disruptive groups, and took protesters to court.

In spring 1970, 10,000 people were arrested in Washington, DC. Although most of the arrests were thrown out of the courts because they violated the demonstrators' civil rights, the litigation kept the protesters too busy and broke (with legal fees) to cause more trouble. When in 1971, 30,000 peaceful students camped out in Washington, DC, the police and military arrested a record 12,000. The most famous court cases were those involving the Black Panthers (see page 112) and the Chicago Eight, who had been arrested in 1968 at the Democratic National Convention. In 1969, the Nixon administration charged these New Left leaders with conspiracy. Among the eight were Tom Hayden of SDS, Abbie Hoffman of the Yippies and Bobby Seale of the Black Panthers. Five were convicted by an exceptionally hostile judge, although their convictions were eventually overturned on appeal.

The incomprehensible counterculture

Middle America observed the counterculture with incomprehension, as with the greatest counterculture happening at the Woodstock rock festival in New York State in 1969. Over 400,000 attended over the three days. Their favourite slogan was 'Make love not war'. The acts were led by Joan Baez, Jefferson Airplane and Jimi Hendrix, who performed the 'Star Spangled Banner'. One enthusiastic participant recalled how 'everyone swam nude in the lake, [having sex] was easier than getting breakfast, and the pigs [police] just smiled and passed out the oats [drugs]'.

Another famous 1969 happening was at Altamont Speedway in Livermore, California. One audience member was stabbed by a member of the Hells Angels, hired by the Rolling Stones to keep order. Another was apparently trampled to death by the crowd.

Where the young people who flocked to Woodstock and Altamont saw liberation and freedom, Middle America saw anarchy and worried about youthful behaviour and role models (several great rock stars, Janis Joplin, Jim Morrison and Jimi Hendrix, all died from drug overdoses within a 10-month period in 1970–1).

What happened to the New Left?

The New Left student movement soon imploded, because:

- The authorities were clearly not going to grant any of their demands.
- SDS, which had always rejected a traditional leadership structure, had dissolved into splinter groups that had different philosophies and preoccupations: the 'Up Against the Wall Motherf***ers' adopted the counterculture, the 'Crazies' advocated anarchy, the Progressive Labor faction favoured Communism, and the Weathermen (a good example of unsuccessful extremism) called for violent revolution.

The aims, methods and achievements of the Weathermen

Aims: The Weathermen's manifesto ('You Don't Need a Weatherman To Tell You Which Way the Wind Blows') said the great contemporary issue was 'between US imperialism and the national liberation struggles against it'. They wanted 'a classless world', and freedom from the 'iron grip of authoritarian institutions' and their 'pigs' (teachers, social workers and the army).

Methods: The 'Weathermen' favoured terrorist violence.

Achievements: In 1969, the Weathermen staged a 'Days of Rage' campaign in Chicago. Three hundred Weathermen turned up, dynamited a statue, smashed windows and stole cars. Most were arrested. After Chicago they went underground, randomly attacking established institutions. In March 1970, the movement was deprived of important leaders when several Weathermen accidentally blew themselves up when building a bomb in New York.

- Some members of SDS lost interest when Nixon ended the draft.
- Some retreated into communes and/or religion. Tom Hayden said, 'There is a race going on between religion and revolution to capture people's minds, and I'm afraid we are losing to the occult.'

The presidential candidate of the counterculture 1972

According to historian Stephen Ambrose (1989), the 1972 Democratic National Convention was 'the high watermark of the New Left's participation in national politics'. Influenced by the protesters at the 1968 National Convention (see page 178), the Democratic Party had reformed its nomination process for the 'maximization of participation', so that in the 1972 convention, more delegates would be under 30 than ever before. This had a massive impact on the 1972 presidential election. As a result of this new nomination process, the Democrats chose their most left-wing option, George McGovern, whom Middle America considered the candidate of the counterculture. Middle America was further alienated when some long-haired young delegates nominated Communist China's leader Mao Zedong as McGovern's running mate, others urged the legalisation of cannabis and

SOURCE D

President Nixon (left) greets Elvis Presley (right) in the Oval Office in 1970. Presley (whose secret addiction to prescription drugs hastened his early death) had offered to help in the war on drugs.

What do you suppose Presley and Nixon each hoped to gain from this photo opportunity in Source D?

the recognition of gay rights, and the party's platform called for the 'equitable distribution of wealth and power' and 'the right to be different'.

Republicans played on conservative fears of McGovern, christening him the '3As' candidate –'**acid, abortion and amnesty**'. Not surprisingly, Nixon won by a landslide, with 60.7 per cent of the popular vote, which historian Michael Heale (2001) described as 'a decisive repudiation of the permissive sixties'. Nixon's victory was assisted by the counterculture and the protests and his decrease of their numbers, accomplished through the prosecutions, surveillance, and the end of the draft (see page 181). Also, many radicals were simply exhausted.

🔑 KEY TERM

Acid, abortion and amnesty Republicans smeared Democratic presidential candidate George McGovern as being in favour of legalizing LSD and abortion, and pardoning Vietnam War draft dodgers.

? What, according to Source E, were the two opposing viewpoints on the 1960s? Which interpretation do you favour and why?

SOURCE E

An extract from *The Sixties in America: History, Politics and Protest* by M.J. Heale, published by Edinburgh University Press, Edinburgh, UK, 2001, pages 2–4.

The New Left and the counterculture have had their critics … their members have been characterised as a 'destructive generation', as naive, utopian and self-dramatising, indulging in fantasies that promoted violence and offered little of a constructive nature … . Many studies of the 60s focus on discord, presenting a picture of a society 'coming apart' or 'unravelling', perhaps even close to anarchy …

But the 60s … have had their defenders too: liberals … did something to improve the quality of American life, particularly for the poor and minorities … The decade as a whole, its admirers have argued, bequeathed a more egalitarian political society and greater respect for a variety of cultural and lifestyle forms. The withdrawal of US troops from Vietnam … [has] been cited as evidence that the political system 'worked' …

The competing interpretations of the 1960s owe something to the continuing relevance of the decade, which still evokes strong emotions. Conservatives deplore sixties … 'permissiveness' … But for many the 1960s … was a time when 'right' and 'wrong' seemed clearly defined, when in particular there could be no doubt that the black and white supporters of the Civil Rights Movement were on the side of the angels … It was a period when both governments and individuals seemed to be moved in part by more than self-interest … Liberation movements of all kinds – African American, women's, gay, grey – trace their origins to the 1960s. Some Americans credit the sixties with releasing them from a Victorian moral code that they had found stifling. Students look with wonder and some envy at the extraordinary youth movement of the 1960s, at the demonstrations which seemed capable of … even bringing down governments.

Student rebellion

Why
- Proportionately more young people and students
- Kennedy appealed to idealism
- Civil Rights Movement inspired activism
- College authorities unpopular
- Pacifism, Vietnam War

How
- Hippies – 'all sex and drugs'
- Counterculture
- Anti-war protests
- SDS – left-wing
- Attempted sabotage of Democrat National Convention
- Bombings

Results
- Destructive?
- Election of Nixon in 1968
- Exit Vietnam?
- More tolerant society?

SUMMARY DIAGRAM

Youth culture and protests in the USA

② Key debate

▶ *Key question: How 'new', effective and widespread was 1960s' US student radicalism?*

Student protests: good or bad?

From the early 1970s, historians began to analyse the 1960s. Many, like Allen J. Matusow (1983), blamed student extremism for damaging the great US liberal tradition, but veterans of the student movement such as Todd Gitlin (1980) wrote books defending and praising SDS and the New Left, and bewailing their ruin at the hands of the counterculture's selfishness and excess.

Were the veterans' accounts accurate?

Eventually the veterans' interpretations were challenged. Ken Heineman (1995) lamented the SDS leaders' accounts' focus on élite universities, and found lots of students from blue-collar backgrounds dominating anti-war protests in non-élite universities such as Penn State. While Gitlin described Kent State as a backwoods university, Heineman pointed out that Kent Staters were protesting a year before the Free Speech Movement at Berkeley supposedly gave birth to white student activism. Kent State's first anti-war group was established one year before Berkeley's, and Kent Staters were among the founders of the Weathermen. Doug Rossinow (1994) challenged the view that 1960s' radicalism had imploded by the end of the decade, arguing that women's liberation emerged at the end of the decade and flourished afterwards.

Thomas Sugrue (1994) also lamented the veterans of the 1960s having 'the corner on the market' and maintaining the focus on the Black Panthers and SDS, which actually had a 'very small membership'. Sugrue said, 'I teach a course on the sixties now, but in 50 years there will be no courses on the history of America in the sixties.' He argued that 1960s' veterans and historians were wrong in claiming 'radical discontinuities' with the 1950s. Mary Brennan (1995) suggested a more productive focus might be the rise of **neoconservatism** and the 'conservative capture of the **GOP**' in the 1960s.

TOK

Are there elements of 1960s' radicalism that are necessarily 'young' in perspective? How so? (Language, Reason, Social Sciences, Perception, History.)

☞ KEY TERM

Neoconservatism Ideology combining traditional conservatism with greater faith in the free market.

GOP Grand Old Party (nickname for the Republican Party).

3 Youth culture and protests in Canada

> ▶ **Key question:** Why, to what extent and with what results did Canadian students adopt the counterculture?

According to historian J.M. Bumsted (2007), 'Revolution was in the air' in 1960s' Canada, 'but it never quite arrived'. Student discontent manifested itself in political activism and personal programmes.

Political activism

Political activism was usually focused in the universities. Many young people joined the New Left movement, which was critical of the current system (for example, capitalism) but not particularly clear on alternatives. Many joined one of the several national organizations established by student activists, such as the student Union for Peace Action (1965). Some campuses were centres of student radicalism, particularly Simon Fraser, York, and the Université de Montréal. Less extreme students tried to radicalize the New Democratic Party (NDP) into supporting social reform.

Sometimes the political activists were violent, as in 1969 at Sir George Williams University (now Concordia) in Montreal. Students occupied the university for two weeks in protest against racial intolerance and Canadian 'imperialism' in the West Indies. They smashed computers and damaged equipment and records worth several million dollars. Ninety occupiers were arrested, including 41 black students, mostly from the Caribbean.

Quebec youth dominated the *Front de liberation du Québec* (FLQ). FLQ was associated with over 200 bombings between 1963 and 1970 and kidnapped two government officials (one of whom was murdered) in the October Crisis of 1970. The Canadian government responded with martial law. In Quebec, the situation was unusual in that French–Canadian adults sympathized with the students, as they too felt oppressed by Anglo-Canadians.

SOURCE F

An extract from *The Penguin History of Canada*, by Robert Bothwell, published by Penguin, Toronto, Canada, 2006, pages 437–8.

Like any other part of Canada afflicted by the baby-boom and the youth or counterculture, Quebec endured a lot of noise, mostly oratorical, during the 1960s and 1970s; but in Quebec, unlike the rest of Canada, there were also bombs.

?

Quoting relevant words, describe the attitude of the writer of Source F towards the counterculture and protests.

Personal fulfilment

Many politicized students were also hippies. Most were from middle-class backgrounds. Manifestations of the counterculture included cannabis smoking, affection for rock music and sexual promiscuity. In their search for their true souls, some hippies lived in communes, close to nature, particularly on isolated islands. Some adopted and adapted Eastern mystical religions. Many took hallucinogenic drugs.

What caused the counterculture?

The great expansion of university education made the universities fertile ground for mass middle-class rebellion. Some of the grievances were very specific to students, including unresponsive administrative structures in schools and universities. The counterculture was a broader movement, a rebellion by young **baby boomers** against the values of the older generation. Much of it was impressed and inspired by the counterculture and Civil Rights Movement in the USA.

KEY TERM

Baby boomers Generation born in the post-Second World War population surge.

The Vietnam War was inspirational and central to Canadian counterculture. The war fuelled Canadian anti-Americanism, as seen in Al Purdy's 1967 book, *The New Romans: Candid Canadian Opinions of the United States*. Anti-war Canadians sent 5000 copies of the paperback *Manual for Draft Age Immigrants to Canada* to the USA to encourage US citizens to leave their country and come to Canada because of Vietnam. Perhaps 100,000 arrived. Most attended Canadian universities or joined hippie communities.

There were some very Canadian concerns. Some Québécois, inspired by the Algerian struggle to be rid of French imperialism, demanded independence for Quebec. Again, US influence was important, as when the US Black Power movement inspired Québécois terrorism.

Why did the youth movement end?

The youth movement ended because:

- In Quebec, many joined a more mainline political party, the *Parti Québécois*, established in 1968.
- Many were shocked and frightened when Kent State (1970) showed how brutal the authorities could be (see page 180).
- The idealistic students simply got older.
- The Canadian government tried to show some sympathy with the protesters and the counterculture.

Canadian government sympathy

After the student protests against racism at Sir George Williams University, the federal government offered to fund organizations such as the Black United Front (BUF), set up in 1968 to combat Canadian racism after an inspirational visit by Stokely Carmichael. Prime Minister Trudeau appointed a commission to investigate non-medicinal drug usage. Its 1970 report did not openly advocate the legalisation of 'soft' drugs such as cannabis, but suggested that it was not the role of the state to enforce morality. Such developments suggest that the counterculture contributed to the liberalization of Canadian society.

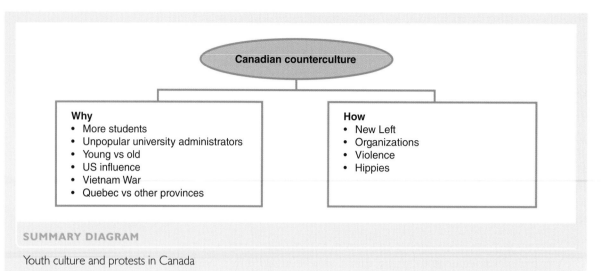

Youth culture and protests in Canada

4 Youth culture and protests in Latin America

▶ **Key question:** *Why, to what extent and with what results did Latin American youth rebel?*

During the 1960s, young people protested in many Latin American countries. Sometimes the issue was the running of the universities, as in Chile (1967–8). Sometimes university issues developed into anti-government protests, as in Mexico and Brazil. In some countries there was little or no youth protest, owing to repressive governments, as in Argentina.

The Mexican student movement

Why and with what results did Mexican students protest?

As Mexico City prepared to host the Olympics in summer 1968, there was student unrest. It was uncoordinated, with varied grievances. On 22 July, the Mexico City police were called out because rival student factions were fighting. On 26 July, students gathered to peacefully celebrate the anniversary of Fidel Castro's first attempt to overthrow the Cuban dictatorship. The police were called to disperse the crowd. The participants reacted and the demonstration became violent. Four people died, and hundreds were wounded. Students seized school buildings, and threw homemade bombs at the police, who used bazookas on them. The students established a National Strike Council and nationwide demonstrations occurred in most high schools and universities. From August, more students became radicalized in response to government repression and police brutality.

The protests then spread to workers tired of authoritarian governments and corruption, and to ousted government bureaucrats who had not been paid for weeks. On 27 August, around half a million people joined in the biggest anti-government demonstration in Mexican history in Mexico City. Mexico was about to host the Olympics, so the government wanted to prove to the world that it was in control. Armed soldiers and tanks broke up the demonstration. Many students were beaten and jailed, and some were killed, which increased the number and size of demonstrations.

Tlatelolco Plaza

On 2 October, 10 days before the Olympics were due to open, around 5000 students protested in Tlatelolco Plaza against the military occupation of the National University, the continued use of the repressive riot police and the cost of the Olympic Games. In among the protesters were people simply passing by, watching the demonstration or sitting in the Plaza and talking to friends, and children playing games.

Viewpoints on what happened next often vary according to political stance. It seems that the demonstrators did not leave when requested, so the soldiers used tear gas, clubs, rifles with bayonets and automatic weapons on them. The government subsequently claimed the students were armed and aggressive, and that the police and soldiers behaved exemplarily in the face of great provocation. According to official reports, 43 died, although some of the foreign reporters in Mexico City to cover the Olympics estimated up to 500 deaths. Hundreds, maybe thousands, were arrested. Some 'disappeared'. An estimated 2500 were wounded. It was subsequently revealed that the police pulled the wounded from ambulances, that military vehicles prevented doctors and nurses from accessing the wounded, and that hospital emergency rooms were invaded by the military who dragged injured people back into the street.

Causes of the protests

The counterculture and political and economic discontent contributed to the protests.

The counterculture

Historian Eric Zolov (1999) attributed student unrest in part to the British and US rock 'n' roll music, popular in Mexico from the late 1950s. When middle- and upper-class young people became influenced by rock 'n' roll's rejection of traditional values, the Mexican press denounced their attitude as *rebeldismo sin causa* (rebellion without a cause). The government attempted to discredit rock 'n' roll, for example, by circulating the rumour that Elvis Presley had said he would 'rather kiss three black girls than a Mexican' and by initiating an advertising campaign entitled 'Die Elvis Presley'. Mexico had its own rock 'n' roll musicians, such as Los Loud Jets and Los Teen Tops, who copied the Beatles, the Doors, Janis Joplin, Jimi Hendrix and the Rolling Stones. By 1965, the rock music focused on Mexico City's coffee houses constituted the centre of the Mexican counterculture. Countercultural heroes included Che Guevara (see page 160), Beat Generation poet Allen Ginsberg and Rolling Stone Mick Jagger. The authorities denounced the coffee houses as 'centres of perversion' corrupted by decadent foreigners and tried to close them down. Border officials were instructed to refuse entry to 'dirty, long-haired North American youth'.

Zolov (1999) linked the counterculture with the protests, pointing out that those who supported the student demands for an end to state repression were initially attracted to the movement because of its association with the rock 'n' roll subculture that had developed over the previous decade. Zolov interviewed one student who confessed that he joined the movement because it consisted of students who 'listen to rock'. Others told Zolov that the student movement recruited supporters by reminding them of state and parental attempts to limit their access to rock music: 'Isn't it true they don't let you listen to rock?' However, it is far more persuasive to see the discontent as generated by political and economic problems in Mexico.

Political and economic discontent

There was considerable popular discontent in 1968. The government of Gustavo Díaz Ordaz, in power since 1963, repeatedly stole elections at all levels. The students were angry that Mexico, supposedly a democracy, had become a single-party state, run for decades by the PRI (Partido Revolucionario Institucional). Students felt the PRI had betrayed the Mexican Revolution of 1910. Half a century after the revolution, most Mexicans and indigenous people lived in poverty. Critics said the Olympics were excessively expensive and taking money away from social programmes.

Results and significance of the protests

The bloody massacre at Tlatelolco Plaza ended the disorder, and the Olympics went ahead. Mexican writer Carlos Fuentes dated the birth of a new Mexico from these events at Tlatelolco Plaza, because it showed that the government only survived on repression. However, the alienated young people of Mexico felt little had changed and some turned to the counterculture.

Hippies and rock 'n' roll

Some students took the 'hippie' route and sought relief in psychedelic mushrooms and the uncorrupted life of indigenous Mexicans. Working-class youth took up the rock 'n' roll culture of which many middle-class and upper-class students tired after 1968. The culmination of urban 'raves' was the Avándaro Rock Festival of 1971, which attracted nearly a quarter of a million young people from all classes. As the older generation denounced the music festival, one of the bands advertised that, 'Rock isn't about peace and love; rock is about Revolution.' The historian Eric Zolov (1999) claimed that, Avándaro 'revealed the political dangers of rock'. The PRI certainly thought so, and worked even harder to stop the music.

Investigations of the Massacre at Tlatelolco Plaza

The government kept details of what became known as the Massacre at Tlatelolco Plaza as quiet as it possibly could until the PRI finally lost power in 2000, after which there was a full investigation of the massacre. In 2006, a judge ordered the arrest of the 84-year-old former president Luis Echeverría because of his responsibility for the deaths of the students and others in 1968. Some felt that President Vicente Fox was simply trying to deflect criticism of his own conservative government's record of abuse, particularly against the indigenous population in Oaxaca and Chiapas (see page 19).

> **Similarities between student movements in the Americas**
> - Impatience with the administration of educational institutions.
> - Some student violence.
> - Some 'dropped out' and adopted the counterculture (especially in the USA).
> - Opposition to the Vietnam War (in USA and Canada).
> - Ethnic separatist movements (in USA and Canada).
> - Opposition to capitalism.
> - Faced repressive governments (especially in Latin America).
> - Student radicalism helped to provoke a conservative reaction (particularly in the USA and Brazil).

Other Latin American protests

Although not of the Mexican magnitude, there were protests elsewhere in Latin America.

> ← **When, where, why and with what results did young people protest in Latin America?**

Student guerrillas

After Fidel Castro came to power in Cuba in 1959, he and his Argentine colleague Che Guevara initially sought left-wing revolutions throughout Latin America. They helped to inspire student guerrillas in countries such as Uruguay and Argentina.

Uruguay

During the 1960s, Uruguay faced unprecedented economic and political instability, which engendered widespread opposition from students and the working class. The students were an important component of an underground guerrilla movement named after the eighteenth-century Inca revolutionary Túpac Amaru II. The 'Tupamaros' robbed banks and food warehouses and distributed the money and the food to the poor. They publicly exposed corruption in the Uruguayan élite. Their tactics became more radical, and in the late 1960s included kidnapping and execution, most famously of a **USAID** public safety officer known for training Latin American police in surveillance and torture methods. They kidnapped a leading bank manager and the British ambassador, demanding the release of

 **KEY TERM**

USAID US Agency for International Development.

political prisoners and a guarantee of fair national elections. Their activities contributed to the collapse of civilian government and an army coup in 1973.

Argentina

During the 1970s, Argentina was politically and economically unstable. A considerable number of university students participated in a guerrilla movement, the Montoneros, established in 1964. They favoured social welfare programmes, citing those advocated and implemented by Eva Perón (see page 208) in the 1940s and 1950s. They earned a great deal of money from bank robberies, kidnappings and from multinational corporations who paid them protection money to avert kidnappings. By 1978, the repressive military regime had crushed them. Many university and high school students 'disappeared' (see page 210). Some had been politically active, but others suffered simply because their name was down in the address book of a political activist.

Brazil

In 1964, an era of democratic government came to an end when the military overthrew the elected government of João Goulart. Despite the repressive government, students mounted what historian Teresa Meade (2010) described as 'huge demonstrations' against Brazil's military government in 1968. Historians such as Boris Fausto (2006) say the trigger event was when the military police killed a high school student protesting for cheaper meals for low-income students in Rio de Janeiro. The protesters were joined by large numbers of the industrial workers in São Paulo and Rio de Janeiro. The government said Brazil was threatened by Communism and became even more repressive and prescriptive (see Source G).

What were the aims of the Brazilian government in Source G? How effectively does the text achieve those aims?

SOURCE G

An excerpt from a 1973 Brazilian textbook quoted in *The History of Brazil* by Robert Levine, published by Palgrave Macmillan, Basingstoke, UK, 1999, pages 129–30.

Brazil ... is an enormous land distinguished by its greatness among the nations of South America; it is a land of hope, destined for power and for world leadership. Its population of 110 millions form a western people forever united in pride and bravery. We are known for our generous character and Christian values ... We speak the same language and are united behind the same flag. ... The very map of Brazil appears in the shape of the human heart ... a heart which incorporates blood from the Indian, Latin and African races ... This is my country; I am proud to call myself Brazilian ... [The] safety of every Brazilian is guarded by the nation's armed forces ... [which] stand vigilant to repel any external threat. There stand other enemies within our midst: terrorists, subversives, and militants of communistic ideologies. The armed forces combat this menace, and remind us of our obligation for hierarchy and discipline ... To subordinate our own freedoms to the common good is the maximum norm of the exercise of liberty in the social order.

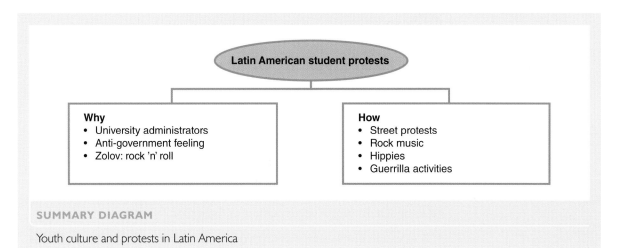

SUMMARY DIAGRAM

Youth culture and protests in Latin America

Chapter summary

Youth culture and protests of the 1960s and 1970s

The 1960s was characterized by protest movements in many countries. US student unrest was due to the rising proportion of young people in college, where they discussed responding to President Kennedy's call to idealism, to the Civil Rights Movement, to the perceived repression by the college authorities, and to the Vietnam War. Some students sought personal fulfilment, dropped out and adopted the counterculture, most famously the hippies. Other students, such as those in the New Left, sought social, political and economic reform. Many students participated in protests, as in Chicago in 1968. Perhaps the most important result of the Chicago riots was their contribution to the election (1968) and re-election (1972) of Richard Nixon to the presidency.

The Nixon administration responded to student violence by trying to discredit the students and by using force and, some say, persecution. The protests eventually died out because of internal divisions, government repression and the exit from Vietnam.

The 1960s remains controversial. Some people look back with affection on the decade as having led to a more liberal USA, others lament the permissiveness.

The Canadian counterculture was also due to the expansion of university education and conservative university administrations. Much of the unrest was due to the generation gap, but the influence of the US student movement and hostility to the Vietnam War were also important. Again, some sought personal fulfilment and became hippies, others became politically active. Some students became violent, especially Québécois separatists. The Canadian government was more tolerant and sympathetic than the US government. This contributed to the petering out of the student unrest.

In some Latin American countries, repressive governments ensured that there was no student protest. Chilean students protested against university administrators, Brazilian and Mexican students against their governments. The Mexican protests were on the largest scale, influenced by rock 'n' roll but especially by discontent with one-party rule, excessive expenditure on the Olympics, and the repressive, brutal government response to protests. Some students avoided political protest and opted out as hippies. Some students' hatred of the government was such that they resorted to terrorism, as in Uruguay and Argentina.

✅ Examination advice

How to answer 'in what ways and with what effects' questions

For questions that contain the command term <u>in what ways and with what effects</u> stay focused on what is being asked. There are really two elements to this question and both should be tackled.

Example

In what ways and with what effects did 1960s' student movements challenge traditional authority in *two* countries of the region?

1 A question of this sort is asking you to do several tasks. You are to discuss *both* the ways student movements challenged authority and the effects of these efforts. Be sure to provide supporting evidence that discusses the two. You might be tempted to divide your essay in two, the first section that deals with the ways and the second section with the effects, but this will not score as highly as an essay that synthesizes the two. In other words, discuss in one paragraph one way a group such as the SDS tried to challenge authority and what resulted from its actions. It is also important that you discuss student movements in two countries, not one. Try to spend roughly equivalent space on each instead of an unbalanced approach.

2 Before writing your essay, take five minutes to make an outline. For this question, you might well choose the USA and Mexico. You are not asked to compare and contrast the student movements although it would not hurt to mention similarities where they exist.

3 In the body of the essay, you need to discuss each of the points you raised in the introduction. Devote at least a paragraph to each one. Be sure to make the connection between the points you raise and the major thrust of your argument. An example of how one of the points could be addressed is given below.

> Mexico in 1968 was shaken by a series of protests and violent repression by the authorities. In July, with the country on the verge of hosting the Olympic Games, students organized a commemoration of Castro's first attempt at overthrowing the Batista dictatorship in Cuba. The police responded violently and several students were killed and hundreds wounded. Outraged students then challenged authority by organizing a National Strike Council and demonstrations. These were crushed by the authorities. Events came to a head on 2 October 1968 at Tlatelolco Plaza in Mexico City. Five

▶

thousand students demonstrated against the military takeover of the National University and the high costs of hosting the Olympics in a country with severe poverty. The military ruthlessly responded to this challenge to their authority and killed hundreds. Their crimes were covered up and it would take decades before the wounds from Tlatelolco would heal. Some students turned to the counterculture, a few became terrorists. The challenge to traditional authority had proved ineffective.

4 Now try writing a complete answer to the question following the advice above.

✎ Examination practice

Below are two exam-style questions for you to practise on this topic.

1 Why did student movements grow dramatically in the USA in the 1960s?
   (For guidance on how to answer 'why' questions, see pages 140–1.)

2 Evaluate the social and political impact of the anti-war movement in the USA.
   (For guidance on how to answer 'evaluate' questions, see pages 171–3.)

CHAPTER 7

Feminist movements in the Americas

This chapter looks at the inequality suffered by women in the Americas. It investigates the reasons behind the increased activism of women after the Second World War, traces the actions they took to remedy their inequality, and assesses the extent to which equality was achieved by the start of the twenty-first century. You need to consider the following questions throughout this chapter:

✪ How and with what success have Canadian women attempted to achieve equality?
✪ How and with what success have Latin American women attempted to achieve equality?
✪ How and with what success have US women tried to achieve equality?
✪ When and why did the modern women's movement start?

① Women's movements in Canada

▶ **Key question:** *How and with what success have Canadian women attempted to achieve equality?*

To what extent did the women's movement of the 1960s have roots in the past?

→ ## Background to 1945

Nineteenth-century Canadian women lacked voting rights, equal employment opportunities and control over their own reproductive systems and property when married. However, they entered the workforce in increasing numbers despite the male-dominated society's conviction that their place was in the home, limited their pregnancies despite an 1892 law criminalizing birth control and abortion, and exhibited a conscious desire to organize separately from men. Pressure from women's organizations gained widows and single women the vote in city elections in several provinces in the 1880s. From 1893, the National Council of Women in Canada (NCWC) was an umbrella organization for groups that campaigned for the vote, better working conditions, free access to the professions (in 1891 only 1.6 per cent of doctors were women) and other social reforms.

The early twentieth century
During the First World War women obtained the vote in most provinces (Quebec held out until 1940) and in federal elections. From the 1920s,

women became involved in party politics and political campaigns. In 1929, the **Judicial Committee of the Privy Council** found that women were 'persons' under the law and therefore entitled to sit in the Canadian Senate, but only a handful did.

Before 1940, most women who worked were in low-paid jobs in offices, shops or domestic service. The better educated could be teachers or nurses, but the orthodoxy was that motherhood was the most suitable occupation. The percentage of female university students was slowly increasing (10 per cent in 1920, 24 per cent by 1940), but they were on a typical 'women's courses' such as nursing, household science and library studies.

The Canadian Federation of Business and Professional Women's Clubs, established in 1930, campaigned for better training and fairer promotions for women, but even among activists, there were those who did not envisage their sex as equal (see Source A).

KEY TERM

Judicial Committee of the Privy Council The final Court of Appeal in Canada.

SOURCE A

Judge Helen Gregory MacGill's response to NCWC president Laura Hardy's suggestion in 1944 that the NCWC should the lobby the provincial and federal governments to establish female training programmes for nurses, laboratory technicians, office assistants for doctors and dentists, household workers, bookkeepers, dressmakers and switchboard operators. Quoted in *History of the Canadian Peoples II* by Alvin Finkel and Margaret Conrad, published by Copp Clark Pitman, Toronto, Canada, 1993, page 444.

But these recommendations are for training women to take subordinate positions, yet the men in the Armed Services are offered full professional courses in medicine, law, pharmacy, social service, personnel, engineering, biology, bacteriology, chemistry, etc., graduating not as assistants, but as fully qualified practitioners.

May I beg to remind you that these professions have been opened to women after great struggle and only recently. No opportunity should be lost to give talented women and girls an opportunity to enter any of the professions should they desire.

What does MacGill's letter to Hardy (Source A) tell us about attitudes to women and employment in 1944?

Women 1945–60

Historians Alvin Finkel and Margaret Conrad (1993) described women as 'still relatively powerless in Canadian society' between 1920 and 1960. Before 1960, there were few women in the House of Commons or the provincial legislatures (see page 41). One exception was Agnes Macphail, elected to the House of Commons (1921–40), then the Ontario legislature (1943–5, 1948–51). She was responsible for the first equal pay legislation in Canada.

Although it was increasingly common for women to undertake paid work, those who worked remained mostly in low-paying jobs in offices and stores. On average, males earned far more, often for the same job or for jobs that required less skill.

How, why and to what extent did women gain greater equality 1945–60?

Women lacked control over their personal circumstances. It remained extremely difficult to get out of unhappy marriages. Abortions were illegal. Post-war **suburbanization** often made upper middle-class **homemakers** feel unfulfilled and disconnected with the outside world. Some sought refuge in tranquillizers and/or alcohol.

The foundations of the political activism of the 1960s were laid in the previous decades, but it was not until the 1960s that women really put their gender grievances on the national agenda.

How, why and to what extent did women gain greater equality after 1945?

Women after 1960

Women gained greater equality after 1945 because the government responded to the women's movement, which questioned gender roles and was the largest and most challenging of the new political pressure groups. Many **feminists** joined organizations. Some put pressure on the government, businesses and community organizations to include women. Others focused on consciousness-raising to bring about deeper changes in behaviour.

The women's movement

The Committee for the Equality of Women was established in 1966 as an umbrella group for all the women's organizations that fought for women's rights. Its threatened protest march on the capital and pressure from Judy LaMarsh persuaded Prime Minister Lester Pearson to set up the Royal Commission on the Status of Women in 1967.

Judy LaMarsh 1924–80

Ontario-born Julia 'Judy' LaMarsh was elected member of parliament (MP) for Niagara Falls in 1960. From 1963 she was a member of Lester Pearson's Cabinet. After an unguarded comment about Pierre Trudeau succeeding Pearson as party leader was broadcast live on television, she left politics for a media career (1968).

SOURCE B

An extract about Judy LaMarsh, from *A History of the Canadian Peoples* by J.M. Bumsted, published by Oxford University Press, Toronto, Canada, 2007, page 421.

*In 1962 she became part of the '**Truth Squad**' … [which] drew her to the attention of the media. A short, overweight woman, she took to wearing obvious wigs and knee-high leather boots. She was an extremely easy target for cartoonists to caricature, with increasing cruelty; and she was by her own account 'publicity prone', a situation hardly aided by a tendency to shoot from the lip. In 1963 she made a famous appearance at a benefit impersonating a gold rush prostitute … In 1963, LaMarsh was made a member of the Pearson Cabinet and became Minister of Health and Welfare, a key portfolio that enabled her to capture many headlines. She personally helped draft the legislation for the Canada Pension Plan that was passed under her ministership. She was probably*

Suburbanization Growth of residential communities outside cities.

Homemakers Mothers staying at home to look after their families, rather than going out to work.

Feminists Advocates of equal political, economic and social rights for women.

Truth Squad Group that that monitored the speeches of Prime Minister John Diefenbaker.

Compare Bumsted's account of Harold Cardinal (see page 42) with his account of Judy LaMarsh in Source B. Do you consider Bumsted to be sympathetic to both Cardinal and LaMarsh? Quote from the sources to explain your judgement.

better known for having given up smoking while Minister of Health and Welfare, however. LaMarsh subsequently became Secretary of State, in charge of Canada's Centennial year, travelling thousands of miles to participate in celebrations and helping to entertain visiting dignitaries … She also was partly responsible for the creation of the Royal Commission on the Status of Women … She subsequently retired from politics, leaving the incoming Parliament extremely short of women members.

The government response

The government responded to the women's movement with the Royal Commission on the Status of Women and the Charter.

The Royal Commission on the Status of Women

The commission centralized and catalysed a great many complaints from all over Canada. It recommended reforms in education, employment, family law, childcare and the abortion laws, and that women should have unlimited access to contraceptive devices and to graduate and professional schools (see Source C).

SOURCE C

An extract from the Report of the Royal Commission on the Status of Women, 1970, quoted in *History of the Canadian Peoples* by J.M. Bumsted, Oxford University Press, Toronto, Canada, 2007, page 420.

In particular, the Commission adopted four principles: first, that women should be free to choose whether or not to take employment outside their homes … The second is that the care of children is a responsibility to be shared by the mother, the father and society … The third principle specifically recognizes the childbearing function of women. It is apparent that society has a responsibility for women because of pregnancy and childbirth, and special treatment related to maternity will always be necessary. The fourth principle is that in certain areas women will for an interim period require special treatment to overcome the adverse effects of discriminatory practices.

What can you infer from Source C as to the ways in which women lacked equality in Canada in 1970?

NAC

In 1972, the National Action Committee on the Status of Women (NAC) was established. NAC lobbied the government to ensure that the Commission's recommendations remained on the agenda. The largest feminist pressure group, it included over 500 member organizations, such as the Canadian Abortion Rights Action League and the Women's Legal Education and Action Fund (LEAF). These organizations lobbied for access to abortion, better welfare provision, better day care, equal pay for equal work, tougher laws relating to sexual assault, sexual harassment, wife beating and pornography, and an end to discrimination against lesbians. Despite NAC lobbying, there was a considerable gap between what the Commission recommended and what was achieved in many areas, as shown with the Charter in 1981.

The Constitution Act and the Charter of Rights and Freedoms

The Canadian Constitution Act (1981) incorporated a Charter of Rights and Freedoms. Section 28 said Charter rights 'are guaranteed equally to male and female persons' and contained the explicit right to reproductive freedom and to equal representation on the Supreme Court. Section 28 owed its existence to concerted pressure from women's groups, as the proposed Charter was initially silent on gender equality. Even when incorporated, the Charter provisions fell short of the demands of women's groups, especially as it gave the provinces the right to opt out on women's rights.

Charter provisions on gender inequality came into force in 1985. A 1989 study prepared for the Canadian Advisory Council on the Status of Women said women were initiating few cases, and early court decisions by male dominated courts favoured men. Feminist lawyers, especially in LEAF, worked to change this, but clearly could not rely on the courts to guarantee equality.

Equality in employment and pay

The 1970 Royal Commission's recommendations for equal pay for equal work prompted equal pay for equal work legislation by the federal and provincial governments.

However, problems with the **'glass ceiling'** and pay disparity continued. Women's full-time earnings were 59.7 per cent that of men in 1971, and still only 64 per cent in 1982. This exacerbated the problems of the many working divorcees or widows who were the sole providers of their family. National Council on Welfare reports of 1975 and 1987 said more than half of adults in poverty were female. Females found it hard to get childcare, and suffered from the **'double day'**. Although the feminist movement encouraged more women to become involved in unions, women in the service industries usually remained unorganized.

Divorce and reproductive rights

The **women's liberation** movement emerged concurrently with the Royal Commission. A militant branch of feminism, they sought women's control over their own bodies (which necessitated access to birth control and abortion) and easier divorce.

In 1969, divorce was made easier, which, coupled with the widely available birth control pill, gave women greater control over their lives. However, access to abortion varied across Canada.

Abortion

In 1988, the Supreme Court ruled that the 1969 law, which required abortion to be approved by a three-doctor panel, violated Charter guarantees (see above) for equal rights. The ruling made abortions more easily available but there was opposition. First, the House of Commons tried to recriminalize abortion in 1990, although the bill was rejected by the Senate. Second,

KEY TERM

Glass ceiling An invisible barrier that stopped women gaining top jobs.

Double day Women had to do housework as well as paid work.

Women's liberation Militant feminists who emphasized male attitudes as the great barrier to equal rights for women.

anti-choice campaigners threatened to take doctors who performed abortions to court, which made many doctors halt the practice. In 1992, a Toronto abortion clinic was bombed. Many **pro-choice** individuals felt that this extremist act had been inspired by actions across the border in the USA.

Political equality
Legislation helpful to women required sympathetic MPs. However, male MPs greatly outnumbered female MPs and were sometimes unhelpful. In 1982, MP Margaret Mitchell spoke on behalf of women's groups who sought to expose male violence against women and children in the House of Commons. Her speech about wife battering elicited laughter and rude comments from many MPs.

Although several women (for example, Rita Johnson) were elected to the leadership of the provincial parties, and Audrey McLaughlin became the leader of a federal party, the New Democrats, women remained under-represented in politics.

Conclusions
Inequality in pay and employment, under-representation in parliament, and increasingly uncertain access to abortion suggested that women had not attained full equality by 2000.

 **KEY TERM**

Anti-choice Those who believe that a woman does not have the right to terminate her pregnancy.

Pro-choice Those who support the right of a woman to choose whether or not to continue a pregnancy.

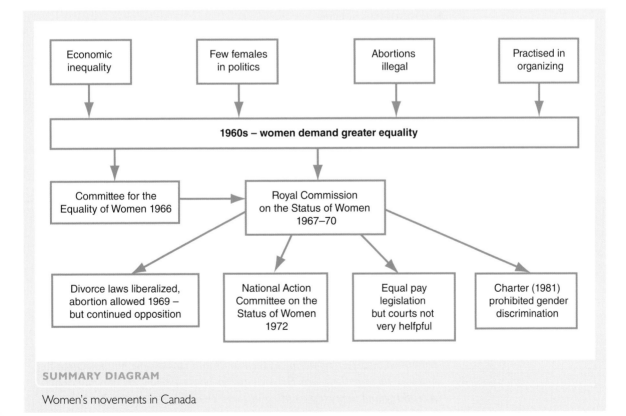

SUMMARY DIAGRAM

Women's movements in Canada

2 Women's movements in Latin America

▶ **Key question:** *How and with what success have Latin American women attempted to achieve equality?*

According to historian Kathryn Sloan (2011), Latin American women shared 'a common history of subordination, initiative, and agency'.

Why and how far had the situation of women improved by the year 2000?

→ The movement towards equality after 1945

In 1945, despite campaigns by women's organizations, women's rights were not yet a major item on Latin American national political agendas. By 2000, their situation had improved greatly, because of:

- the reaction to blatant gender inequality
- gaining the vote
- improved education
- participation in labour unions, organizations, political protest and revolutionary wars
- regional and transnational influence
- government policies
- using the vote.

Blatant gender inequality

While slowly increasing numbers of Latin American women could vote by 1945, the 'homemaker' ideal persisted, even as more women went out to work. In many Latin American nations it was difficult to get a divorce or an abortion, women's pay and working conditions were far worse than men's, and many women were victims of domestic violence and sexual harassment. Women therefore campaigned for improvements.

SOURCE D

? How does Source D account for the exploitation of women?

Colombian feminist Ofelia Uribe de Acosta (1963) explaining the exploitation of women, quoted in *Women in Latin American History – Their Lives and Views* edited by June Hahner, published by UCLA Press, Los Angeles, USA, 1984, pages 120 and 122.

Their husbands are employees, day labourers or agriculture workers. When these men arrive home exhausted they want peace and quiet; a clean, comfortable home; and a good meal. Their wives, who have put up all day with the children's nonsense and mischief, who have mended clothes, swept and cleaned, done the shopping at the market with prodigious economy, and prepared the dinner, must remain on their feet, rendering to their lords and masters the multiple attentions and care that are their due. The men are the ones who supplied the money for everything and they keep pointing this out. Their wives are parasites because they do not earn money, merely living with their children at the men's expense. Women share this erroneous concept because they never stop to think that their work at home is worth as much as or more than that of their husbands …

Women's subservience and ignorance of the law have combined to work against them … Since women are convinced they are inferior beings, they believe they should earn less. This undervaluing of themselves leads them to regard as a gift whatever miserable job they managed to obtain by pleading with men, the supreme arbiters and distributors of public and private employment. Under such circumstances, it is only natural that they should be exploited. They are also unaware that the first step a female worker must take when starting on a job is to join a union in order to obtain protection to which she is entitled.

Gaining the vote

By the 1960s, all Latin American countries had granted women the vote (see the table), although not without a struggle. Their enfranchisement was opposed by religious and social conservatives who feared that family life would suffer. Some politicians were more interested in gaining support from women voters than in the promotion of women's rights, but whatever the motivation, in periods of democracy, the vote gave women the opportunity to elect more sympathetic politicians.

Enfranchisement of Latin American women

Country	Year women enfranchised
Argentina	1947
Brazil	1932
Chile	1949
Colombia	1954
Costa Rica	1949
Cuba	1934
Mexico	1953
Peru	1963
Uruguay	1967
Venezuela	1958

Improved educational opportunities

After the Second World War, Latin American student populations rocketed. For example, Mexico had 76,000 university students in 1960, and 1.3 million in 1987. Among the students were increasing numbers of females. This new generation was more confident and articulate in demanding equality.

Labour unions and organizations

During the twentieth century, the proportion of waged women increased, as in Brazil where women constituted 10 per cent of the workforce in 1900 but around 50 per cent by 2000. Many working-class women were empowered and politicized by participation in trade unions and other organizations, such as the Catholic Church's Christian Base Communities (CEBs), established to help the oppressed poor. Women were allowed to rise to positions of authority in these organizations, which empowered them to seek leadership roles in other ways.

Political protest

In the 1960s and 1970s, many Latin American regimes were exceptionally repressive. The perceived apolitical and inferior status of women sometimes enabled them to protest more effectively than men. Because of the lack of trade unions and political parties and the murder or disappearance of thousands of male activists, women took the lead against the military dictators in Argentina, Chile and Uruguay in the early 1970s.

Revolutionary wars

Women were important in and empowered by guerrilla revolutionary movements in countries such as Argentina, Uruguay, Nicaragua and El Salvador.

Nicaragua

The Somoza dynasty ruled Nicaragua for nearly half a century before its overthrow in 1979 in a revolution led by the Sandinista National Liberation Front (*Frente Sandinista de Liberación Nacional* or FSLN). According to historians Keen and Haynes (2009), women played 'a large role, militarily, economically and politically' in the Sandinista movement. Nearly one-third of the Sandinista armies were female, some only 13 years old. Battalions such as the Juana Elena Mendoza Infantry Company were all female and there were a considerable number of female officers. Three women were guerrilla commanders, two were on the general staff. The revolutionary experience made the women more assertive (see Source E, page 207).

El Salvador

In the revolution against a brutal regime in El Salvador (1980–92), women constituted 30 per cent of guerrilla fighters, and 20 per cent of the military leadership. Guerrilla María Serrano said, 'We grew up with a mentality … that a woman is no more than a person to look after the house, raise the children. But with the revolution this stopped; women found that they could do the same things as men.' However, once peace was restored, many women felt relegated to inferiority again (see Source E, page 207).

El Salvador illustrates how some housewives began as human rights activists on behalf of 'disappeared' family members, then developed into feminists. In 1977 the Catholic Church helped to establish CO-MADRES (Mothers and Relatives of Political Prisoners, Disappeared, and Assassinated in El Salvador). The women staged demonstrations, hunger strikes, and sit-ins in government buildings. Government forces bombed their offices five times and kidnapped, tortured or raped over 40 members. After the civil war, CO-MADRES focused on gender inequality.

Regional and transnational influence

In 1975, the United Nations (UN) proclaimed the decade of women and Mexico City hosted the first of many UN conferences on women. Conferences brought women together to debate and network. The UN Convention on the Elimination of All Forms of Discrimination Against Women (1979) was ratified by many Latin American governments and contributed to legislation to prevent and punish violence against women, as in Peru. Regional organizations also raised consciousness, especially the Inter-American Commission on Human Rights.

Government policies

By 2000, governments paid more attention to women. Some established government departments devoted to women's issues. The Fujimori administration (1990–2000) in Peru set up a Ministry of Women and a Public Defender for women, and passed laws against domestic violence and to establish quotas for women in party lists of candidates. Countries such as Costa Rica offered day care for workers, Chile gave maternity and paternity leave for new parents, and Brazil tried to give women more power in labour negotiations. Many governments eroded discriminatory family and labour laws.

The use of the vote

Women voters became increasingly important, as in the late twentieth-century 'Pink Tide' (see page 15) that saw socialist Luiz Inácio Lula da Silva (Lula) gain the Brazilian presidency in 2002, and the progressive nationalists Evo Morales and Rafael Correa become presidents of Bolivia (2005) and Ecuador (2007), respectively. Such leaders were more likely to support gender equality.

Women and political office

The election of women potentially contributed to gender equality. From the 1990s, women moved into government office at an unprecedented rate. By 2009, the Bolivian cabinet was 50 per cent female, along with 25 per cent of the lower chamber and 47 per cent of the upper chamber. By 2010, 39 per cent of the seats in Costa Rica's lower chamber were held by women, and in Argentina 39 per cent of the lower chamber and 40 per cent of the upper chamber were women. Late twentieth-century Ecuador had a woman president, Rosalía Arteaga, for a few days in 1997. Although Presidents Mireya Moscoso of Panama and Cristina Kirchner of Argentina owed much to their husbands' prior presidencies, Michelle Bachelet of Chile (see page 215) did not. However, women leaders were not necessarily progressive: Violeta Chamorro was president of Nicaragua from 1990 to 1996, but according to historian Kathryn Sloan (2011), she 'recommended policies that set women back decades. She thought women should be in the home and dismantled day care and other services that allowed working women to enjoy security and freedom.'

What factors retarded progress?

Obstacles to change

Forces that hindered change included unhelpful governments, problems with quotas, conservatism, and divisions among women.

Unhelpful governments

In the 1990s, according to sociologist Rosa Geldstein, gender discrimination, conditions in the workplace and pay worsened, owing to government economic policies that favoured deregulation of the economy. Also, government ministries were often underfunded and disconnected from women's organizations, and enforcement of laws to help women varied from country to country. According to historian Jane Jaquette (2009), the new laws 'are rarely adequately implemented'.

Problems with quotas

In the 1990s, countries such as Peru, Venezuela and Bolivia adopted quotas to ensure that parties gave opportunities to female candidates. However, problems remained. Thirty per cent of any Venezuelan party's candidates had to be women, but most Venezuelan women did not know about the rule and, even when informed, voted for men instead. In Bolivia, the 30 per cent quota was taken up by élite and right-wing women, and indigenous and rural women often remained unengaged.

Political scientists Jutta Marx, Jutta Borner and Mariana Caminotti (2009) compared gender quota laws in Argentina and Brazil and concluded that the Argentine quota laws were far more successful because of particular features of Argentina's electoral system and loopholes in the Brazilian law. Historian Michelle Taylor-Robinson (2005) showed that despite quotas, women were excluded from powerful committees and leadership roles in Latin American legislatures.

Conservatism

Feminist scholars Christine Bose and Edna Acosta-Belén (1995) describe women as the 'last colony', with unwaged or low-wage labour, great poverty and 'structural subordination and dependency'. Cuba's Communist regime always prided itself on its programme for gender equality, but even there discrimination still exists (see page 218). Although women played a key role in the guerrilla movements in El Salvador and Nicaragua, feminist demands for reproductive rights and employment equality have not been met. Former Nicaraguan guerrilla Gioconda Belli said that traditional male dominance undermined the feminist agenda in those countries (see Source E).

Reproductive rights

Conservatism is most in evidence with regard to reproductive rights. Many Latin American women still lack control over their own bodies, as their countries are bitterly divided over abortion. Under pressure from pro-life groups, El Salvador (1997) and Nicaragua (2006) made abortion illegal, even though polls showed public support for the right to choose in cases such as

SOURCE E

An extract from *A History of Latin America: Independence to the Present, Volume 2*, eighth edition by Benjamin Keen and Keith Haynes, published by Houston Mifflin, Boston, USA, 2009, page 299.

*Despite their services [in revolutionary struggles], women in Cuba, Nicaragua, and the countries of the **Southern Cone** had not achieved full recognition of their equality. Gioconda Belli, a former Nicaraguan guerrilla leader, complained, 'We'd led troops into battle, we'd done all sorts of things, and then as soon as the Sandinistas took office we were displaced from the important posts. We'd had to content ourselves with intermediate-level positions for the most part.' The complaint was echoed by a Uruguayan trade unionist who had taken part in the struggle against the military dictatorship. 'When the men came out of prison or return from exile,' she lamented, 'they took up all the spaces, sat down on the same chairs, and expected the women to go back home.' And Rosa, one of the Chilean working-class women who played key roles in the resistance to the military dictatorship, remembered, 'When the democratic government took over, the men around here said, "It's okay, Rosa, you can leave it to us now." We thought, "Have they forgotten everything we did during the dictatorship?" ' Consciously or unconsciously, the old prejudices persisted in the thought patterns of men – even radicals and revolutionaries – from one end of the area to the other.*

> **?** Source E cites women who had fought against military dictatorships. Would you have any reason to doubt the inequality under the new governments that they describe?

> 🔑 **KEY TERM**
>
> **Southern Cone** Argentina, Brazil, Chile, Paraguay, Uruguay.
>
> **Machismo** Exaggerated sense of masculinity and belief in male domination of women.

rape and where the mother's health was endangered. In Uruguay, the 2005 electoral victory of the Broad Front (*Frente Amplio*) was expected to bring about reproductive rights legislation, supported by 63 per cent of the population. However, President Tabaré Vásquez hesitated to decriminalize abortion and excluded the prohibition of gender-based discrimination and domestic violence from his reforming programme. Some critics ascribed this to the strong influence of the Catholic Church.

According to Jane Jaquette (2009), women's movements 'appear to have lost momentum' on reproductive issues, because of other successes, 'persistent **machismo**', and the opposition of the Catholic Church and other conservative sectors of society, including some women, such as Laura Chinchilla, elected president of Costa Rica in 2010.

Churches

Along with the Catholic Church's opposition to reproductive rights, some attribute Nicaraguan President Daniel Ortega's conservatism since his election in 2007 to his newfound fundamentalist Christianity. Previously, as a Sandinista guerrilla and as president, he had been pro-women's rights.

Divisions

Women's progress has been retarded by divisions between women. Working-class women frequently criticized traditional feminist organizations as middle class and uninterested in their practical needs. When around 500

Central American women met in Nicaragua in 1992, class divisions emerged as they talked about women's issues. According to a Chilean woman activist, 'We have things in common with middle-class women, but we also have other problems that middle-class women don't have, like the housing shortage, debt problems, unemployment.' Some conservative women do not seek gender equality and/or oppose some aspects of it, such as reproductive rights.

How do Argentina, Brazil, Chile, Cuba and Mexico illustrate how, why and to what extent women attained greater equality?

→ Case studies of women in post-1945 Latin America

Argentina: wife and mother power

In the early twentieth century, Argentine women's organizations were influential, particularly in the 1920s' legislation that cut working hours, provided facilities for nursing mothers in factories, and allowed married women to sign contracts and pursue careers without permission from their husbands. Progress was temporarily retarded by the military regime after 1930, but resumed under the populist regime of Juan Perón (1943–55).

Perón's Argentina 1943–55

Perón gave women full voting rights in 1947, and increased their access to education. The number who attended university was doubled within the decade. Perón improved women's working conditions and by 1949 had established a minimum wage for the piecework many women did at home and for the food and textile industries. By 1955, the wage differential between males and females was down to around 11 per cent, one of the lowest differences in the non-socialist world. Perón also legalized prostitution, which gave workers legal protection.

Perón's second wife Eva, whom the people called 'Evita' or 'little Eva', was his unofficial minister for women. 'Just as only workers could wage their own struggle for liberation, so too could only women be the salvation of women', she said. After women gained the vote in 1947, she was important in the foundation of the Perónist Feminist Party, which aimed to mobilize women's support for her husband. She established the Eva Perón Foundation, which financed women's centres that gave social, medical and legal services and drummed up support for Perón. Such policies paid political dividends. In the first presidential election in which women voted in 1951, 90 per cent of Argentine women voted and 65 per cent of them voted for Perón. They also ensured that the Argentine Congress contained the largest number of elected female representatives in the Americas.

The early death of Evita in 1952 decreased her husband's interest in women's rights, to which neither of them was fully wedded. He sought women's support, she only gained prominence because of him (she always claimed that to be a complete woman, she needed him). Nevertheless, together they did a great deal for women.

SOURCE F

An extract from *My Mission in Life* by Eva Perón, quoted in *Women in Latin American History* edited by June Hahner, published by UCLA Press, Los Angeles, USA, 1984, pages 107–11.

I confess I was a little afraid of the day I found myself facing the possibility of starting on the 'feminist' path … I was not an old maid, nor even ugly enough [to be the usual kind of feminist leader, who were] … women whose first impulse undoubtedly had been to be like men … They were resentful of women who did not want to stop being women. They were resentful of men because they would not let them be like them … the immense majority of feminists in the world … never seemed to me to be entirely womanly!

Every day thousands of women forsake the feminine camp and begin to live like men. They work like them … Is this 'feminism'? I think, rather, that it must be the 'masculinization' of our sex … The number of young women who look down upon the occupation of homemaking increases every day. And yet that is what we were born for …

Even if we are chosen by a good man, our home will not always be what we dreamt of when we were single. The entire nation ends at the door of our home, and other laws and other rights begin … The law and the rights of man – who very often is only a master, and also, at times, a dictator. And nobody can interfere there. The mother of the family is … the only worker in the world without a salary, or a guarantee, or limited working hours, or free Sundays, or holidays, or any rest, or indemnity for dismissal, or strikes of any kind. All that, we learned as girls, belongs to the sphere of love … but the trouble is that after marriage, love often flies out of the window, and then everything becomes 'forced labor' … obligations without any rights! … That is why the first objective of the feminine movement which wishes to improve things for women – which does not aim at changing them into men – should be the home.

How does Source F perceive feminists? To what extent could Eva Perón be described as a feminist?

When Juan Perón died during his second period in office in 1974, his third wife, Isabel Perón, became president. However, both wives were prominent because of him and not indicative of any great change in the role of women.

The Mothers of the Plaza de Mayo

Isabel Perón quickly lost power, and Argentina was soon under a military regime, at its most oppressive between 1976 and 1982. The only public opponents were a handful of mothers and grandmothers who, from 1977, regularly marched outside the Plaza in front of the presidential palace, demanding to know what had happened to their disappeared children. Despite daily harassment by the military, these Mothers of the Plaza de Mayo were a great and international embarrassment to the brutally repressive Argentine military regime, which promoted motherhood as the most admirable role for women.

SOURCE G

Extracts from statements from some of the Argentine Mothers of the Plaza De Mayo, quoted on womeninworldhistory.com/contemporary-07. html

One of the things that I simply will not do now is shut up. The women of my generation in Latin America have been taught that the man is always in charge and the woman is silent even in the face of injustice … Now I know that we have to speak out about the injustices publicly. If not, we are accomplices. I am going to denounce them publicly without fear. This is what I learned. María del Rosario de Cerruti

We realize that to demand the fulfillment of human rights is a revolutionary act, that to question the government about bringing our children back alive was a revolutionary act. We are fighting for liberation, to live in freedom, and that is a revolutionary act … To transform a system is always revolutionary. Madres of the Plaza de Mayo

SOURCE H

The Argentine Mothers of the Plaza de Mayo protesting in Buenos Aires in the 1970s about the disappearance of their children. The white scarves symbolized their children's nappies.

Women further contributed to the weakening of the military dictatorship when the Housewives of the Country campaigned against high prices and organized shopping boycotts, and others campaigned for joint custody of children, reproductive rights and sex education. However, general Argentine conservatism was demonstrated by the fact that even with the return of democracy, divorce was only allowed as late as 1987.

Cristina Kirchner

Historian Teresa Meade (2009) claimed that prominent lawyer and senator Cristina Kirchner was elected to the leadership of Argentina in 2007 'because a vital feminist movement has been organizing to break down traditional gender barriers that excluded women from positions of authority', However, the popularity of her husband Néstor Kirchner, who had preceded her as president, was surely far more important. Significantly, Kirchner referred to Eva Perón while campaigning for the election of her husband and of herself.

Brazil: from unions to presidency

Some early twentieth-century Brazilian women were active in their own cause. In 1917, women weavers initiated the first Brazilian general strike in the city and state of São Paulo. In 1922, women's rights activists set up the Brazilian Federation for Feminine Progress (FBPF).

The Vargas years 1930–45 and 1951–4

Women's groups persuaded Getúlio Vargas (1930–45) to incorporate FBPF's '13 Principles' (which included the vote for women, legal equality, equal pay for equal work, paid maternity leave and affirmative action in government employment) in the 1934 constitution.

In 1932, Vargas gave the vote to literate working women (only five per cent of Brazilians were literate). However, when he became a dictator (1938), he no longer needed women's votes and his policies changed. Women workers were encouraged to stay in the home, and single and childless women were penalized by the tax code.

The impact of war

During the Second World War, Vargas' dictatorship could not stop the development of raised consciousness within the Women's Division of the League for National Defence, out of which developed the Women's Committee for Amnesty, which demanded greater freedom.

Women workers

In summer 1945, the women textile workers of São Paulo led another strike, which gained thousands of supporters and forced Vargas to call an election. The historians John French and Mary Lynn Cluff (1999) described the years 1945–8 as years of 'important breakthroughs' for Brazilian women thanks to the activism of the working-class left.

João Goulart 1961–4

President João Goulart introduced a civil code that prohibited gender discrimination in employment and gave married women legal control of their earnings and shared ownership of jointly acquired property. However, right-wing women's groups played an important part in Goulart's overthrow when they led protest Marches of the Family with God, in which thousands participated.

SOURCE I

An extract from *Women's Roles in Latin America and the Caribbean* by Kathryn Sloan, published by ABC-CLIO, Santa Barbara, USA, 2011, page 182.

Rightist women did not act on their own initiative; men orchestrated their political strategy.

Military dictatorship

Despite the demise of democracy, women's activism continued. Influenced by liberation theology and CEBs (see page 16), Brazilian women organized community and neighbourhood groups in the 1970s that began by demanding better water and housing but became far more politicized and eventually demanded democracy. Concessions to women were few, although from 1977 the military dictatorship allowed divorce.

Democracy restored

The restoration of democracy in 1985 slowly increased women's participation in politics. In the early twenty-first century, Benedita da Silva, the most prominent Afro-Brazilian activist, became the first slum dweller to be elected as a senator. The Coalition of Black Brazilian Women pressed President Luiz Inácio Lula da Silva (Lula) to increase black representation in government, education and business and he responded with affirmative action, the María da Penha Law that protected women from domestic violence, and a Special Secretariat on Policy for Women. Constitutionally prohibited from running for a third term, Lula supported Dilma Rousseff in her successful run for the presidency in 2010 (she belonged to the Workers' Party).

Chile: conservatives and a female president

One-quarter of the early twentieth-century Chilean workforce were women, mostly employed in dirty, unsafe sweatshops for meagre wages. Feminists demanded a minimum wage, equal pay, a 48-hour week, the abolition of night work, pre-natal healthcare, paid maternity leave and subsidized on-site childcare.

Although illegal, abortion was widely practised and frequently botched: in 1936, five hospitals registered over 10,000 abortions that left the mother in need of hospital care. The leftist feminist Women's Liberation Movement (MENCH) complained about 'compulsory motherhood' and the 'slavery of unwanted children' and sought 'the economic, juridical, biological, and political emancipation' of women.

The impact of the Second World War

During the Second World War, the Chilean Federation of Feminine Institutions (FECHIF) represented 213 women's organizations and mobilized huge street demonstrations that demanded the vote for women in national elections. Radical President Gabriel González Videla (1946–52) granted women the vote in 1949 and organized women's centres that provided education, training and career services.

The 1960s: Conservatives versus Socialists

When Eduardo Frei won the 1964 presidential election, he asked women to preserve the sacred Catholic family and set up 6000 women's centres to encourage domesticity. Left-wingers were more sympathetic. President Salvador Allende (1970–3) established a Ministry of the Family and community day-care centres. As the Chilean economy deteriorated, Allende's opponents mobilized middle-class women to protest by banging together empty pots, which contributed to his overthrow. Such was the importance of the female vote that by this time women were known as *hacedoras de presidentes* (makers of presidents).

The Pinochet years 1973–90

During Augusto Pinochet's dictatorship:

- the husband's legal control over the wife and her property was restored
- labour legislation that protected women was eliminated
- women's access to employment was restricted
- women were prohibited from holding elected office
- women's income was reduced to 68 per cent to 36 per cent that of men.

Pinochet encouraged The Feminine Power (EPF), a middle- and upper-class organization that had opposed Salvador Allende. He emphasized family values and established a National Ministry of Women. His wife, Lucia Hiriart, revitalized clubs for homemakers that eventually claimed a quarter of a million members.

Pinochet's politicization of women

Pinochet politicized many women. His economic policies were unpopular with working-class women and a women's trade union group, the Women's Department (DF), organized the first anti-Pinochet demonstration on International Women's Day in 1978. Encouraged by the Catholic Church, Chilean women imprisoned under the repressive Pinochet regime developed three-dimensional textile pictures, the *arpilleras,* in which were hidden scenes of the torture and abuse that they were suffering. Prison guards failed to realize that the women were hiding messages about their sufferings. By the 1980s, the opposition to Pinochet had mushroomed. The women's politicization had led them to:

- hide victims of the terror
- make and distribute bread containing messages about opposition activities
- circulate information about the 'disappeared'
- create critical *arpilleras* (see Source J, page 214)
- participate in hunger strikes
- chain themselves to public buildings such as the Supreme Court and Pinochet's house.

SOURCE J

One of the original and most typical *arpillera* designs created by women unhappy with the Pinochet dictatorship in Chile.

By the late 1980s, the Feminist Movement (MF) called for democracy in the nation and in the home, civil equality, protection for women workers and affirmative action to establish 30 per cent female employment.

The democratic 1990s

When democracy was restored in the early 1990s, the position of women improved. However, a UN report noted, 'Chile's women had played a leading role in the battle against the dictatorship and human rights, yet they had no divorce law, were under-represented in decision-making positions and faced severe constraints on reproductive health.' Laws still described the husband as 'head' of the family.

Socialist Ricardo Lagos was elected president in 2001 and one of his campaign promises was to promote equality for women and indigenous people. Despite a reluctant Senate, workplace discrimination was made illegal. In 2004 divorce was finally allowed.

Women became increasingly prominent in politics. Between 1990 and 2006 the percentage of women in the Chilean Senate rose from 2.6 to 5.2 per cent, and from 5.8 to 15 per cent in the Chamber of Deputies. In those years, the number of women in the president's Cabinet rose from one to five, including Michelle Bachelet, elected president of Chile in 2005.

President Bachelet 2006–10

Feminist Michelle Bachelet's election was a somewhat surprising development, given the strength of Chilean Catholicism and cultural conservatism. Many upper-class women remained at the heart of the pro-Catholic, conservative opposition to a more equal society. Bachelet was a socialist, atheist, unmarried mother of three children, each with a different father. Her narrow electoral victory was variously attributed to feminists, her charisma, greater tolerance and the vagaries of the electoral system. In her first annual address to the Chilean Congress she said, 'I am here as a woman, representing the defeat of the exclusion to which we were subjected for so long.' Even so, despite great UN pressure, in 2008 Chile remained one of only three Latin American countries that did not allow abortions, even in cases of rape or when the mother's life was in danger.

Key debate: what was the role of gender in Bachelet's election?

According to historian Kathryn Sloan (2011), 'There is no doubt that Bachelet was elected on a wave of women demanding a greater share of the political discourse.' Similarly, according to historian Teresa Meade (2010), 'Her very election reflected greater tolerance of a more radical, feminist agenda on the part of the electorate, or a least a willingness to consider a more radical cultural make-up.' On the other hand, Marcela Rios Tobar (2009) concluded that 'feminist political mobilization had only an indirect influence on Bachelet's election', which owed more to 'the particularities of a close and contentious electoral competition'.

Socialist Cuba

From 1952 to 1959, Cuba was ruled by the dictator Fulgencio Batista. Following an unsuccessful rebellion in 1953, Fidel Castro returned from exile in 1956. By 1959, Castro and the revolutionaries had overthrown Batista.

Women such as Haydée Santamaría and Celia Sánchez played an important part in the revolt against the Batista dictatorship. The Association of United Cuban Women and the Women's Martí Civic Front created a network of lawyers, medical aids, grassroots organizers, educators, spies, messengers and soldiers (the Mariana Grajales Brigade was an all-female combat unit) that was vital to the success of the revolution. Women revolutionaries initially lived charmed lives thanks to the sexism of the Batista regime, but suffered arrests, torture and jail when Batista became more desperate and brutal after 1957.

Castro's socialist regime 1959–

Castro's socialist regime aimed to improve the situation of women. The most important female in the new revolutionary government was Vilma Espín (1930–2007), daughter of a rich Bacardí rum company executive, anti-Batista revolutionary, and wife of Fidel Castro's brother Raúl since 1959. She was a member of the Central Committee of the Communist Party and the Political Bureau.

In 1960, the Cuban Women's Federation (FMC) was set up under Espín. The FMC monitored women's progress and established a childcare system for working women, vocational education and healthcare programmes for peasant women, and schools that taught maids and prostitutes other trades. In 2000, the FMC remained Latin America's biggest women's organization, with over three million members.

? How and why does Source K criticize the feminist movement?

SOURCE K

Vilma Espín, head of the Cuban Women's Federation, talked about feminism in a 1972 interview, quoted in *Women in Latin American History* edited by June Hahner, published by UCLA Press, Los Angeles, USA, 1984, pages 167–8.

In my opinion, the liberation of women cannot be separated from the liberation of society in general. There can be no liberation for a social group constituting half of humankind, as long as exploitation of man by man continues, as long as the means of production are owned by an exploiting minority.

… Historically, the feminist movement has put forth partial solutions, struggling for political rights – as did the suffragettes – but in my opinion, it has not attacked the roots of the problem, which is a capitalist society.

Of course, the feminist movement as such was progressive in its time, at the start of this century, because it helped to create consciousness in the woman, to take her out of the narrow confines of the home … Unfortunately many feminist groups take away forces that could strengthen the genuinely revolutionary movement. We even know of some capitalist countries where the ruling class stimulates those movements, they do not persecute them, they let them grow because to a certain extent these movements are playing into the hands of the so-called democracies. Let's not forget that women make up half of the electorate.

The problem of the liberation of women is a class problem and we can't speak of women's liberation as long as the oppressed classes do not free themselves from the exploitation of the oppressing classes.

'Rights unparalleled in Latin America'?

Cuban women benefited greatly from the Castro regime, with complete freedom of choice about abortion and birth control, assistance with childcare and generous maternity leave. They obtained what historian Teresa Meade (2010) evaluated as 'rights unparalleled in Latin America – or most of the world'. The 1974 Maternity of the Working Woman law gave women six weeks of paid leave before birth and one year of job security after birth if the mother chose additional unpaid leave. The 1975 Cuban Family Code outlawed discrimination against females, recognized the right of women to have an education and employment, made it law for husbands to assist in household labour and childcare, and made divorce easier. However, Vilma Espín admitted that the law was difficult to enforce (see Source L). Particularly problematic was the double day. According to a 1988 survey, men only did 4.52 hours per week in the home, while women did 22.28. On the other hand, the survey said that the ratio was improving.

SOURCE L

Vilma Espín's assessment of the success of the Cuban Family Code, quoted in *A History of Latin America: Independence to the Present, Volume 2*, eighth edition by Benjamin Keen and Keith Haynes, published by Houghton Mifflin, Boston, USA, 2009, page 298.

Tradition is very strong. But we have advanced. Before, the machismo was terrible. Before, the men on the streets would brag about how their wives took care of them and did all the work at home. They were very proud of that. At least now we have reached the point where they don't dare say that. That is an advance. And now with the young people you can see the difference.

To what extent does Source L give a useful assessment of the success of the Family Code?

When Soviet subsidies ceased in the 1990s, there were cutbacks in assistance to women. Prostitution, racial exploitation of black women and general gender discrimination all revived, even though they had supposedly been wiped out after 30 years of socialism. According to historian Teresa Meade (2010), this was 'indicative that Cuba had not fully equalized gender responsibilities'. On the other hand, few countries in the world even tried to enforce strict gender equality and statistics demonstrated that women gained enormously from the Cuban revolution.

Statistics to show progress in Cuba
- In 1953, 20 per cent of women were illiterate; by the early 1960s, all were literate and able to access free education.
- In 1956, 45 per cent of university students were women; by 1990 it was 57 per cent in a university population that had increased ten-fold.
- Before the Revolution, women constituted 13 per cent of the workforce, and one-third of those workers were in domestic service. By 1990, they constituted 38.6 per cent of the workforce, 58 per cent of technical workers, 85 per cent of administrative workers, and 63 per cent of service workers, and had equal pay.
- By 1990, women achieved equality in local government positions.
- In 1990 women comprised only 27 per cent of the Communist party leadership, 16 per cent of the National Assembly members, and 17 per cent of People's Power delegates. By 2006 they comprised nearly half of the National Assembly of the People's Power.

The statistics for Cuba (see the box on page 217) were generally far better than for the majority of Latin America, but in 2000 Castro admitted that Cuba was still not 'a perfect model of equality and justice' and that prejudice persisted even though 'we established the fullest equality before the law and complete intolerance for … sexual discrimination in the case of women, or racial prejudice'. In 2012 women only held around 25 per cent of high-level administrative positions in government. When Castro became ill in 2006, not one of the dozen possible successors discussed was female.

Mexico: revolution without enfranchisement

Women played a part in the Mexican Revolution (1910–20). Dolores Jiménez, working-class leader of the feminist Daughters of Cuauhtémoc, was one of the two main leaders of Mexico City's 1914 urban revolt, which demanded indigenous rights, equal pay for equal work and equal access to education. Women also fought in and supported Emiliano Zapata's peasant armies.

Women revolutionaries demanded the right to vote but many males at the 1916 **constitutional convention** felt they would vote wrongly because only 17 per cent were waged and many would be influenced by the conservative Catholic Church. Women were denied political rights in the new constitution, but gained civil rights earlier than in any other Latin American country. They obtained easier divorce, alimony rights, equal custody rights, the ability to enter into contracts and to control their property and money, childbirth benefits and childcare provisions in factories. However, in practice, divorce was generally considered socially unacceptable and in contrast to male adultery, female adultery was frowned on.

The government came under great pressure from the increasingly well-organized and united women's movement, in the vanguard of which was the Communist Maria del Refugio 'Cuca' García's United Front for Women's Rights. It incorporated over 800 women's groups, had over 50,000 members, and demanded the right to vote and to hold office, protective legislation for women workers, legal equality, and centres for vocational and cultural training and education.

The effectiveness of women's organizations

In 1953, Mexican women finally got the vote, 'largely due' to pressure from the Alliance of Women of Mexico, according to historian Kathryn Sloan (2011). On the other hand, historian Carmen Ramos Escandón (1994) said that late date demonstrated the 'lack of effectiveness' of the women's movement, which she contended remained ineffective until the emergence of a new wave of feminism in the 1970s. The participants in this new wave were young professionals, students and middle-class women, who focused on inequality in everyday life, at home and at work. The particularly depressed state of the Mexican economy from 1976 to 1986 gave a filip to these women's organizations (see Source M).

KEY TERM

Constitutional convention Meeting to create a constitution for revolutionary Mexico.

SOURCE M

A Mexican woman who joined an organization protesting against increasing poverty in 1988, quoted in *The Women's Movement in Latin America: Participation and Democracy* edited by Jane Jaquette, Westview Press, Boulder, Colorado, USA, 1994, page 210.

Since I've been here I've felt a very important change. Before I had only my home and my work and went from one to the other. Now it's not only my home and my work, it's the group. I think that women are useful not only at home, and that's one of the main things I've learned in this organization.

> What effect did participation in an organization have upon the writer of Source M?

Mexican conservatism was evident in that until a 1991 reform of sexual crime laws, a Mexican male could get away with abducting an unwilling minor for sex, so long as he agreed to marry her.

The USA and the maquiladoras

Mexican women were further inspired to militancy by employers who frequently ignored the 1972 law that granted women equality in employment, pay and legal standing. That remained a problem in the 1980s when, between 1982 and 1988, the number of **maquiladora plants** rocketed from 455 to 2000. In 1998, two-thirds of the half million plant workers were women, poor, uneducated, low waged and often harassed. Mexican laws mandated maternity leave, but these US companies frequently rejected pregnant job applicants, forced women employees to take the pill, checked their menstrual cycles and either fired pregnant women or gave them physically demanding tasks designed to result in resignation or a miscarriage. The American Medical Association said the maquiladoras had created 'a virtual cesspool' on the border.

> 🔑 **KEY TERM**
>
> **Maquiladora plants**
> Factories owned by multinational and US companies, mostly located near the US border.

Reproductive rights

In 1970, President Luis Echeverría became the first president to call for a decrease in the Mexican population. He supported family planning clinics and educational programmes. By 1988 annual population growth had halved. In the face of opposition from the Catholic Church and from Felipe Calderón's conservative government (2006–12), Mexico City passed a pro-choice abortion rights law unique in the Americas (tens of thousands of women had died from post-abortion complications). It enabled females to abort without parental or spousal consent. Placing reproductive choice in the hands of the woman alone in this manner is not widespread, although it exists in Cuba, European countries and some US states. The law was upheld in the courts despite a challenge from anti-abortion campaigners in 2008.

Are Latin American women equal?

→ # Conclusions

SOURCE N

An extract from *Women's Roles in Latin America and the Caribbean*, by Kathryn Sloan, published by ABC-CLIO, Santa Barbara, California, USA, 2011, pages xxiv–xxv.

In fact, Latin American women have surpassed many other regions in their levels of political participation, in part due to legislated quotas. This is an especially significant accomplishment considering their relatively late achievement of the franchise. However, modern Latin American and Caribbean women still experience many of the same inequities suffered by their colonial sisters. Female gender subordination continues to plague women. Women earn less for the same work; they suffer gender discrimination in hiring. Domestic abuse continues to be a salient concern of many women's lives as does the threat of sexual abuse. Simply put, the historian must recognize that women have achieved significant advances over more than 500 years of history, but at the same time, they face some of the identical tensions, struggles, and injustices of their counterparts half a millennium ago.

? Do you consider the conclusions in Source N to be fair?

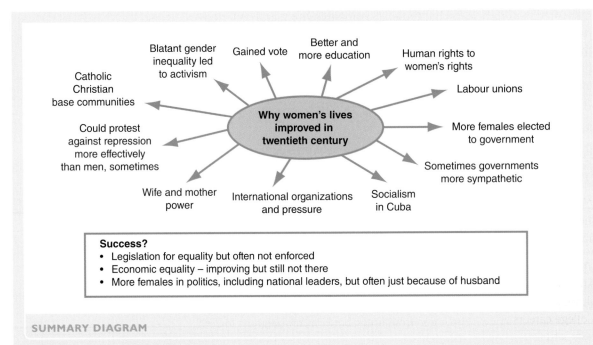

Success?
- Legislation for equality but often not enforced
- Economic equality – improving but still not there
- More females in politics, including national leaders, but often just because of husband

SUMMARY DIAGRAM

Women's movements in Latin America

③ Women's movements in the USA

▶ **Key question:** *How and with what success have US women tried to achieve equality?*

Historian Michael Heale (2001) opined that unlike the student protest movements and the counterculture, which expired soon after the 1960s.'One of the great triumphs of the 60s ferment, [feminism] became an all but irresistible force in the 70s.'

US women in 1945

Women gained the vote in 1920, but the homemaker remained the'ideal' woman. The federal government encouraged women to join the workforce during the Second World War (1941–5), but although the National War Labor Board declared approval of equal pay for equal work, the principle was never enforced. In 1945, women working in manufacturing still earned only 65 per cent of what men earned and although many working women needed childcare, the federal and state governments did not provide it.

The war did not alter majority attitudes about gender equality. Even Secretary of Labor Frances Perkins said,'Legal equality … between the sexes is not possible, because men and women are not identical in physical structure or social function.'However, the director of the Women's Bureau of the Department of Labor noted'doubts and uneasiness'about 'a developing attitude of militancy or a crusading spirit on the part of women leaders'.

← **What was the situation of women in the USA by 1945?**

Reasons for the development of the feminist movement

← **Why did more women become activists in the 1960s?**

Women's activism burgeoned in the 1960s because of persistent inequality, the activist tradition, economic pressures, Betty Friedan, other protest movements and consciousness-raising.

Inequality

After the war, increasing numbers of women joined the paid workforce, although mostly as waitresses, cleaners, shop assistants or secretaries. College careers advisers steered educated women toward'female occupations'such as nursing and teaching. In the mid-1960s, Congresswoman (1955–74) Martha Griffiths told an airline that had fired stewardesses when they married or reached age 32,'You are asking … that a stewardess be young, attractive and single. What are you running, an airline or a whorehouse?'

Statistics were telling. In the early 1960s, women constituted:

- 80 per cent of teachers, but 10 per cent of headteachers
- 40 per cent of university students, but 10 per cent of the faculty
- two-thirds of the federal workforce, but two per cent of senior managers
- seven per cent of doctors and three per cent of lawyers
- 50 per cent of voters, but under four per cent of state legislators and two per cent of judges.

Gender inequality was often enshrined in law or practice. Eighteen states refused to allow women to be jurors, 17 forbade them from being bartenders, and six said they could not enter into financial agreements without a male co-signatory. Schools expelled pregnant girls and fired pregnant teachers. Some states prohibited married women from accessing contraception. Daniel Patrick Moynihan, a leading figure in the Nixon administration (1969–74), admitted that 'male dominance is so deeply a part of American life the males don't even notice it'. Articulate middle-class women began to agitate for equal pay for equal work, equal opportunities and equal respect.

The activist tradition

The 1960s women's movement did not come out of the blue. The National Women's Party, established in 1916, was still active, and 'social feminists' such as labour unionists were influential in the Democratic Party and helped persuade President Kennedy to establish a Presidential Commission on the Status of Women. The commission called for equal pay but also for special training for women for marriage and motherhood. It rejected feminist demands that an Equal Rights Amendment to guarantee gender equality be inserted in the Constitution.

Economic pressures

Twice as many women were employed in 1968 as in 1940. Working women were naturally more aware of and inclined to discuss inequality in the workplace.

Betty Friedan and domesticity

Women's magazines, films and advertisements of the 1950s promoted domesticity as the norm and the ideal. Sociologists pointed out how girls were trained to play with dolls and later felt under pressure to emphasize their femininity and hide their intelligence. Some women took refuge in tranquillizers (the quantity taken more than doubled between 1958 and 1959) and/or alcohol.

In her early 40s, Smith College graduate and suburban housewife Betty Friedan wrote about what she described as 'the problem that has no name' (see Source O). Her *The Feminine Mystique*, published in 1963, averred that women were imprisoned in a 'comfortable concentration camp', taught that 'they could desire no greater destiny than to glory in their own femininity'. Friedan urged women to break out of the camp and fulfil their potential. Her book tapped into women's discontent and was a bestseller, particularly among college students. Friedan was perhaps motivated by her husband, a wife-beater, whom she divorced in 1969.

SOURCE O

An extract from *The Feminine Mystique* by Betty Friedan, published by Penguin Classics, London, UK, 2010 (first published in 1963), page 1.

The problem lay buried, unspoken, for many years in the minds of American women. It was a strange stirring, a sense of dissatisfaction, a yearning that women suffered in the middle of the twentieth century in the United States. Each suburban wife struggled with it alone. As she made the beds, shopped for groceries, matched slipcover material, ate peanut butter sandwiches with her children, chauffeured Cub Scouts and Brownies, lay beside her husband at night – she was afraid to ask even of herself the silent question – 'Is this all?'

For over 15 years there was no word of this yearning in the millions of words written about women, for women, in all the columns, books, and articles by experts telling women their role was to seek fulfilment as wives and mothers …

By the end of the nineteen-fifties, the … proportion of women attending college in comparison with men dropped from 47 per cent in 1920 to 35 per cent in 1958. A century earlier, women had fought for higher education; now girls went to college to get a husband. By the mid-fifties, 60 per cent dropped out of college to marry, or because they were afraid too much education would be a marriage bar …

Then American girls began getting married in high school. And the women's magazines, deploring the unhappy statistics about these young marriages, urged that courses on marriage, and marriage counsellors, be installed in the high schools. Girls started going steady at 12 and 13, in junior high. Manufacturers put out brassieres with false bosoms of foam rubber for little girls of 10. And an advertisement for a child's dress, sizes 3–6x, in the New York Times *in the fall of 1960, said: 'She Too Can Join the Man-Trap Set.'*

In Source O, what is 'the problem that has no name' and what other problems did women face?

The impact of other protest movements

Several protest movements had an impact on women.

The Civil Rights Movement

The Civil Rights Movement provided the catalyst for feminism, in several ways:

- It publicized that groups could be discriminated against on grounds of culture and physical characteristics.
- It showed the power of pressure groups in gaining legislative reform (see Chapter 2).
- Women faced discrimination and sexual harassment in organizations such as SNCC, SCLC and CORE, which inspired many female civil rights activists to campaign for gender as well as racial equality.

The SDS

Many female students joined SDS (see page 177) but even that radical organization was sexist. 'Women made peanut butter, waited on table, cleaned up and got laid. That was their role', confessed one SDS male. In 1964 females constituted 33 per cent of SDS members but only six per cent of the executive. The anti-war slogan 'Girls say yes to guys who say no' said it all. Whenever women in SDS tried to raise the issue of gender inequality, they got nowhere. Although SDS approved a pro-women's rights resolution, the accompanying debate was characterized by ridicule and contempt. SDS politicized many young women, some of whom moved on to women's organizations.

The Vietnam War

Some of the many women who participated in the anti-war movement (see page 176) moved into further protests. In early 1968, hundreds of women attended an anti-war meeting in Washington then marched to Arlington National Cemetery and staged a mock 'Burial of Traditional Womanhood'.

How did women demonstrate their discontent?

The actions of the women's movement

The women's movement organized, litigated and lobbied.

National Organization for Women (NOW)

The government's Equal Employment Opportunities Commission (EEOC) publicly refused to enforce **Title VII** of the 1964 Civil Rights Act, which contained a ban on discrimination in employment on the basis of sex as well as race. This prompted Betty Friedan, pioneers of the labour movement, business women, professional women and participants in the civil rights organizations to form the National Organization for Women (**NOW**). NOW aimed to monitor the enforcement of the legislation, to demand an amendment to the Constitution that affirmed women's right to equality in all areas and, according to its Statement of Purpose (1966):

to break through the silken curtain of prejudice and discrimination against women in government, industry, the professions, the churches, the political parties, the judiciary, the labour unions, in education, science, medicine, law, religion, and every other field of importance in American society. There is no civil rights movement to speak for women, as there has been for Negroes and other victims of discrimination. The National Organization of Women must therefore begin to speak.

NOW's tactics

NOW's tactics included litigation, political pressure, public information campaigns and protests. In 1970, NOW organized a national women's strike for equality. Thousands marched with 'Don't iron while the strike is hot' banners. Some dumped their children on their husbands' desks. NOW produced a Bill of Rights for Women, which sought the enforcement of

KEY TERM

Title VII The anti-sex discrimination section of the 1964 US Civil Rights Act.

NOW National Organization for Women, established in 1966, is a US pressure group for equal rights for women.

Title VII, equal access to education and employment, maternity leave, federally funded childcare and reproductive rights.

The spread of women's liberation

The movement of the women who sought equal rights became known as known as women's liberation or 'women's lib'. It spread quickly across campuses and cities, through 'consciousness-raising' grassroots meetings.

Consciousness-raising

From 1967, women discussed discrimination and inequality in consciousness-raising meetings in colleges (where women's studies became a popular course) and in the community. One group wrote *Our Bodies, Ourselves* (1973), a bestseller with practical information on anatomy, sexuality, rape, self-defence, sexually transmitted diseases, birth control, abortion, pregnancy, childcare and the menopause. Gloria Steinem published *Ms.*, a magazine that explored issues such as female sexuality and the glass ceiling. Women began to use the prefix 'Ms' in protest against the differentiation between 'Miss' and 'Mrs' that had no counterpart for unmarried and married males. Only around a quarter of women said they felt discriminated against in a 1960 opinion poll. The proportion rose to two-thirds by 1974, due to consciousness-raising.

Increased radicalism

Women's lib protests in 1968

In 1968, a group of over 100 women who objected to the swim-suited parade at the Miss America pageant in Atlantic City, disrupted the proceedings with a stink-bomb and crowned a live sheep 'Miss America'. They threw bras, girdles, curlers, false eyelashes, wigs and other 'women's garbage' into a 'freedom trash can', singing 'Atlantic City is a town without class, they raise your morals and they judge your ass.'

Too radical?

By 1977, NOW had nearly 70,000 members. They demanded 'a fully equal partnership of the sexes, as part of a worldwide revolution of human rights', childcare assistance for working mothers, legalized abortion ('the right of women to control their reproductive lives'), and particularly the Equal Rights Amendment (ERA).

Feminists had demanded an ERA since the 1920s but abortion was a radical demand that alienated some women. However, for breakaway groups such as the Radicalesbians, NOW was not radical enough.

During the 1970s, conservative opposition to feminist demands grew. Opponents of the ERA said it would lead to the end of the nuclear family, the conscription of women, and unisex toilets. However, despite the conservative opposition, politicians had to take feminists seriously.

→ # The government response

President Johnson (1963–9) responded to feminist lobbying with an executive order that banned gender discrimination in federal-connected employment. Women's groups monitored enforcement: NOW fought over 1000 legal cases on discrimination.

The Nixon years 1969–74

President Richard Nixon made it clear that he opposed the ERA even as Congress overwhelmingly voted for it. He also opposed abortion, and vetoed the 1971 Child Development Act, a bill passed by the Democrat-controlled Congress for a national system of childcare centres for poor working mothers, for which feminists had long lobbied. His veto pleased those who valued the nuclear family and believed that mothers should stay at home and look after the children, and those who felt the system would be too expensive.

Nixon and many others feared the impact of change on family life. The availability of the pill from 1961 gave women control over unwanted pregnancies and in the more relaxed atmosphere of the 1960s many defied traditional conventions about extramarital sex. The divorce rate doubled between 1960 and 1980 to over 40 per cent as women gained the confidence to exit unhappy marriages. Some women did not even bother to get married, and married women had fewer children. The birth rate nearly halved between 1955 and 1975, because women concluded that larger families were more expensive and could limit the mother's personal development. Not all women lived happily ever after in this new world. Some felt they were neglecting their familial duties, some felt inadequate without a career and some struggled to juggle work and family.

Concessions to feminists

Despite his social conservatism, Nixon had to recognize that gender inequality had become an important political issue. He was concerned when an anxious adviser pointed out that only 3.5 per cent of his appointees were women.

Others too paid attention. Television commercials that women found demeaning were removed. The EEOC took enforcement increasingly seriously and by 1971, NOW had won $30 million in back pay for women. Most importantly, the Supreme Court seemed sympathetic to women's rights.

> **Violent women**
>
> Nixon's adviser, Daniel Moynihan, feared there would be violence if women were not granted equality because 'by all accounts, the women radicals are the most fearsome of all'.

SOURCE P

An extract from African American Congresswoman Shirley Chisholm's speech in the House of Representatives, 1969, quoted at gos.sbc.edu/c/chisholm.html.

Why is it acceptable for women to be secretaries, librarians, and teachers, but totally unacceptable for them to be managers, administrators, doctors, lawyers, and Members of Congress? The unspoken assumption is that women are different. They do not have executive ability orderly minds, stability, leadership skills, and they are too emotional …

As a black person, I am no stranger to race prejudice. But the truth is that in the political world I have been far oftener discriminated against because I am a woman than because I am black.

Prejudice against blacks is becoming unacceptable although it will take years to eliminate it. But it is doomed because, slowly, white America is beginning to admit that it exists. Prejudice against women is still acceptable. There is very little understanding yet of the immorality involved in double pay scales and the classification of most of the better jobs as 'for men only.'

More than half of the population of the United States is female. But women occupy only 2 percent of the managerial positions. They have not even reached the level of tokenism yet. No women sit on the [American Federation of Labour– Congress of Industrial Organizations] council or Supreme Court. There have been only two women who have held Cabinet rank, and at present there are none. Only two women now hold ambassadorial rank in the diplomatic corps. In Congress, we are down to one Senator and 10 Representatives … this situation is outrageous.

It is true that part of the problem has been that women have not been aggressive in demanding their rights. This was also true of the black population for many years. They submitted to oppression and even cooperated with it. Women have done the same thing. But now there is an awareness of this situation particularly among the younger segment of the population…

According to Source P, what problems did women face in the USA in 1969?

The Supreme Court 1971–3

The greatest successes of the women's liberation movement came through the Supreme Court:

1. In *Reed v. Reed* (1971), the Supreme Court ruled against the state of Idaho's preference for men over women as executors of the estates, saying that laws differentiating men and women had to be 'reasonable not arbitrary'.
2. NOW played a big part in the 1972 Supreme Court unanimous ruling that the **equal protection clause** of the 14th Amendment applied to women.
3. The court cited the 1964 Civil Rights Act and the 1973 Equal Pay Act when it ruled against hiring that discriminated against mothers with small children (*Phillips v. Martin Marietta*, 1971) and for equal pay in the armed forces (*Frontiero v. Richardson*, 1973).

 **KEY TERM**

Equal protection clause
Clause of the 14th Amendment to the US Constitution that forbids denial of equal protection of the law to citizens.

Abortion and *Roe v. Wade*

For many feminists, the right to abortion was the most important of women's rights. Many states made abortion a felony, which led to risky backstreet abortions, where many unqualified practitioners used primitive instruments and harsh chemicals. By the 1960s, college students could usually obtain safe abortions performed by sympathetic doctors, but poor women lacked such access. One feminist said, 'When we talk about women's rights, we can get all the rights in the world … And none of them means a doggone thing if we don't own the flesh we stand in.' In 1971, the National Abortion Rights Action League (NARAL) was set up to lobby state legislatures to review traditional anti-abortion laws. NARAL established crisis centres for victims of rape and physical assault.

In 1973, the Supreme Court looked at the case of an impoverished Texas woman who did not want to bear a child that would grow up in poverty. Abortion in Texas was punishable by fines and imprisonment, regardless of the circumstances. The feminists' lawyers argued that the rights of privacy established in *Griswold v. Connecticut* (which allowed contraception) should be extended to abortion. In *Roe v. Wade*, the Supreme Court ruled that women could abort in the first 13 weeks when a foetus could not sustain life on its own.

Roe v. Wade thrilled organizations such as NOW and Planned Parenthood, but the ruling mobilized conservatives who established the National Right to Life Committee, and campaigned in the courts, in elections and in the streets. Republican Representative Henry Hyde led Congress in the passage of a law that banned the use of federal funds for abortion. In 1977, the Supreme Court ruled Hyde's bill constitutional and the following year, Congress extended the ban on federally funded abortions to military personnel and members of the Peace Corps. Anti-abortion activists were highly effective at fund raising and recruitment. Their mailings (see Source Q) were particularly successful.

SOURCE Q

? Why do you think some people found the Source Q mailing persuasive?

Extracts from a 1978 anti-abortion mailing that also contained graphic pictures, quoted in *Unfinished Journey* by William Chafe, published by Oxford University Press, New York, USA, 1991, page 463.

STOP THE BABY KILLERS … These anti-life baby killers are already organizing, working and raising money to re-elect pro-abortionists like George McGovern. Abortion means killing a living baby, a tiny human being with a beating heart and little fingers … killing a baby boy or girl with burning deadly chemicals or a powerful machine that sucks and tears the little infant from its mother's womb.

Phyllis Schlafly

Catholic lawyer and mother of six, Phyllis Schlafly, 'Sweetheart of the Silent Majority', mobilized opinion against the ERA and abortion. Her 'Stop ERA' organization, the Eagle Forum, established in 1972 was joined by 50,000 people. When 20,000 feminists met in Houston, Texas, for a National Women's Conference in 1978, Schlafly organized a counter-rally that attracted 8000 supporters. She said, 'The American people do not want the ERA, and they do not want government-funded abortion, lesbian privileges, or … universal childcare.' Symptomatic of a strong anti-feminist backlash, Schlafly campaigned for women's skirts to be two inches (50 mm) below the knee.

SOURCE R

A cartoon from a 1973 flyer in support of the ERA, produced by the League of Women Voters.

How effective is the cartoon shown in Source R?

The Ford years 1974–7

By the time Gerald Ford became president in 1974, women's lives had changed dramatically from the early 1960s. Over two-thirds of female college students agreed that 'the idea that the woman's place is in the home is nonsense'. Most women now expected to work for most of their lives, even with young families. More women entered traditionally masculine occupations such as medicine and law, although they only received 73 per cent of the salaries paid to professional men.

First Lady Betty Ford championed the ERA and *Roe v. Wade* ('great, great decision'), but her husband did nothing to help women.

Ratification Amendments to the US constitution require ratification (approval) by three-quarters of the states.

New Right Right-wing voters who became influential in the late 1970s. Their beliefs were a reaction to the counterculture of the 1960s, and included opposition to abortion and feminism.

The Carter years 1977–81

President Jimmy Carter was sensitive to women's rights. He appointed two female cabinet members and more women to high-level posts than any previous president. He supported the ERA, which Congress had passed in 1972, but which still needed **ratification** by four more states.

Carter was a conservative on abortion, opposing federal funding except in cases of the endangerment of the mother's life, incest or rape. Women now spoke much more openly of rape. Each year an average 50,000 were reported, although far more were not. Self-defence courses became popular and there were protests against police treatment of complainants.

The **New Right** or Religious Right played a significant part in Carter's defeat in the presidential election of 1980. They favoured the Republican presidential candidate Ronald Reagan, the apostle of the nuclear family.

The Reagan years 1981–9

'Women's Lib' went quieter in the 1980s when the ascendancy of Reaganite conservatives was demonstrated by the defeat of the ERA in 1982. Fashion reflected the conservative trend. Suits were out, frills and high hemlines came back: 'Girls want to be girls again', said one designer. Magazines reflected the change. *Newsweek* magazine lamented divorce rates and wondered whether working 'Supermums' were damaging their kids. Even *Ms.* magazine switched from feminism to celebrity coverage. However, liberals felt much remained to be done. Although the statistics were improving, women still earned only 72 per cent of what men earned.

Abortion battles

The most divisive social issue in the Reagan years was abortion. Anti-abortionists joined Operation Rescue (established 1988), a militant new organization that used sit-ins to block access to abortion clinics. Thousands of members were jailed in 1988–99 and a few of the most extreme bombed clinics and killed medical practitioners. Increased social conservatism was evidenced in 1988, when federal-funded family planning centres were forbidden to discuss abortion with patients, and the Supreme Court ruling *Bowen v. Kendrick* denied federal funding to pro-choice programmes. Reagan said 'chastity clinics' that encouraged women to avoid sex would render abortion unnecessary, but he failed to persuade the Democrat-controlled Congress to pass a constitutional amendment to ban abortion.

In *Webster v. Reproductive Services of Missouri* (1989), the Supreme Court ruled that states could deny women access to public abortion facilities. *Webster* did not overturn *Roe v. Wade* (only three states followed Missouri's example), which was reaffirmed by a 1992 Supreme Court decision.

Bork battles

In 1987, Reagan nominated Robert Bork for the Supreme Court. Bork opposed abortion, claimed women's rights were not included in the 14th

? Give arguments for and against the unelected justices of the Supreme Court being able to rule on issues such as abortion.

Amendment, defended a Connecticut law that would have denied contraception to married couples and criticized the principle of racial equality. Organizations such as NAACP (see page 55) and NOW mounted an exceptionally aggressive congressional lobby drive and played a big part in the Senate's rejection of Bork by 58 votes to 42, the largest ever defeat for a Supreme Court nominee.

> **A female president?**
> During the 1984 presidential election campaign, Reagan's Democrat opponent Walter Mondale chose Geraldine Ferraro as his running mate. Some were concerned at the prospect of a woman 'a heartbeat away from the presidency'. The *Denver Post* asked, 'What if she is supposed to push the button to fire the missiles and she can't because she's just done her nails?' Vice President George H.W. Bush's wife Barbara dubbed Ferraro 'something that rhymes with witch'.

The Bush years 1989–93
Earlier in his career, President George H.W. Bush had been pro-choice but in the 1988 presidential election campaign he changed his mind and said 'abortion is murder', which pleased conservative Republicans. As president he forbade doctors working in federal-funded clinics to give advice on abortion, stopped military hospitals performing abortions, and cut off US funding to UN agencies that tried to decrease the population of impoverished countries through the use of contraceptives and abortion.

Clarence Thomas and the revitalization of feminism
In 1991, Bush nominated conservative Clarence Thomas as the replacement for retiring African American Supreme Court Justice Thurgood Marshall. Thomas had expressed public doubts about a woman's right to abortion but anyone who criticized or rejected him would be open to charges of racism.

Thomas's confirmation hearings became big news when Anita Hill, a black Oklahoma University law professor, testified that he liked pornographic movies, discussed his sexual prowess with female aides and had sexually harassed her when they both worked for the EEOC. Republican committee members subjected Hill to a brutal cross-examination and confirmed Thomas's nomination by 52–48.

The feminist movement had gone quiet. In 1975, even pioneer feminist Betty Friedan had abandoned NOW, criticizing it as anti-male, anti-family, anti-feminine and preoccupied with gay and lesbian issues. However, Hill's ordeal mobilized women on the issue of sexual harassment: many campaigned for laws and regulations to protect women, particularly on college campuses, and unprecedented numbers stood for local, state and national office in 1992, pointing out that the 98 per cent male Senate had brushed aside Hill's accusations.

The Clinton years 1993–2001

Charismatic and pro-choice, Bill Clinton was highly popular with women voters. By his presidency, the focus of feminism had changed.

'Second-stage feminism'

First-stage feminism concentrated on equality under the law and in the workplace. In the 1990s, NOW and other groups continued to litigate successfully to enforce compliance to Title VII and the 14th Amendment (see page 227). Several corporations had to compensate women for discrimination. By the early 1990s, six states had passed 'pay equity laws'.

However, some women felt that such 'progress' simply made women into successful men and that a new emphasis was needed. Most feminists agreed that women ought to go beyond first-stage feminism. Paid work was increasingly important to women owing to the rising divorce rate and the number of single mothers, which made many women heads of households. Feminists now wanted to focus on the problems in combining work and homemaking. They wanted to make it easier for women by means of the provision of good childcare facilities in the workplace, longer paternity and maternity leave, and harsher penalties for divorced fathers who were remiss in paying child support.

President Clinton was important in the passage of the 1993 Family and Medical Leave Act, which increased employers' flexibility over parental leave. While Clinton himself was more of a **New Democrat**, his wife Hillary and congressional **Old Democrats** sympathized with second-stage feminism and (unsuccessfully) sought state-supervised childcare centres for the working poor, which conservatives derided as 'government babysitting'.

More abortion battles

Clinton quickly signed executive orders reversing President Bush's abortion policies and a 1993 Supreme Court decision rejected a Louisiana state law that prohibited the vast majority of abortions. Polls showed that a majority of Americans were pro-choice, although extremism flourished. For example, in 1993 pro-life activists shot and killed a Florida gynaecologist outside an abortion clinic where he worked.

KEY TERM

New Democrat Member of the Democratic Party who believed that the party needed to move more to the centre to be electable.

Old Democrat Member of the Democratic Party who believed in large-scale government intervention and expenditure to ameliorate social and economic ills.

Was there equality by 2000?

Women at the end of the twentieth century

Economic equality?

Statistics demonstrated progress in employment. In 2000, women held nearly 50 per cent of executive and managerial positions (compared to 32 per cent in 1983). Although under-represented in the boardrooms of the largest companies and in the professions (only 20 per cent of doctors and lawyers were women), they constituted around 50 per cent of students entering law and medical schools. Full-time female workers' earnings were still only 76 per cent of men's in 2000, although the incomes of childless young women were virtually the same as those of comparable males. Continuing inequality reflected both sexism and the desire of some women to interrupt their careers to give time to homemaking.

Political equality?

Although increasing numbers of women were elected to the House of Representatives (62 in 2000, compared to 28 in 1991) and in the Senate (13, compared to three in 1991), the numbers remained depressingly low.

Sexual harassment

Toleration of sexual harassment in the workplace had decreased. Inspired by sympathetic Congressional legislation and Supreme Court rulings, groups such as NOW (see page 224) filed many successful lawsuits on behalf of sexual harassment plaintiffs. However, after a municipal courthouse employee claimed that the exhibition of an impressionist painting of a nude constituted sexual harassment, and won her case, a backlash set in. By 2000, 58 per cent of men and 53 per cent of women agreed, 'We have gone too far in making common interactions between employees into cases of sexual harassment.'

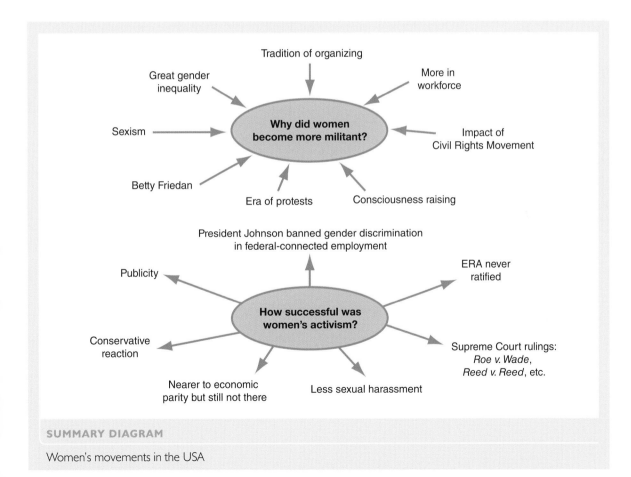

SUMMARY DIAGRAM

Women's movements in the USA

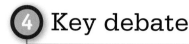

4 Key debate

▶ **Key question:** *When and why did the modern women's movement start?*

Historian William Chafe (1972) argued that women's views were crucially transformed by the Second World War, 'a watershed', 'a catalyst which broke up old modes of behavior and helped forge new ones'. Others date the women's movement from the 1950s. Joanne Meyerowitz (1994) argued that the domesticity ideal was already undermined before Betty Friedan. Historians of the Civil Rights Movement emphasized black women's activism in the 1950s (Vicki Crawford, 1990), and historians of the labour movement have noted women's militancy in the 1950s (Nancy Gabin, 1990). Leslie Reagan (1997) pointed out that ordinary women had been pressing for abortions long before the women's movements of the 1960s and *Roe v. Wade*, and that pressure from these ordinary women had led sympathetic doctors to campaign for the legalization of abortion. Sara Evans (1979 and 2000) took the more conventional line that it was the 1960s, especially the Civil Rights Movement and the New Left, that stimulated white women activists to begin the real struggle for gender equality.

The wage gap

What are some examples of language used by men (and some women) to oppose the women's movement? (Language, Reason, Perception, History.)

TOK

Nancy MacLean (2006) considered the puzzle as to why the USA, which had 'the world's strongest women's movement', also had one of the largest wage gaps between the sexes. She argued that this was more to do with the general existence and acceptance of economic inequalities within the USA than with gender inequality. That continuing wage gap is also a reminder that while most historians (for example, Ruth Rosen, 2000) agree that the women's movement was one of the most (if not the most) influential social movements in modern US history, they perhaps overestimate the movement's success.

Chapter summary

Feminist movements in the Americas

After the Second World War, Canadian women had the vote but had not attained equality in education and employment. Divorce was difficult, abortions were illegal. In the great decade of protest, the 1960s, Canadian women became far more organized and militant, forcing Lester Pearson set up the Royal Commission on the Status of Women (1967), which recommended great changes, including equal pay legislation. Although divorce was made easier (1969) and abortion was legalized, the latter remained controversial. Male domination of the political and legal systems ensured that even when pressure from women's groups led to the prohibition of gender discrimination in the new constitution of 1981, women's groups believed women's rights had not been fully attained. Women's pay improved but remained on average less than men's.

The situation of Latin American women improved during the twentieth century, due to the reaction to blatant gender inequality, to gaining the vote, to more and better education, to participation in leftist movements, labour unions and political protest, to international organizations and to sympathetic governments. However, women who participated in struggles against oppressive governments in countries such as El Salvador and Nicaragua found themselves marginalized by male co-revolutionaries once peace was restored. Effective enforcement of laws against discrimination varied from country to country. Several women were elected to national leadership roles, although some owed their position to politically prominent husbands, and some were unsympathetic to women's rights. Reproductive rights and economic equality had not been fully attained by the early twenty-first century. In many societies the belief that domesticity was the most appropriate role for women remained strong. Even socialist Cuba failed to totally eradicate gender discrimination.

In post-Second World War USA, many people considered that the ideal woman was a homemaker, working women were usually in low-paid jobs and women lacked full reproductive rights. The women's movement developed because of inequality, the activist tradition, economic pressures, Betty Friedan, and the impact of the Civil Rights Movement, SDS and the Vietnam War. The federal government granted some concessions, for example over abortion, but conservatives waged a fierce and sometimes successful rearguard action. The Equal Rights Amendment was never enacted. Women still had problems with the double day and childcare for working mothers. The proportion of female politicians remained low. However, women made considerable progress in equality in education and employment, and sexism was frowned on.

✅ Examination advice

How to answer 'compare and contrast' questions

For compare and contrast questions, you are asked to identify both similarities and differences. Better essays tend to approach the question thematically. It is best not to write half of the essay as a collection of similarities and half as differences. Finally, straight narrative should be avoided.

Example

Compare and contrast the social and political impact of feminist movements in *two* countries in the region after 1960.

1 Your first step will be to decide which two countries you wish to discuss. Be sure to choose examples for which you have plenty of supporting evidence. It also helps to put your answer into context. In other words, if you choose the USA and Canada, for example, you will want to discuss what was occurring in each country that might have affected the political and social impact of the women's movements. Furthermore, you will find that in some cases there were stark differences between the two countries' movements while in others very close similarities. Answers that will receive higher marks often will explain why there were differences and similarities instead of just stating what these were.

2 Take five minutes before you begin writing your essay to jot down examples of political and social impacts of feminist movements in both the USA and Canada. Your notes might look something like this:

USA

Political impact:

- *1963: Betty Friedan published* **The Feminine Mystique.**
- *National Organization of Women founded in 1966: group wanted to enforce legislation; organized protests; consciousness raising.*
- *Supreme Court issued important rulings on equal protection (**Reed v. Reed**, 1971) and reproductive rights (**Roe v. Wade**, 1973).*
- *Movement to pass Equal Rights Amendment failed in 1982, but politicians were taking more notice.*
- *Backlash from social conservatives.*
- *Under-representation in politics.*

Social impact:

- *Women became better educated.*
- *Women had greater control over their bodies but controversial.*
- *Working and pay conditions improved.*
- *Women were better organized; gender consciousness raised.*

Canada

Political impact:

- *Women joined movements in greater numbers.*
- *Judy LaMarsh: member of Truth Squad; Minister of Health and Welfare (1963) and then Secretary of State.*

- *1966: Committee for the Equality of Women formed. Umbrella group.*
- *1967: Government forced by pressure from women's groups to set up Royal Commission on the Status of Women.*
- *1972: National Action Committee on the Status of Women (NAC) created. Umbrella group of over 500 organizations.*
- *1981: Canadian Constitutional Act. Incorporated Charter of Rights and Freedom.*
- *Under-representation in politics.*

Social impact:

- *Slow progress made after release of report from Royal Commission.*
- *1969: divorce made easier.*
- *1988: greater access to abortion, but divisive.*
- *Improvement in pay disparities.*

3 In your introduction, clearly state the areas in which the political and social impact of feminist movements were similar and different in the USA and Canada. Don't worry if there are more similarities or differences. You will be judged on the evidence you present.

4 In the body of the essay, you need to discuss each of the points you raised in the introduction. Devote at least a paragraph to each one. It would be a good idea to order these in terms of which ones you think are most important. Be sure to make the connection between the points you raise and the major thrust of your argument. An example of how one of the points could be addressed is given below.

The formation of women's political pressure groups in both Canada and the USA helped put pressure on their respective governments. The creation of the Committee for the Equality of Women in Canada in 1966 was mirrored by the establishment of the National Organization of Women (NOW) in the USA, also founded in 1966. Both groups lobbied politicians and brought attention to the disparities in income and opportunity for women. In the case of Canada, the government felt compelled to set up the Royal Commission on the Status of Women. The Commission's report was published several years later and was slow to be implemented. In the case of the USA, NOW pushed for the enforcement of ignored legislation and brought pressure to bear on politicians through marches, petitions and demonstrations. As in Canada, the results were slow in coming. Nonetheless, in both countries, politicians were served notice that they could no longer take women's votes for granted and that change was coming.

5 In your conclusion, you will want to summarize your findings. This is your opportunity to support your thesis. Remember not to bring up any evidence that you did not discuss in the body of your essay. An example of a good concluding paragraph is given below.

In conclusion, feminist movements had significant political and social impact in both the USA and Canada. While the two neighbouring countries shared similar results from pressure by women's groups, as well as backlashes and under-representation in the political system, there were differences. In Canada, women were guaranteed political rights that US women were not, especially with the failure of the Equal Rights Amendment.

6 Now try writing a complete answer to the question following the advice above.

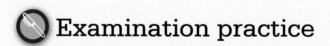 Examination practice

Below are two exam-style questions for you to practise on this topic.
1 To what extent have women achieved equal rights in the Americas?
(For guidance on how to answer 'why' questions, see pages 140–1.)

2 Evaluate the role of women in Latin American politics after 1945.
(For guidance on how to answer 'evaluate' questions, see pages 171–3.)

Timeline

Pre-19th century	Europeans conquered indigenous inhabitants of the Americas and imported African slaves
1787	Constitution of new USA enshrined African American and Native American inferiority
Early 19th century	Establishment of Latin American republics; non-whites oppressed throughout Americas
1861–5	US Civil War ended slavery
Late 19th century	Segregation laws restored white supremacy in US South; US and Canadian 'Indians' placed on reservations; Latin American indigenous population lacked land and rights; women lacked rights throughout Americas
1920	19th Amendment to the US Constitution ratified. Women allowed to vote
1920s	Latin American *indigenismo* movement
1933	Gilberto Freyre declared Brazil a racial democracy
1933–45	Roosevelt administration helped African Americans and Native Americans
1939–45	Second World War helped to trigger civil rights activism throughout the Americas
1947	Truman's commission recommended civil rights legislation ('To Secure These Rights')
1952	Land redistributed to indigenous population in Guatemala and Bolivia
1953	Eisenhower administration planned reservation termination; Mexican women enfranchised a quarter of a century after the Mexican Revolution
1954	US Supreme Court ruled against segregated education (*Brown*)
1955	Montgomery bus boycott triggered US civil rights movement
1957	Nine African American students tried to enter Central High School in Little Rock, Arkansas
1959	Socialist Castro regime gained power in Cuba, promising racial and gender equality
1961	National Indian Youth Council (NIYC) established, more radical than National Congress of American Indians (NCAI)
1963	Martin Luther King Jr's 'I have a dream' speech during the March on Washington; King masterminded Birmingham campaign; publication of Betty Friedan's *The Feminine Mystique*
1964	Civil Rights Act ended segregation in US South; first of four years of US ghetto riots; Free Speech Movement at Berkeley
1965	Voting Rights Act enabled Southern African Americans to vote; Malcolm X assassinated
1966	Chants of 'black power' on the Meredith March; National Organization of Women (NOW) established (USA); Bolivian Military–Peasant Pact

1967	New Left students organized anti-Vietnam War demonstration in Washington; Royal Commission on the Status of [Canadian] Women	1978	Bolivian indigenous activist Domitila Barrios de Chúngara's *Let Me Speak!* published
1968	Student protests in Chicago important trigger of conservative reaction; liberation theology prominent at Catholic Bishops conference at Medellín, Colombia; most radical Native American organization, American Indian Movement (AIM), established; student protests led to massacre in Tlatelolco Plaza, Mexico City; students demonstrated against Brazilian government; Dr Martin Luther King Jr assassinated	1980	Shining Path guerrillas encouraged indigenous Peruvians to seize land; US Supreme Court upheld affirmative action (*Bakke*)
		1982	US Equal Rights Amendment finally rejected
		1989	Many Latin American states ratified Convention 169 of International Labour Organization, which required governments to ensure indigenous equality
		1988	Centenary of abolition of slavery in Brazil
1969	Trudeau's White Paper confirmed First Peoples assimilation not viable; student violence in Montreal	1990	Mohawk militancy in Quebec
		1992	Guatemalan indigenous leader Rigoberta Menchú awarded Nobel Peace Prize
1969–71	Militant Native Americans occupied Alcatraz	1994	Mayan rebellion in Chiapas, Mexico
1970	Student protests led to violent response at Kent State (USA)	1995	Black organizations marched on Brazilian capital to demand enforcement of anti-discrimination legislation
1973	Canadian Supreme Court ruled Aboriginal title to land could not be extinguished; US Supreme Court legalized abortion (*Roe v. Wade*), triggering conservative backlash; Wounded Knee incident	1997	UN report on genocide of Guatemalan indigenous population
		1998	Pardo Hugo Chávez elected president of Venezuela (part of Pink Tide)
1975	Indian Self-Determination Act (USA); UN proclaimed decade of women; Cuban Family Code outlawed discrimination against women and prescribed male housework	1999	Nunavit established; Bolivian water wars began
		2001	Indigenous march on Mexico City
		2005	Aymara Evo Morales elected president of Bolivia
1977	CO-MADRES established in El Salvador; Mothers of the Plaza de Mayo first protest in Argentina	2006	Feminist Michelle Bachelet elected president in Chile

Glossary

Aboriginal Canadian term for the indigenous populations.

Aboriginal title Claim to land based on centuries of residence by the indigenous population.

Accommodationism Booker T. Washington's philosophy, which advocated initial black concentration on economic improvement rather than on social, political and legal equality.

Acid, abortion and amnesty Republicans smeared Democratic presidential candidate George McGovern as being in favour of legalizing LSD and abortion, and pardoning Vietnam War draft dodgers.

Affirmative action Positive discrimination to help those who have had a disadvantageous start in life.

Afro-Latin Americans Residents of Latin America with black ancestry, including those of mixed race.

Agency In this context, where black actions were influential, as opposed to black history being determined by white actions.

Agrarian reform The Latin American indigenous population owned a disproportionately small amount of land. Sometimes governments redistributed the land to remedy this inequality.

Amendment The US Congress could amend the Constitution if 75 per cent of the states approved.

Andes South American mountain range running through Colombia, Venezuela, Ecuador, Peru, Bolivia, Argentina and Chile.

Anti-choice Those who believe that a woman does not have the right to terminate her pregnancy.

Aymara Member and language of an indigenous ethnic group in Peru, Bolivia, Argentina and Chile.

Aztecs Central Mexican people conquered by Spain in the sixteenth century.

Baby boomers Generation born in the post-Second World War population surge.

Bands First Nations tribes.

Beat Generation Post-Second World War writers who rejected materialism and experimented sexually and with drugs.

Black nationalist Favouring a separate black nation either within the USA or in Africa.

Black Power A controversial term, with different meanings, such as black pride, black economic self-sufficiency, black violence, black separatism, black nationalism, black political power, black working-class revolution, black domination.

Bureau of Indian Affairs (BIA) Established in 1824, the BIA had responsibility for Native Americans. From the late twentieth century, it focused more on advice and less on control.

Caciques Local leaders of indigenous groups.

Campesinos Peasants.

Carnaval Annual festival before the deprivations of Lent.

Central Obrero Boliviano (COB) National labour union set up in the early days of the revolutionary MNR government to represent the general voice of Bolivian workers.

Chaco War War between Bolivia and Paraguay 1932–5.

Chapters Local branches of a national organization.

Che Guevara An Argentine Communist who promoted revolution in Latin America and Africa.

Cheyenne Native American tribe in the western USA.

Cholos Bolivian mestizos or indigenous Bolivians who are city dwellers or more prosperous farmers, speaking both Spanish and an indigenous language.

Civil Rights Movement Movement for legal, social, political and economic equality for African Americans.

Coca Leaf that can be used as a mild sedative or processed into cocaine. Coca tea is a traditional drink for most Andean natives.

Cold War The state of extreme tension between the capitalist USA and Communist USSR and their allies 1945–91.

Communist Believer in the economic system under which capitalism and the private ownership of property are rejected and the land and industry are controlled by the state in order to attain economic equality.

Confederacy The 11 Southern states that left the Union became the Confederate States of America.

Congress Legislative branch of US government, consisting of the Senate and the House of Representatives.

Constitution The rules and system by which a country's government works.

Constitutional convention Meeting to create a constitution for revolutionary Mexico.

Counterculture Alternative lifestyle to that of the dominant culture.

De facto segregation Segregation of the races in fact rather than in the law.

De jure segregation The legal segregation of the races, set down in laws in the South until 1964.

Democrat The Democratic Party favours government intervention on behalf of the less fortunate.

Department of Indian Affairs Canadian government department set up under the 1880 Indian Act to regulate First Nations peoples.

Direct action Physical protest, such as occupation of land.

Dixiecrat Breakaway Southern Democrat party founded in 1948.

Double day Women had to do housework as well as paid work.

Draft Conscription; compulsory call-up to the nation's armed forces.

Equal protection clause Clause of the 14th Amendment to the US Constitution that forbids denial of equal protection of the law to citizens.

Favelas Shantytowns in Brazil.

Federal government The USA is a federal state, where political power is divided between the federal government (consisting of the President, Congress and the Supreme Court, all located in Washington, DC) and the states.

Feminists Advocates of equal political, economic and social rights for women.

Filibuster Use of tactic to delay congressional voting on a bill.

First Nations Indigenous peoples in Canada. More recently, members of the various nations refer to themselves by their tribal or national identity.

First-come, first-served Southern buses were divided into black and white sections. Sometimes black people would be standing while the white section was empty. They therefore sought seating on a first-come, first-served basis.

Founding Fathers The men who drew up the US Constitution in 1787.

Freedom Summer SNCC voter registration campaign in Mississippi in 1964.

Genocide Deliberate destruction of an ethnic group.

Ghettos Areas in cities inhabited mostly or solely by (usually poor) members of a particular ethnicity or nationality.

Glass ceiling An invisible barrier that stopped women gaining top jobs.

Globalization Increasing internationalization of national economies, finance, trade and communications.

GOP Grand Old Party (nickname for the Republican Party).

Grandfather clause Southern state laws allowed the illiterate to vote if they could prove an ancestor had voted before Reconstruction, which no African American could do.

Great Depression Worldwide economic depression which began in 1929 and lasted for around 10 years.

Great migration Early twentieth-century northward movement of black Southerners.

Great Society President Johnson in 1965 declared a 'war on poverty' and called for a revolutionary programme of social welfare legislation that involved unprecedented federal expenditure on education, medical care for the elderly and an expanded Social Security Program.

Guerrillas Groups of fighters who use tactics such as sabotage, raids and assassination, usually against governments.

Haciendas Great landed estates.

Happenings Events with large, youthful crowds, such as Woodstock.

Hash A resin prepared from cannabis.

Hippies Young people (often students) in the 1960s who rejected the beliefs and fashions of the older generation, and favoured free love and drugs.

Hispanics Spanish-speaking people in the USA, usually of Latin American origin.

Homemakers Mothers staying at home to look after their families, rather than going out to work.

Howard Prestigious African American university in Washington, DC.

HUAC House Un-American Activities Committee, which pursued Communists in the 1940s and 1950s and others considered to threaten internal security in the 1960s and 1970s.

Inca Indigenous Peruvian; the Inca Empire stretched from Ecuador to Chile before the Spanish conquest.

Indian Act The 1876 Indian Act said how reserves and tribes should operate and who should be recognized as 'Indian'. It was amended on many occasions.

Indian Agents Canadian government representatives with ultimate authority over reserves.

Indigenismo Latin American movement that revered indigenous culture as a source of what was best in national values.

Indigenous Original/native inhabitants.

Integrationist Desirous to participate in the 'American dream' without separation of the races.

International Labour Organization (ILO) An agency of the United Nations which seeks the promotion of social justice and internationally recognized human and labour rights.

Inuit Indigenous people in Canada, formerly known as Eskimos.

Jim Crow A popular 1830s' comic, black-faced, minstrel character developed by white performing artists. Post-Reconstruction Southern state laws that legalized segregation were called 'Jim Crow laws'.

Judicial Committee of the Privy Council The final Court of Appeal in Canada.

Justice Department Branch of the federal government in Washington, DC with special responsibility for enforcing the law and administering justice.

Katarismo Bolivian movement to re-create Aymara ethnic solidarity.

Korean War The USA, South Korea and the United Nations fought against Communist North Korea and China in 1950–3.

Ku Klux Klan Violent, white supremacist organization.

Labour union An organization of workers seeking improved pay and working conditions.

Latin America The countries in Central and South America that gained their independence from Spain and Portugal in the nineteenth century.

Left wing Those sympathetic to the ideas of socialism, under which system the national economy is controlled by the government to prevent extremes in wealth or poverty.

Liberation theology Latin American Catholic clergy movement, inspiring parishioners to work for change in this life, rather than waiting for their reward in heaven.

Lynching Unlawful killing (usually by hanging).

Machismo Exaggerated sense of masculinity and belief in male domination of women.

Mao Zedong Leader of Communist China 1949–75.

Maquiladora plants Factories owned by multinational and US companies, mostly located near the US border.

Marxist Someone who believes in Marx and Engels' political, economic and social principles.

Maximum leader Recognition of one leader as superior to all other tribal leaders.

Mayan Indigenous person(s) of southern Mexico or parts of Central America.

Merengue Music and dance created by Afro-Dominicans.

Mestizos Offspring of Europeans and native peoples.

Métis Of mixed European and First Nations or Inuit blood.

Mexican Revolution A revolt against the dictatorship of Porfirio Díaz began in 1910 then developed into a struggle between several different Mexican groups that lasted until about 1920.

Mi'kmaq Aboriginal of eastern Canada.

Middle America A term invented by the media to describe ordinary, patriotic, middle-income US citizens.

Minority leader Leader of the party with fewer members in Congress.

Miscegenation The mixing of races through marriage and interbreeding.

Miskitos Indigenous population resident on the Nicaraguan and Honduran coasts.

Mobilization Being inspired/roused into activism.

Mohawk Native American, resident on the US and Canadian east coasts.

Moratorium In this context, suspension of normal activities to facilitate nationwide anti-Vietnam War protests in 1969.

Mulatto Of European–African descent.

Narrangansetts Native American tribe of eastern USA.

National Convention Before the presidential election, the Republicans and Democrats hold conferences in which each party selects or confirms its candidate for the presidency.

National Guard State-based US armed forces reserves.

Navajo and Hopi Native Americans of Arizona, Utah and New Mexico.

Neoconservatism Ideology combining traditional conservatism with greater faith in the free market.

Neoliberal Proponent of an economic system that promotes free trade and private business rather than government intervention to deal with inequality.

New Democrat Member of the Democratic Party who believed that the party needed to move more to the centre to be electable.

New Left Term used by SDS to differentiate themselves from the Communist Old Left of the 1930s.

New Right Right-wing voters who became influential in the late 1970s. Their beliefs were a reaction to the counterculture of the 1960s, and included opposition to abortion and feminism.

NOW National Organization for Women, established in 1966, is a US pressure group for equal rights for women.

Old Democrat Member of the Democratic Party who believed in large-scale government intervention and expenditure to ameliorate social and economic ills.

Oligarchy Government by a privileged few.

Pardo Mixed-race.

Passive resistance Non-violent refusal to comply with a particular policy.

Pentagon Home of US Department of Defense.

Pink Tide The left-wing governments elected in many Latin American countries from the end of the twentieth century.

Poll tax Tax levied on would-be voters that made it harder for blacks (who were usually poor) to vote.

Popular front Alliance of several leftist parties.

Populist regimes Governments that courted support from large groups such as labour unions and the poor.

Potlatches Ceremonial exchange of gifts by coastal First Nations peoples of British Columbia.

Primaries Elections to choose a party's candidate for elective office.

Pro-choice Those who support the right of a woman to choose whether or not to continue a pregnancy.

Pueblo Native American tribe of the West.

Quechua Member/language of an indigenous ethnic group in Peru, Bolivia, Colombia, Ecuador and Chile.

Radical left Communists, militant labour unionists.

Ratification Amendments to the US constitution require ratification (approval) by three-quarters of the states.

Reconstruction When the 11 ex-Confederate states were rebuilt, reformed and restored to the Union.

Republican The Republican Party tends to favour minimal government intervention in the economy and society.

Reservation An area of land set aside for Native American tribes in the nineteenth century.

Reserves Areas officially designated as living space for Canada's indigenous population.

Rights revolution Increasingly assertive movements for equal rights for minorities and women in the 1960s.

ROTC College-based programme to train officers for armed forces (Reserve Officer Training Corps).

Scorched-earth campaign Destruction of crops so the population lacks food.

Separatism Desire for African Americans to live separate but equal lives from whites, in all-black communities or even in a black state or Africa.

Sioux Native American tribe, mostly resident in the Great Plains.

Sit-ins African American protesters sat in and refused to move from white-only restaurants in the mid-twentieth century.

Socialism Political philosophy that society should be as equitable as possible in terms of economic and social standing.

Southern Cone Argentina, Brazil, Chile, Paraguay, Uruguay.

Status Indians Also known as registered Indians; listed on Indian Register and entitled to benefits under the Indian Act.

Suburbanization Growth of residential communities outside cities.

Sun Dances Religious ceremonies of prairie First Nations peoples.

Supreme Court The judicial branch of the federal government, which rules on the constitutionality of actions and laws.

Survival schools Under Title IV of the Indian Education Act (1972), Native Americans could control their children's education.

Title VII The anti-sex discrimination section of the 1964 US Civil Rights Act.

Treaty Indian Status Indian.

Truth Squad Group that monitored the speeches of Prime Minister John Diefenbaker.

Uncle Tom Uncle Tom in Harriet Beecher Stowe's novel *Uncle Tom's Cabin* (1852) was perceived as excessively deferential to whites by twentieth-century African Americans, who described obsequious contemporaries as Uncle Toms.

USAID US Agency for International Development.

USSR Union of Soviet Socialist Republics, the name given to Russia from 1922, also known as the Soviet Union.

Vietnam War War between non-Communist South Vietnam (supported by the USA) and Communist North Vietnam and its allies in the South (1954–75).

War on children Brazilian street children were seen as a threat to the property and life of the more prosperous classes, who employed security forces to be rid of them, sometimes resulting in murder.

War on Poverty President Johnson's programmes to help the poor, e.g. Social Security Act (1965).

Welfare dependency Reliance on federal aid.

White-collar worker Person who performs professional or office work rather than manual labour.

Women's liberation Militant feminists who emphasized male attitudes as the great barrier to equal rights for women.

Yanomamis Amerindian tribe living in the Amazonian rainforest.

Yippies Radical student group that wanted to pit the politics of freedom and disorder against the machine-dominated politics of the Democratic Party at Chicago in 1968.

Zapotec Indigenous people in Mexico's Oaxaca province.

Further reading

Latin American history: general

John Chasteen, *Born in Blood & Fire: A Concise History of Latin America*, third edition, Norton, 2011
An engaging overview of Latin American history. Students find Chasteen's approach interesting and informative.

Marshall Eakin, *The History of Latin America: Collision of Cultures*, Palgrave, 2007
A stimulating overview.

Benjamin Keen and Keith Haynes, *A History of Latin America: Independence to the Present*, Houghton Mifflin, 2009
An easy read that recognizes the need to balance generalizations about Latin America with specific case studies. There is a related useful website: college.hmco.com/pic/keen8e

Eduardo Galeano, *Century of the Wind*, Norton, 1998
An interesting approach to the history of the 20th century in the Americas. Galeano presents his interpretation in small vignettes organized by date and place.

Teresa Meade, *A History of Modern Latin America: 1800 to the Present*, Wiley-Blackwell, 2010
The author admits that it is very difficult to sustain the reader's focus when flitting between 20 Latin American countries, and even more difficult to cover all 20 countries in one book, but if the reader is patient and able to systematize the content, Meade is particularly good on women and the indigenous population.

Edwin Williamson, *The Penguin History of Latin America*, Penguin, 2009
Excellent overview that copes well with the problems of handling so many different countries.

Chapter 1

Greg Grandin *et al.* (editors), *The Guatemala Reader*, Duke University Press, 2011
All the volumes in this Duke series (Argentina, Brazil, Costa Rica, Cuba, Ecuador, Mexico, Peru) contain stimulating extracts from contemporaries and historians.

Howard Zinn, *A People's History of the United States*, Longman
Multiple editions attest that this is a good read, particularly sympathetic to and strong on Native Americans.

Chapters 2 and 3

Taylor Branch, *Parting the Waters: America in the King Years, 1954–63*, Simon & Schuster, 1989
An exhaustive look at the formative years of the Civil Rights Movement.

John Dittmer, *Local People: The Struggle for Civil Rights in Mississippi*, University of Illinois Press, 1994
Local studies such as this are always a useful corrective to the 'national' narrative.

Adam Fairclough, *Race and Democracy: The Civil Rights Struggle in Louisiana 1915–1972*, University of Georgia Press, 1999
Another useful local study.

Adam Fairclough, *Better Day Coming: Blacks and Equality, 1890–2000*, Penguin, 2002
Probably the best single-volume history of the African American story.

David Garrow, *Bearing the Cross*, William Morrow, 1986
Excellent biography of Martin Luther King Jr, full of contemporary quotations that give the reader a real 'feel' for the Civil Rights Movement.

Peniel Joseph, *Waiting 'Til the Midnight Hour: A Narrative History of Black Power in America*, Henry Holt, 2006
As with Manning Marable (below), raises the interesting question as to whether African Americans write the best histories of African Americans.

Michael Klarman, *From Jim Crow to Civil Rights: The Supreme Court and the Struggle for Racial Equality*, Oxford University Press, 2006
A much-needed overview of the role of the Supreme Court and the quest for equality.

Steven Lawson and Charles Payne, *Debating the Civil Rights Movement, 1945–1968*, Rowman & Littlefield, 2006
Insightful analyses accompanied by relevant documents.

Manning Marable, *Malcolm X*, Penguin, 2011
Currently considered the definitive biography.

Chapter 4

Stephen Ambrose, *Eisenhower: Soldier and President*, Simon & Schuster, 1990
Biographies of presidents are usually a good introduction to government actions and preoccupations in any particular period. Ambrose's writing holds the reader's interest.

Stephen Ambrose, *Nixon: The Triumph of a Politician, 1962–72*, Simon & Schuster, 1989
Exhaustive but not exhausting, balanced insight into one of America's most hated presidents.

Stephen Ambrose, *Nixon: Ruin and Recovery, 1973–90*, Simon & Schuster, 1993
As above.

Irving Bernstein, *Guns or Butter? The Presidency of Lyndon Johnson*, Oxford University Press, 1996
Useful, balanced account.

David McCullough, *Truman*, Simon & Schuster, 1992
Another biography that brings the president alive.

Waltraud Morales, *A Brief History of Bolivia*, Facts On File, 2010
Far easier read than Herbert Klein's *A Concise History of Bolivia*, text enlivened by author's sympathy for the indigenous population and a reader-friendly layout, nicely broken up by subheadings, photographs and interesting information boxes.

Chapter 5

George Reid Andrews, *Afro-Latin America: 1800–2000*, Oxford University Press, 2004
Detailed, solid.

Henry Louis Gates Jr, *Black in Latin America*, New York University Press, 2011
Summarizes the author's investigations for a television series of the same name. Much of it is inevitably in the rather irritating style of 'I met this expert and [s]he said …' and 'As an African American I felt …', but many interesting insights.

Chapter 6

William Chafe, *The Unfinished Journey: America Since World War II*, Oxford University Press, 2003
Liberal author, with excellent selection of interesting points and contemporary quotations that bring the account to life. Raises the interesting question as to whether only a liberal reader can enjoy and believe a liberal historian.

Michael Heale, *The Sixties in America: History, Politics and Protest*, Edinburgh University Press, 2001
Easy and balanced read.

Eric Zolov, *Refried Elvis: The Rise of the Mexican Counterculture*, University of California Press, 1999
Fascinating read. The claim that rock 'n' roll provoked the 1968 student riots again raises interesting historiographical questions – do historians sometimes try too hard to be 'cool' and radical, and is that good history?

Chapter 7

June Hahner, *Women in Latin American History: Their Lives and Views*, University of California, 1980
Difficult to find but excellent examination of the contribution of women in Latin American History.

Jane Jaquette (editor), *Feminist Agendas and Democracy in Latin America*, Duke University Press, 2009
Jaquette's introductory overview is good; as always with collections of articles, some are far better than others. Marcela Rios Tobar on Michelle Bachelet and Chile is one of the better ones.

Kathryn Sloan, *Women's Roles Through History: Women's Roles in Latin America and the Caribbean*, Greenwood, 2011
Has some really useful nuggets of information, but within the thematic organization (family, law, religion, work, culture, politics), poorly balanced chronological

coverage. The emphasis is really pre-twentieth century, and there it gives useful and interesting detail.

Nancy MacLean, *The American Women's Movement, 1945–2000: A Brief History With Documents*, Bedford/St. Martin's Press, 2008
Excellent coverage of the women's movement in the USA, accompanied by essential documents.

Internet resources

- Library of Congress portal with thousands of sources on African Americans, Native Americans and Women:
http://memory.loc.gov/ammem/index.html
- Native Americans, First Nations, Amer-Indians: A portal with many links to websites on North American native peoples: www.multcolib.org/homework/natamhc.html
A Brazilian website devoted to the many indigenous tribes in Brazil: http://pib.socioambiental.org/en
- African-Americans and the Civil Rights Movement:
An excellent site with transcripts, film and interviews:
www.teachersdomain.org/special/civil/
US National Archives resources for teachers. Many excellent sources on the Civil Rights Movement: www.archives.gov/education/index.html
Interesting links to important sources on the Civil Rights Movement: www.hartford-hwp.com/archives/45a/index-b.html
- Martin, Malcolm and the Black Power movement:
From the World History Archives site, many links to articles about Martin Luther King Jr, as well as documents by King: www.hartford-hwp.com/archives/45a/index-bc.html
An interesting collection of sources relating to Malcolm X: www.malcolm-x.org/docs/
- Afro-Latinos:
Many resources for the African diaspora in Latin America, some in English, especially those in the International Resources section:
http://lanic.utexas.edu/la/region/african/

- Role of government:
For students (and teachers) who wish to read the full decisions of the Supreme Court that relate to the civil rights of African Americans:
http://civilrights.findlaw.com/civil-rights-overview/civil-rights-u-s-supreme-court-decisions.html
- Youth movements:
Links to student and anti-war movements in the 1960s: www2.iath.virginia.edu/sixties/HTML_docs/Sixties.html and www.jaysleftist.info/directory/subjects/history.htm
- Women in Latin America:
Also from the excellent University of Texas portal on all things Latin American: http://lanic.utexas.edu/la/region/women/

Films

There are several documentaries that fit in well with this book. Among them are:

- *Eyes on the Prize: America's Civil Rights Years, 1954–1965.* This six-hour series covers important events in the early years of the movement.
- *Eyes on the Prize II: America at the Racial Crossroads, 1965–1985.* Eight hours of documentary film which includes sections on Martin Luther King Jr, Malcolm X and the Black Panthers.
- *We Shall Remain: America Through Native Eyes.* Seven-and-a half hour series on Native Americans. Of particular interest is the last episode. It details the 1973 standoff at Wounded Knee.
- *Black in Latin America.* The Afro-Latino experience in Haiti, Cuba, Brazil, Mexico and Peru is explored.

All of the above are from pbs.org

Internal assessment

The internal assessment is a historical investigation on a historical topic. Below is a list of possible topics on Civil Rights and Social Movements that could warrant further investigation. They have been organized by chapter theme.

Native Americans and civil rights in the Americas

1 How was the Peruvian government able to defeat the *Sendero Luminoso*?
2 Why did the American Indian Movement seize and occupy the town of Wounded Knee?
3 What cultural impact did Canadian residential schools have on First Nations children in the twentieth century?

African Americans and the Civil Rights Movement

1 How did the NAACP contribute to the Civil Rights Movement?
2 What impact did the Freedom Riders have on public opinion?
3 Why did the US Supreme Court agree to hear civil rights lawsuits in the 1950s?

Martin, Malcolm and Black Power

1 Why was Malcolm X assassinated?
2 What factors led to the demise of the Black Panthers?
3 Why did Malcolm X break from the Nation of Islam?

Afro-Latin Americans

1 To what extent was Gilberto Freyre's thesis that Brazil was a racial democracy a myth?
2 What impact did the Cuban revolution have on the Afro-Cuban community after 1959?
3 What led to the growth of Afro-Brazilian groups in the 1970s?

Role of governments in Civil Rights Movements in the Americas

1 How was President Johnson able to pass the Civil Rights Act of 1964?
2 Why did the Sandinista government persecute the Miskito tribe in Nicaragua?
3 How effective were President Eisenhower's race policies?

Youth culture and protests of the 1960s and 1970s

1 What factors led the Mexican government to carry out the Tlatelolco Massacre?
2 Why did the Chicago police attack protesters at the 1968 Democratic National Convention?
3 Why was the 1969 Moratorium the USA's 'greatest ever anti-war protest'?

Feminist movements in the Americas

1 What role did women play in the Nicaraguan revolution?
2 To what extent did the National Organization for Women improve working conditions for women in the USA?
3 Why was Quebec the last Canadian province to allow women the vote?

Index

A

African Americans
  education 53, 54, 55, 56, 59–60, 83, 90, 92, 93, 106–7, 109, 116, 143, 145, 150
  historical tensions 53–4
  impact of Second World War 56
  origins of Civil Rights Movement 54–5
  see also individuals and specific movements; Civil Rights Acts; USA
Abortion 200–1, 202, 206–7, 212, 215, 216, 219, 225, 226, 228–9, 230–2, 234
Afro-Latin Americans
  Civil Rights Movement 128–31, 133–9
  cultural developments 127
  education 126, 129, 134
  effect of slavery 123
  employment opportunities 126
  ideology 127
  labour unions 126
  populations 131–3
  sympathetic regimes 125–6
Alcatraz Island 31
American Indian Movement (AIM) 30–2, 40, 46
American Indian Religious Freedom Act (1978) 36
Árbenz, Jacobo 21–2
Arévalo, Juan José 21
Argentina
  student protests 192
  women's rights 208–11
Aymara 15, 18, 154, 155, 160, 161, 162, 164–5, 167
Aztecs 10

B

Barrios de Chúngara, Domitila 16
Biographers
  Bernstein, Irving 84
  Clegg, Claude Andrew 105, 118
  Haley, Alex 108, 118
  Marable, Manning 118
  Pearson, Hugh 114
  Perry, Bruce 118
  White, John 67
Black muslims, *see* Nation of Islam
Black Panthers 112–15, 116, 119, 180, 181, 185
Black Power 94, 96, 97, 98, 99, 101, 102, 104, 105, 108–19, 149, 150, 187
Bolivia
  Agrarian Reform Law 158

coca and cocaine 14, 161, 162, 163, 165, 168
education 126, 154–5, 156, 157, 159, 162
gas dispute 164–6
indigenous population 154–7, 160–8
military governments 159–61
National Revolution 157–9
protests 16
water wars 162–3, 164–5
Brazil
  employment opportunities 126
  racial democracy 127
  racism 124, 134–6, 136, 138–9
  student protests 192
  women's rights 211–12
Brown v. Board of Education (1954) 59–60, 64, 65, 68, 70, 71, 72, 98, 145–6
Bush, George H.W. 36, 152, 231, 232

C

Canada
  counterculture 186–7
  government 40, 41–3, 46–7
  Supreme Court rulings 40, 41, 44–5, 46, 49
  women's rights 196–201
  youth culture 186–7
  see also First Peoples
Cardinal, Harold 42, 43, 198
Castro, Fidel 125, 129, 137, 188, 191, 215–18
Catholic Church 13–14, 15, 23, 131, 134, 204, 207, 213, 218, 219
Chiapas 12, 19–21, 24, 191
Chicago riots 178–80
Chile
  Pinochet dictatorship 213–14
  women's rights 212–15, 217, 218, 226, 230, 232
Civil Rights Acts
  (1957) 71–2
  (1960) 72
  (1964) 68, 78, 80–2, 83–4, 98, 148–9, 224, 227
  (1968) 33
  see also individual countries and civil rights movements
Clinton, Bill 18, 36, 153, 232
Coalition of Workers, Peasants and Students (COCEI) 19
Cold War 18, 29, 101, 109, 144, 178
Congress of Racial Equality (CORE) 56, 72, 74–5, 92, 95, 96, 98, 105, 108, 110, 111, 115, 116, 177, 223

Counterculture 176–7, 178, 181, 182, 183, 184, 185, 186–7, 189–90, 191, 221
Cuba 125, 188
  education 126
  foreign visits 129, 130
  racism 123, 137
  women's rights 206–7, 215–18

D

Divorce 200, 202, 210, 212
Du Bois, W.E.B. 55

E

Ecuador, enfranchisement of indigenous people 17
Education Acts
  Canada 38
  USA (1972) 31, 33–4, 83–4
Eisenhower, Dwight D. 28–9, 70, 71–2, 145–6
Enfranchisement 12, 15, 17, 40, 53, 54, 56, 58, 61, 68, 71–2, 76, 80, 82–3, 94, 95, 96, 98, 99, 148–9, 158, 196, 202, 203, 208, 211, 212–13, 218, 221
Essays 4–5
Examination questions 3–4, 6
  'analyse' questions 51–2
  'assess' questions 121–2
  'compare and contrast' questions 235–8
  'evaluate' questions 171–3
  'in what ways and with what effects' questions 194–5
  'to what extent' questions 86–8
  'why' questions 140–1
  see also Essays

F

Farmer, James 56, 74, 111, 116
Feminism, *see* Women's movement
First Peoples
  discrimination 39, 43–4, 44–6
  education 38, 40, 44, 48
  effect of European settlement 38–9
  living conditions 38–9, 43, 48–9
  militancy 38, 40
  residential schools 47–8, 49
  self-government 46–7
  White Paper (1969) 40, 41–3, 48
  see also Canada; Land rights
Freedom Rides 74–5, 77
Friedan, Betty 221, 222–3, 224, 231, 234

G

García Pérez, Alan 18
Garvey, Marcus 55, 101–2, 114, 118
Ghettos 30–1, 43, 55, 82, 90, 91–3, 94, 95, 97, 98, 99, 102, 103, 104, 105, 107–10, 114, 116, 149, 150, 151
Guatemala 16, 21–4, 142, 166
Guerrilla groups 15, 18, 20, 21, 22, 129
    involvement of women 204, 206–7
    student 191–2

H

Hampton, Fred 114–15
Hippies 176–7, 186–7, 190
Historians 7, 101, 117–18, 127, 147, 185
    Ambrose, Stephen 71, 182
    Andrews, George Reid 125, 127, 131, 134, 137, 139
    Arocha, Jaime 169
    Badger, Anthony 100
    Bracey, John 117
    Brennan, Mary 185
    Brock, Lisa 135
    Bumsted, J.M. 42, 43, 45, 47, 186, 198, 199
    Carson, Clayborne 64, 100, 101, 118
    Chafe, William 68, 179, 180, 228, 234
    civil rights movement 67–8
    Cluff, Mary Lynn 211
    Conrad, Margaret 39, 40, 197
    Cornell Stephen 37
    Crawford, Vicki 101, 234
    Debo, Angie 28
    Deloria Jr, Vine 30, 32–3, 37
    Dittmer, John 67
    Dudziak, Mary 101
    Escandón, Carmen Ramos 218
    Evans, Sara 234
    Fairclough, Adam 55, 67, 101
    Fausto, Boris 139, 192
    Finkel, Alvin 39, 40, 197
    Fixico, Donald 28, 36, 37
    French, John 211
    Gabin, Nancy 234
    Garrow, David 68, 91
    Gates Jr, Henry Louis 127, 130, 138, 139
    Gitlin, Todd 185
    Gott, Richard 129, 130
    Hale, C.R. 170
    Harley, Sharon 119
    Haynes, Keith 17, 21, 204, 207, 217
    Heale, Michael 183, 184, 221
    Heineman, Ken 185
    Jaquette, Jane 206, 207, 219
    Joseph, Peniel 118, 119
    Keen, Benjamin 17, 21, 204, 207, 217
    Kicza, John 25
    Kirk, John 67

Kirkwood, Burton 21
Klein, Herbert 154, 157
Lawson, Steven 100, 101
Lytle, Clifford 37
MacLean, Nancy 234
Marks, Paula 34
Meade, Teresa 25, 135, 139, 166, 192, 211, 215, 216, 217
Meier, August 17
Meyerowitz, Joanna 234
Morales, Waltraud 157, 162, 163, 165
Morris, Aldon 67, 68, 101
Matusow, Allen J. 185
Newman, Mark 67, 68, 100
Oates, Stephen 83
Ogbar, Jeffrey 119
on Martin Luther King Jr 63
Parman, Donald 37
Patterson, James 101
Payne, Charles 68
Pearcy, Thomas 24
de la Peña, Guillermo 13, 25
Powledge, Fred 100
Reagan, Leslie 234
Rosen, Ruth 234
Rossinow, Doug 185
Rout, Leslie 138
Rudwick, Elliot 117
Sitkoff, Harvard 67
Sloan, Kathryn 202, 205, 212, 215, 218, 220
statistics, use of 11
Sugrue, Thomas 185
Taylor-Robinson, Michelle 206
television, impact of 79
Tobar, Marcela Rios 215
Tuck, Stephen 67, 101
Tyson, Timothy 119
Van Cott, Donna Lee 169
Van Deburg, William 119
Wade, Peter 169
Williams, Yohuru 119
women's movement 234
Zolov, Eric 189–90

I

Incas 11, 154, 191
Indian Self-Determination Act (1974) 33
International Labour Organization (ILO) Convention 169: 14–15, 18

J

Jim Crow laws 54, 55, 59, 64, 73, 98, 100, 143, 145, 148, 151
Johnson, Lyndon 30, 33, 80–1, 82, 83–4, 91, 94, 95, 96, 98, 99, 109, 144, 148–51, 226

K

Katari, Tupac 160, 161, 162
Kataristas 160
Kennedy, John F. 29, 77–8, 80–1, 84, 98, 99, 104, 146–8, 151, 174–5, 222
Kennedy, Robert 29, 75, 76, 78, 82
King Jr, Martin Luther 53, 62, 63, 64, 65, 67, 68, 69, 80, 103, 104, 109, 110, 112, 129, 139, 149
    assassination attempt 97–8
    Chicago campaign 91–5
    comparison with Malcolm X 105–8
    importance to Civil Rights Movement 98–100
    Vietnam War 94–5, 97
    Where Do We Go From Here? 97
    see also Chicago riots; Watts riots
Klarman, Michael 68
Ku Klux Klan 60, 65, 112, 116

L

Land rights
    First Nations people 38, 40, 41, 42, 44–6, 47, 48, 49
    Latin America 9, 11, 12, 13, 14, 15–16, 18, 19–20, 21–2, 24, 25, 128, 154, 155–6, 157–60, 162, 163, 164, 167
    Native Americans 27–8, 30, 32–3, 34, 36, 37
Latin America indigenous population
    activism 12–17, 169–70
    conquerors and attitudes towards them 9, 10, 11
    culture 10, 11
    independence from conquerors 9
    inequality 9, 10–11, 12–15, 17–18, 25–6
    land rights 9, 11, 12, 13, 14, 15–16, 18, 19–20, 21–2, 24, 25, 128, 154, 155–6, 157–60, 162, 163, 164, 167
    proportion of population 11, 12
    racial divisions 10
    women's rights 202–8
    see also specific countries and individuals
Liberation theology 13–14

M

Malcolm X 77, 79, 102, 103–5, 110, 113, 118, 129, 135
    comparison with Martin Luther King Jr 105–8
Mayans 20
    guerrilla group in Guatemala 21–4
Menchú, Rigoberta 16, 24, 25
Meredith March 94, 96–7, 110, 111
Mestizos 9, 11, 19, 166
Mexico
    Afro-Latin Americans 130, 138
    counterculture 189–90, 191

education 203
effect of revolution 10
mestizo domination 18–21, 127
national identity 9, 10
student movement 188–91
women's movement 203, 205, 218–19
Mississippi Freedom Democratic Party (MFDP) 80, 110
Montgomery bus boycott 62–5, 67–8, 71, 72–3, 94, 98, 100, 101, 146
Morales, Evo 161, 163–9, 205
Mothers of the Plaza de Mayo 209–10

N

Nation of Islam 102–4
National Association for the Advancement of Colored People (NAACP) 29, 54, 55–6, 59–61, 62, 63, 64–6, 67, 68–71, 72–3, 76, 78, 80, 81, 83, 92, 94, 96, 98, 100–1, 105, 107, 109, 110, 112, 114, 119, 126, 143–4, 145, 146, 231
National Congress of American Indians (NCAI) 29–30
National Indian Youth Council (NIYC) 30
National Organization for Women (NOW) 224–5, 226, 228, 231, 232, 233
Native American Housing and Self-Determination Act (1996) 36
Native Americans
effect of European settlement 27
Eisenhower years 28–9
impact of Second World War 28
increased assertiveness 29–37
land rights 27–8, 30, 32–3, 34, 36, 37
litigation 33
populations 34, 35
Roosevelt years 27–8
Truman years 28
victims of racism 27
writers 32
see also Indian Self-Determination Act (1974); Native American Housing and Self-Determination Act (1996)
Newton, Huey 112, 113–14
Nicaragua 132
black groups 169
rebellions 15, 18, 20–1, 142, 204
women's rights 205, 206–7
Nixon, E.D. 62, 67
Nixon, Richard 30, 32, 33, 110, 115–6, 151, 179–81, 182, 183, 222, 226

O

Occupation 30, 31, 32, 161, 175
Oil and gas 18, 28, 45, 164

P

Parks, Rosa 56, 60, 62–3, 64, 65, 135
Perón, Eva 192, 208–9
Perón, Isabel 129
Perón, Juan 126, 208–9
Peru
enfranchisement 17, 203
government sympathetic to indigenous population 14, 18
oil and gas 18
politicization of the peasants 13
rebellion 15
unionization 16
women's rights 203, 205, 206
see also Shining Path
Pinochet, Augusto 213, 214
Powell, Adam Clayton 56, 92, 97

Q

Quechua 14, 15, 18, 154, 155, 156, 159, 161

R

Racism
African Americans 65, 68, 75, 77, 143, 175, 178, 231
Afro-Latin Americans 123, 124, 128, 131, 133–7, 138–9
First Nations people 44, 187
Latin America 17, 165, 166
Native Americans 27, 30
see also Enfranchisement
Rainforests 15, 17, 18
Randolph, A. Philip 55, 56, 58, 62, 67, 78, 98, 109, 144
Reagan, Ronald 36, 37, 151–2, 177, 230–2
Red Power 30–1
Richardson, Gloria 119, 227
Rivera, Diego 10
Roe v. Wade 228, 229, 230, 234

S

Sandinista National Liberation Front 18, 142, 204, 207
Seale, Bobby 112, 113–14, 181
Second World War 2, 28, 55, 56, 57, 67, 73, 94, 128, 203, 211, 212–13, 221, 234
Shining Path (*Sendero Luminoso*) 15
Southern Christian Leadership Conference (SCLC) 65, 68, 72–5, 76, 77–8, 80, 82–3, 91–5, 96, 100, 101, 105, 110, 112, 223
Student Non-Violent Co-ordinating Committee (SNCC) 73–4, 76, 80, 82–3, 96, 98, 105, 108, 110–11, 112, 115, 116, 146, 147, 177, 178, 223
Suárez, Hugo Banzer 160
Subcomandante Marcos 20–1

T

Till, Emmett 61
Tlatelolco Plaza 189, 190, 191
Toledo, Alejandro 18
Trail of Broken Treaties 32
Truman, Harry S. 28, 57–8, 144–5, 146
Tupamaros 191

U

Unión de Comuneros Emiliano Zapata (UCEZ) 19
United Nations 16–17, 22, 114, 131, 161, 166, 167, 205, 214, 215, 231
Uruguay 191–2
USA
affirmative action 151–2
counterculture 176–7, 178, 181, 182–3, 184, 185, 221
education 27, 29, 31, 33, 37, 53, 54, 55, 56, 59–60, 83–4, 90, 92, 106–7, 187, 223, 225, *see also* African Americans, education
ERA amendment 225, 226, 228–9, 230
federal system of government 24
New Deal 55, 67, 144
New Left 175–6
Second World War 2, 28, 55, 56, 57, 67, 73, 221, 143, 145, 150, 234
student protests 174–6, 178–82
Supreme Court rulings 30, 34, 36, 54, 55–5, 227–8, 230–1, 232, 233
women's movement 221–34
see also African Americans; Native Americans

V

Venezuela 125
education 126
Voting Rights Act (1965) 68, 82–3, 98, 107, 148–9, *see also* Enfranchisement

W

Washington, Booker T. 55
Watts riots 91, 109, 149
Whitening 123, 127, 138
Williams, Robert 119
Women's movement
Canada 196–201
Latin America 202–20
USA 221–34
Wounded Knee 32

Z

Zapatista Army of National Liberation (EZLN) 20, 21

The publishers would like to thank the following for permission to reproduce material in this book:
Oxford University Press for extracts from *A History of the Canadian Peoples* by J.M. Bumsted, 2007. SR Books for an extract from *The Indian in Latin American History: Resistance, Resilience and Acculturation* edited by John Kicza, 1999. University of Mississippi for extracts from transcripts of interviews with Freedom Riders (© The University of Mississippi).

The publishers would like to acknowledge use of the following extracts:
Curtis Brown for an extract from *The Feminine Mystique* by Betty Friedan, Penguin Classics, 2010. Edinburgh University Press for an extract from *The Sixties in America: History, Politics and Protest* by M.J. Heale, 2001. UCLA for extracts from *Women in Latin American History – Their Lives and Views*, edited by June Hahner, 1984. Houghton Mifflin for extracts from *A History of Latin America: Independence to the Present* by Benjamin Keen and Keith Haynes, 2009. © 2009 Wadsworth, a part of Cengage Learning, Inc. Reproduced by permission. Pearson for extracts from *A People's History of the United States* by Howard Zinn, 1996.

Acknowledgements:
ABC-CLIO, *Women's Roles in Latin America and the Caribbean* by Kathryn Sloan, 2011. www.bolivianconstitution.com, *Constitution of the Plurinational State of Bolivia … 2009* translated by Luis Francisco Valle. Copp Clark Pitman, *History of the Canadian Peoples II* by Alvin Finkel and Margaret Conrad, 1993. Duke University Press, *The Guatemala Reader* edited by Greg Grandin *et al.*, 2011. Facts on File, *A Brief History of Bolivia* by Waltraud Morales, 2010. http://foundsf.org, Proclamation of the 'Indians of All Tribes' from Alcatraz, 1969. Peniel Joseph (www.penielejoseph.com), 'Black Power's powerful legacy', 2006. Longman, *Sweet Land of Liberty* by Robert Cook, 1998. Mercer University Press, *Twentieth Century Shapes of Baptist Social Ethics* by Larry McSwain and William Lloyd Allen, 2008. Monthly Review Press, *Let Me Speak!* by Domitila Barrios de Chúngara, 1978. William Morrow, *Bearing the Cross*, by David Garrow, 1999. New York University Press, *Black in Latin America* by Henry Louis Gates Jr, 2011. Orbis Books, *Martin and Malcolm and America* by James Cone, 1991. Oxford University Press, *Afro-Latin America: 1800–2000* by George Reid Andrews, 2004; *Lone Star Rising: Lyndon Johnson and his Times*, Volume I, by Robert Dallek, 1991; *The Unfinished Journey: America Since World War II* by William Chafe, 2003. Palgrave, *The History of Latin America* by Marshall Eakin, 2007. Palgrave Macmillan, *The History of Brazil* by Robert Levine, 1999. Penguin, *The Autobiography of Malcolm X* by Malcolm X, 1965; *The Penguin History of Canada* by Robert Bothwell, 2006. *Playboy* , Martin Luther King's interview with Alex Haley, 1965. Presidential Recordings Program, University of Virginia, An extract from President Johnson's words to Walker Stone, prominent conservative editor of the Scripps Howard newspapers, quoted in http://whitehousetapes.net. Public Broadcasting Service. *Saturday Evening Post*, Extract on Malcolm X's autobiography, 1964. Simon & Schuster, *Truman* by David McCullough, 1992; *Eisenhower* by Stephen Ambrose, 2003. Stanford University. http://teacher.scholastic.com. Texas A&M University Press, *The Modern Presidency and Civil Rights* by Garth Pauley, 2001. University of California Press, *The Papers of Martin Luther King Jr., III* edited by Clayborne Carson,1997. Westview Press, *The Women's Movement in Latin America: Participation and Democracy* edited by Jane Jaquette, 1994. Yale University Press, *Cuba: A New History* by Richard Gott, 2004.